THE WORD DETECTIVE

A Life in Words: From Serendipity to Selfie

JOHN SIMPSON

Little, Brown

LITTLE, BROWN

First published in Great Britain in 2016 by Little, Brown

Copyright © 2016 by John Simpson

The moral right of the author has been asserted.

A CIP catalogue record for this book
is available from the British Library.

Hardback ISBN 978-1-4087-0660-2
C Format ISBN 978-1-4087-0673-2

Designed by Cynthia Young

Printed and bound in Great Britain by
Clays Ltd, St Ives plc

Papers used by Little, Brown are from well-managed forests
and other responsible sources.

MIX
Paper from
responsible sources
FSC® C104740

Little, Brown
An imprint of
Little, Brown Book Group
Carmelite House
50 Victoria Embankment
London EC4Y 0DZ

An Hachette UK Company
www.hachette.co.uk

www.littlebrown.co.uk

For Hilary

It wasn't until the day I finished the first draft

that I realised that this was for you.

I should have known earlier.

———

There are many voices that can be used to tell a story.

These are just a few of them.

CONTENTS

INTRODUCTION

The Background to the Case

Ever since I started as a cub lexicographer on the majestic *Oxford English Dictionary* (*OED*) in 1976, I've tried to pick away at the stereotypes imposed on lexicographers by the media, by the public, and—worse still—by lexicographers themselves. These days, dictionary entries have to be stone-cold sober and analytical, not occasionally spry and whimsical, as they could be in the days of Samuel Johnson (for whom a lexicographer was "a writer of dictionaries; a harmless drudge, that busies himself in tracing the original, and detailing the signification of words"). And so it's hardly surprising that the public perception of lexicographers is of a rather dull, plodding crew caught in an endless cycle running from *A* to *Z*, and then often turning tail and scampering right back again to the beginning, as we desperately try to capture minor changes from the fringes of language that need to be assessed and defined. And sadly, these stereotypes aren't wholly wrong. Writing a dictionary is, after all, a serious business.

Many books have been written about the *OED*, almost all of which concentrate on the tussle between the publishers at the University Press in Oxford and the heroic dictionary editors, or alternatively, between the heroic and long-suffering executives of the publishing house and the awkward, argumentative, and closed-minded lexicographers. That's mainly because those are the facts that you can extract fairly easily from the archives, depending on which tint you've put on your glasses that day. And I suppose there's something to that side of the narrative.

What the archives don't contain—and what you have no hope of appreciating unless you come at things from another angle—is the fun and excitement of historical dictionary work. If you need to, step back a few paces and draw a deep breath. This excitement derives equally from the detective work involved, from recovering information which has been lost for maybe hundreds of years (new etymological stories and connections, new first usages, links that you never knew existed between words), and from seeing exactly how words arise out of the culture and society in which they are used. Because words do tell us about the people and cultures that use them.

This is a very specific kind of excitement. It's different from the knockabout excitement portrayed in *Ball of Fire*, my favourite film about reference books. I used to play a few minutes of this 1941 screwball comedy to groups of summer-schoolers I taught years ago. I expect they thought it was the best part of the course. In the film, the erudite(-looking) Gary Cooper is the grammarian in a team of gnome-like editors engaged in the noble task of writing an encyclopaedia. The professors have led quiet lives, of the sort that quite unfits them for the vibrant work of reference editing. In particular, they are unfamiliar with the new vocabulary of jive talk and the hepcats. As luck would have it, Gary Cooper stumbles across Barbara Stanwyck (disguised as the night-club singer "Sugarpuss" O'Shea), and he and his fellow editors take rather a shine to her. They sneak out at night to listen to her vocabulary at a nightclub. Gary Cooper's article on slang for the encyclopaedia benefits from his entanglement with Sugarpuss, and Sugarpuss is eventually rescued from numerous potential mishaps by the kindly hearted editors. This is not exactly how things worked at the *Oxford English Dictionary*. Certainly, we never knowingly employed anyone called "Sugarpuss."

I joined the staff of the *Oxford English Dictionary* as an editorial assistant in 1976, and I remained with the dictionary for thirty-seven years, until my retirement in 2013. For the last twenty of those years, I was chief editor. From my first days at the *OED*, I found myself fascinated by the work of creating a dictionary. What captivated me was the English language and its history: how it arose in obscurity 1,500 years ago, and how it grew to define the nations that spoke it. The *OED* is a historical dictionary: it addresses the whole sweep of English from the earliest times right up to the present day—in Britain, America, wherever it is spoken. And yet we have forgotten so much of our heritage. Every day while I was working on the *OED*, as a junior editorial assistant or as the chief editor, I could rediscover facts about the English language that had been forgotten for years—just little facts, but ones which need to be remembered to create an accurate picture of English. Or I could write a definition that captured precisely a meaning that had previously only shimmered uncertainly. My colleagues working on etymologies (word derivation) or pronunciations could crack a problem that had confused scholars and researchers for ages past. The lexicographer sees English as a mosaic—consisting of thousands of little details. Each time one of the tiny tiles of the mosaic is cleaned and polished, we see the mosaic more clearly. It's something of this excitement that I hope to convey in the rest of this book.

The *OED* is also a descriptive dictionary: it monitors the language, and tells you how language *is* used, from real-life, documentary evidence. It doesn't try to tell you—prescriptively—how to use the language. If you don't like *hopefully* as a sentence-adverb ("Hopefully, I'll see you tomorrow"), then the *OED* will tell you that many writers avoid this usage, but ultimately, it will leave it up to you whether you choose to use it yourself. The dictionary will give you the background: that it arose in the United States in the 1930s—as far as the evidence goes—and has been used steadily since then. And it will tell you that the older meaning ("in a hopeful manner; with a feeling of hope") dates back to the seventeenth century. And it will doubtless hope, hopefully, that if you find any better evidence, you'll send it along to the editors for consideration. I liked the way the *OED* describes but doesn't hector.

I didn't expect to become a lexicographer. I studied English literature at university (York), but I probably spent more time on the various bumpy sports fields of the university than was good for me—as captain and then president of the university hockey team. I certainly did not spend a moment dreaming of a career as a lexicographer. In fact, I'm sure I didn't know what the word meant.

It was pure chance that I ended up working at the *OED*, but once I began I never left. I haven't left now, really—you just don't. Language continually changes, and every change is a puzzle. The lexicographer is the historical word detective trying to identify and explain these puzzles. If you don't find the answer now, just set it aside and wait for more information to present itself later. But if you do latch on to a clue, then pursue it until the truth is revealed. The puzzles are inexhaustible, and every answer brings a thrill.

Lexicographers—at least in my opinion—have to come at language sideways. If they don't, they just see what everyone wants them to see. They need to disbelieve everything they thought they knew about a word and about its context, and start again—building a picture up from the documentary evidence they discover. I found all of this rather bewildering when I first started working on the *Oxford English Dictionary*, as you'll see. But gradually I started to gain a more panoramic view of the work and of the language.

Nothing, of course, is perfect. As I continued to work on the dictionary, I—along with many of my colleagues—became more and more aware of cracks in the wallpaper. Back then, the *OED* was a late nineteenth-century dictionary which had hardly changed in a hundred years. As editors, we were adding new meanings to it, but really it needed a complete overhaul and update. Would we ever be able to address this monster project? The *OED* was an intensely scholarly beast, consulted in whispers in university or public libraries. Could we somehow make it more accessible to a wider audience? Oxford itself felt—in those days—very much like an exclusive club, and ordinary people regarded the dictionary as part of this private world, to which they were not invited. Would that ever change? Could we—as dictionary editors—ever help to bring that change about?

The longer I worked on the dictionary, the more I wanted to move the dictionary from being the preserve of the scholar to becoming a modern, dynamic work that kept pace with language. My impression, when I first set foot inside the *OED* offices, was that the dictionary was dominated by the past. It had a crusty, antiquated air. Where were the *real* language creators—the mass of English speakers, the everyday poets and writers and conversationalists in whose mouths the language had changed from day to day over the centuries? Could we somehow give them a voice in the *OED* of the future?

I came to appreciate that there were other ways, too, of opening up pathways into the dictionary. My time at the *OED* coincided with the great shift from reference works as books to reference works as dynamic, online resources. Oxford was at first slow to notice that the world was changing, and much of this book is about how my colleagues and I put the *OED* in the forefront of this revolution. Suppose the massive volumes of the Victorian dictionary could be digitised, comprehensively updated, published online, and made searchable in ways that traditional dictionary users had never imagined—we could learn so much more about the language, and about ourselves. And then suppose users could post their own discoveries about the dictionary on an *OED* wiki and help change the dictionary in the future. The technology was emerging, and immediately we wanted to see how the *OED*—and its users—might benefit.

Although the main story concentrates on life at the dictionary, and on what struck me as interesting, curious, or remarkable over that period, I've also used words that crop up in the narrative itself as jumping-off points for digressions into stories about word history and usage. There is a reason for this, as I want to tell the stories of words from a historical perspective. The *OED* is—crucially—a "historical" dictionary: one that observes language historically (language change, language patterns, language growth, the relationship between words and the societies that use them over time) and doesn't simply look at words from the viewpoint of the definer of contemporary English.

I chose not to select these words for discussion on a rigid chronological or conceptual basis. What I want to show is that any word can have an interesting history, if you just take a few moments to look behind the scenes. The words I discuss often have some resonance with my own life (or they wouldn't be here), but they also give glimpses into how English has emerged and developed over the centuries, from the early days of the Anglo-Saxons, when English was effectively just a Germanic dialect, through the pervasive influence of the Norman Conquest, and on to the present day. I hope—naturally—you may be **intrigued** by some of these facts and coincidences, to use a regular word in one of its more modern meanings.

We can be quite confident that we know the meaning of a word only to discover that "our" meaning is the last in a long line of meanings that the word has had over the centuries. The English first encountered *to intrigue*—according to the *OED*—back in the early seventeenth century (the first evidence currently dates from 1612, in the anonymous *Trauels of Foure English Men*), and the verb meant "to trick or deceive (someone)" or to place them in an embarrassing situation. The dictionary records nine words meaning "to deceive" entering English in the first half of the seventeenth century (*to cog*, *to nosewipe*, etc.). The four Englishmen employed a bit of guesswork in spelling their new word, plumping for *intreag*. It can take a while for the spelling of a new word to settle down.

From deceit we move on to entanglement. The "learned and reverend" seventeenth-century clergyman John Scott sagely observed, in his *Christian Life* (1681), as regards sin: "How doth it perplex and intrigue the whole Course of your Lives, and intangle ye in a labyrinth of Knavish Tricks and Collusions." In the same passage, Scott noted that we find it very difficult to *extricate* ourselves from wrongdoing, and he will have known that *extricate* and *intrigue* are etymologically close cousins. We understand the sense of entanglement more easily in *extricate* today than we do in *intrigue*.

Intrigue entered English as a borrowing from French around 1600. The French themselves only knew it from 1532, when they borrowed the word from Italian (*intrigare*)—and didn't give it back, of course. So it wasn't available in French for borrowing earlier, along with the mass of French words entering English immediately after the Norman Conquest. The Italian word is a late rendering of the classical Latin *intricare* (parallel to *extricare*, as in *extricate*). Latin *tricae* are trifles, tricks, toys, quirks, or perplexities, as the dictionary dutifully tells us.

To intrigue was on the move in English in the late seventeenth century. After entanglement came the meaning "to carry on underhand plotting or scheming." The meanings of the word seem to have intrigued the clergy: Bishop Gilbert Burnet, in his *History of the Reformation* (1679), reported that (in 1527) "the cardinal of York was not satisfied to be intriguing for the Popedom after his death, but was aspiring to it while he was alive."

We waited quietly for another two centuries before *to intrigue* made its next move and became the word we know today: "to excite the curiosity or interest of," or "to puzzle, fascinate"—in the 1890s. This was another French meaning, though the English did not add it to the semantic arsenal of *intrigue* until the late nineteenth century. But we've forgotten all that now, and treat all of its meanings as quite English.

If you happen to spot a word in bold type in this book, like *intrigued* above, it's more or less a sure sign that I will soon talk briefly about the word, its usage, and its history. Although this book is not intended to be a traditional history of English, by the end I'd like to feel that you might be more curious about language and the words you use every day than you were at the beginning.

But first we must get to the beginning. The story starts in the long, hot summer of 1976, before the thought of becoming a lexicographer had first flittered into my head.

ONE

Serendipity, Perhaps

Nobody thinks dictionaries are written. They are just there, and have been since the dawn of time: on your desk, on your parents' bookshelves, just behind the surface of your computer screen. They are the naughty step to which you are sent when you display even the slightest ignorance about the meaning of a word. But somebody has to write them. Can you imagine a job where you arrive at work each morning and start planning how to define the next word in the alphabet? Back in 1976, that is precisely how Hilary thought I might earn a living. I thought I was more interesting than that, but it just goes to show that I must be a bad judge of character.

Hilary and I had met four years earlier, when a mutual friend realised that we were both heading off to the University of York to study English literature, and thought we might like to meet up in advance. **Serendipity**, perhaps. So we got together in a pub in south London, talked about the course we were soon to embark on, and wondered where the future would take us. I was at a disadvantage, as, even though I had been accepted on the course—and it was a tough, well-respected one—I had omitted to consult the university prospectus in advance, relying entirely upon my teacher's recommendations. Hilary already knew all the course modules, and which ones she was likely to take.

Nevertheless, we kept in occasional touch, and several months later we decided to travel up to university together. Even then, eighteen years old to my nineteen, Hilary was naturally talkative, self-confident, artistic, and aware of the big picture, while I—at least to the casual observer—was self-deprecating to the point of self-effacement. In those days, that was an attitude to which you could aspire. She was very smart, but not depressingly intellectual. If I had a criticism of her—as I came to know her better—it was that she displayed no interest in sport. She didn't regard this as a criticism, but more of a positive endorsement of her lifestyle and outlook. I, on the other hand, had balanced my time at school as equally as possible between work, hockey, and cricket. She was faintly amused that I might think studying on the same English course as her the best way to spend the next three years of my life.

Serendipity is, according to the *Oxford English Dictionary*, "the faculty of making happy and unexpected discoveries by accident." Its history is similarly unexpected. The word was coined in English by the eighteenth-century man of letters and art historian Horace Walpole, son of Prime Minister Robert Walpole, and best known today for his Gothic novel *The Castle of Otranto* (1764). *Serendipity* predates his Gothic foray by at least ten years. In 1754 he wrote a long letter to his friend, Sir Horace Mann, in the course of which he describes a fortuitous discovery he had just made linking the Capello family with the Medicis, remarking, "This discovery, indeed, is almost of that kind which I call *Serendipity*." He goes on to explain that he once read "a silly fairy tale, called 'The Three Princes of Serendip.'" The princes "were always making discoveries, by accidents and sagacity, of things which they were not in quest of." The fairy tale was of Middle Eastern origin, and it had been translated into various European languages from the sixteenth century onwards. The word serendipity itself derives from a former name for Sri Lanka, *Serendip*. Walpole simply added the regular English ending *-ity* to create serendipity. What is surprising (to me, at least) is that the *OED* can't find the adjective *serendipitous* until into the twentieth century. On this point the dictionary sagely but evasively notes of the earlier *serendipity*: "Formerly rare, this word and its derivatives have had wide currency in the 20th century."

At university, I soon gravitated towards the older periods of literature (Old English, Middle English, the Early Modern period), and Hilary naturally listed towards the relevant (the modern novel, feminist approaches to literature, even some critical theory). These were remarkable, idyllic years, set in a time capsule where what came next never really seemed to matter.

After York, we moved to Reading as postgraduates. I was following up my interest in the literature of the past by studying for an MA in medieval studies, and Hilary was maintaining her interest in the relevant themes of the day by working towards a PhD in English literature, focusing on D. H. Lawrence and early twentieth-century feminism. At the same time she was concerned about my future. There was no doubt that I was diligent, hard-working, and curious (intellectually), but at the same time I had not developed any ideas about how I might support myself when the one-year MA reached its natural conclusion.

Work was something that had never been spoken about much when I was growing up at home. My father worked for what used to be described as the "Foreign Office," but which was actually the Government Communications Headquarters in Cheltenham (GCHQ, the British government's "listening post" and Secrets Emporium), and then after that for MI6 in London. I never really knew what his job involved. You weren't supposed to know. He certainly never discussed it, and deflected any innocent questions about what he'd got up to on any particular days you might ask. I can say with near certainty that he wasn't a code-cracking linguist, or if he was, he covered it up pretty well. He used to say curtly that he was a data-processing manager, which, in the days before personal computing, meant very little to me.

Similarly, my English degree meant very little to him, and when I graduated from university, he was fairly confident that I wouldn't land a secure job without his help. To rectify this, he regularly sent me newspaper advertisements for jobs as junior and middle managers at car-manufacturing companies.

Fortunately for other potential employers, one afternoon in 1976 in the common room at the University of Reading, Hilary stumbled upon an advertisement in the *Times Literary Supplement* placed by the Personnel Department of Oxford University Press. The advertisement stated enigmatically that "the Editor of the *Pocket Oxford Dictionary* requires an Assistant to work full time in Oxford, starting not later than 1 July 1976, on the revision now in progress."

Hilary asked whether I'd seen the ad. I hadn't, of course.

Had I ever thought about working with words? I had certainly not considered working as a lexicographer. Most arts students at the time wanted to write the great English novel, but I was normally attracted to details and patterns rather than to the panoramic overview—and that (I assumed) meant that I wouldn't have the necessary credentials to be a novelist. But I had spent time studying language during my MA, the high point of which (for me, at least, and perhaps for the handful of people who have ever read it) involved writing a glossary of and commentary on Scandinavian words borrowed into English in the complicated Middle English poem *Sir Gawain and the Green Knight*. The dissertation had required me to spend afternoons checking meanings and etymologies in the *Oxford English Dictionary*. I was fascinated by the details and how they formed networks: how you could identify which words came from the Scandinavian languages, how they might differ in quality from the bedrock of Germanic vocabulary in English, and how this conflict produced remarkable poetry.

My work on *Gawain* wasn't my first encounter with the *OED*: as an English literature undergraduate I had at one point taken it into my head to investigate all of the words in John Milton's *Paradise Lost* which had to do with the notion of rising and falling (as in the gulf between heaven and hell). The project involved hours of ploughing through the *OED* in the university library in the days when it was only available as a series of large, heavy, and tightly printed volumes. I wanted to see whether Milton's actual uses of any of these words were innovative (i.e., if they were the first-ever examples of the terms that the *OED* had collected). And if so, I wanted to know if that told us anything about Milton's creative use of language.

And so I thought that I had considerable experience of the *OED* by the time Hilary came across that ad. But I'd never contemplated a career as a lexicographer, even though I had spent the previous three months critiquing a historical glossary. For Hilary, coming across the ad was fortuitous; for me, it sealed my fate.

But I was hesitant about applying for the post. I was, after all, only twenty-two and had my whole life ahead of me, and didn't need to tie myself down to what I assumed must be the dreary life of a lexicographer. On the other hand, I was confident that I wouldn't make a good teacher, and there was little else on offer at the time for an occasional medievalist.

"Applicants should have a keen interest in lexicography and usage, and should preferably hold an honours degree (First or Second Class) in English with special qualifications in English Philology."

I don't want to give the impression in any way that I wasn't interested in language at the time, but it's just that I didn't know that I was, or hadn't accepted it. So—as usual—I was circumspect. This approach had always worked before as a defensive mechanism, so why shouldn't it now? In reality, I thought that an advertisement for editors on the Oxford Dictionaries would attract so many bright Oxford graduates that an upstart from somewhere else would not stand a chance. There was something about the "special qualifications in English Philology" that disturbed me. I knew that "philology" was the study of the history of and relationship between words, but "special qualifications"? How on earth might I have set about acquiring these? Were there people who had dedicated their entire university careers to obtaining such qualifications? Wouldn't they be much more likely to land the job than me? Why would I want to set myself up for inevitable disappointment?

The promised salary wasn't large—in fact it was only moderate—but in comparison with a student grant it suggested undreamt-of affluence. Eventually I decided to throw my hat in the ring. I noticed that the salary was "in accordance with qualifications and experience," which was not particularly in my favour (my experience was rock bottom), but I did have qualifications in English literature and (if things went as planned) in medieval studies. Within days I had submitted my application to the Personnel Department, Oxford University Press.

To my great surprise, an imposing letter arrived shortly afterwards inviting me to travel over to Oxford for an afternoon of interviews—in the company of the director of personnel and the mysterious denizens of the dictionary department. Suddenly, the prospect of my future employment became serious. I found that I dreaded being required to discuss my hopes and achievements with the intellectual grandees of Oxford, who—I presumed—had spent centuries raising barriers to exclude all-comers from elsewhere. It wasn't that I lacked confidence, but that I had been schooled to hide my confidence behind a show of indifference.

Although I found the academic cloisters of Oxford intimidating, I didn't necessarily include the Oxford dictionaries in this bracket. They were the public face of Oxford to all of us at school and university in the 1960s and 1970s. We had all used a *Pocket Oxford Dictionary* or one of its larger brothers and sisters as we grew up. They provided advice, but didn't threaten. They showed you knowledge you might aspire to, without needing to cross swords with the scholars themselves. In my slight preparation for my Oxford visit I had read up about the *OED* and now knew something of its history.

It had all begun way back in 1857, with the Philological Society of London. The learned scholars of the society had discussed the state-of-the-art dictionaries available to educated gentlemen of the 1850s, and had found them sadly deficient. The charge was led by Richard Chenevix Trench, later archbishop of Dublin, who delivered two papers to the society decrying the fact that modern English dictionaries missed out on so many important words (old ones, scientific ones), didn't pay enough attention to the history of the language, and generally scored only a B+ in terms of editorial effort.

The society members took up the challenge and began collecting materials for a new English dictionary which would knock all of its predecessors into a tin hat or paper bag. But it needed more than the good wishes and earnest endeavour of a London word society to bring the dictionary to life. The society was fortunate in that it managed to inveigle a Scottish schoolmaster working at Mill Hill School in north London to lead the project. He took some convincing, as also did most publishers when confronted with the project. When publishers were first approached, they mostly ran in the wrong direction—Macmillan, Cambridge, Oxford. But then Oxford wavered: they could see the problem from both sides—the potential scholarly prestige, but also the risks and uncertainties of the project. They stopped running away. To cut a very long story short, by 1879 the society had found someone, in the form of the aforementioned schoolmaster, a tall Lowland Scot named James Murray, willing to accept the daunting task of editing this dictionary, and—in Oxford University Press—the ideal publisher for the worthy work.

The key idea was that the dictionary would be based on the real evidence of the language, and not just on impressions, guesswork, and the contents of previous dictionaries. It would provide a potted biography of English words, providing accurate definitions of their meanings, detailed information on word origins, and—crucially—quotations showing real, documentary examples of any word or meaning from its earliest recorded use right up to the present day (or the point at which the term vanished from the language).

To assemble material for the project, Murray perfected a new methodology. People all around the world were badgered and cajoled—by way of international appeals—to copy out useful snippets of language from literary sources, journals, newspapers, etc., on to index cards, and then to post them to the dictionary. Once sufficient documentation had been collected, by the early 1880s, Murray and his colleagues began to work their way through the alphabet, classifying and defining and ordering information. The dictionary was published in instalments, and the first instalment, all the way from *A* to *Ant*, appeared in 1884, at which point the scholarly public recognised the new dictionary as one of the wonders of the age, and eagerly began to look forward to its completion.

It was accepted that several volumes would be needed to contain this mass of information about the language, and that the project would last perhaps a decade or more. Instalments were sent to subscribers as they were published, and at first good progress was made—it all took longer than expected, but not frighteningly so. By 1903 the editors had reached the letter *R*, and it was hoped that the end was in sight. But they had calculated without the enormous letter *S*, before which even the bravest lexicographer has shivered. The letter *S* saw them into the First World War. The war slowed production to a trickle as staff left for military service. Momentum was hard to regain, and the final sections of the dictionary appeared in slow succession through the 1920s. The final instalment was published in 1928. The remaining editors swept some more words, newcomers to the language, into a one-volume *Supplement* published five years later, in 1933, and then the dictionary department was closed down and the University Press got on with the rest of its life, satisfied that it had captured the language for the foreseeable future.

The foreseeable future was shorter than expected. Fortunately for me—as it turned out—in 1957 the Press decided that it needed to revive and expand the original supplement of modern words, in the interests of keeping the *OED* up to date. They appointed a New Zealander, Robert Burchfield, to shoulder this work as its editor. There was an illogicality about the original plan, which was to take the large, single-volume *Supplement* and replace it with another, larger single-volume *Supplement* that included the important new words and meanings of the middle years of the twentieth century. It was envisaged as an add-on to the main dictionary, done in the same editorial style and with the same editorial objectives, but treating modern accessions to the language from Britain, America, and around the world. But the one-volume *Supplement* of 1933 was already too big to be enlarged within the covers of a single volume, and there were interminable arguments within the University Press in the 1960s as one volume turned into two, which in turn became three, as the number of new words to be added kept growing. By 1972 the *Supplement to the OED*, as it was known, had published only one of its eventual four volumes, and much work would be needed to bring it to completion. At the same time, other, smaller Oxford dictionaries were creating a secondary stream of incessant work for editors. And so it came about that in 1976—in order to speed up editorial production on all fronts—the masters of the University Press were advertising for a new editor to help the next edition of the *Pocket Oxford Dictionary* see the light of day.

There were problems with contemplating work on the *OED*: by the 1970s, any arts student or academic knew that it was something of an antiquated **juggernaut**—the home of old-world scholarship. It was the smaller Oxford dictionaries that people loved and respected most. The University Press had published a *Concise Oxford* in 1911, edited by the Fowler brothers and derived in part from the ongoing *OED*, well before the first edition of the big one had been completed (so how could it truly be concise?). The *Concise Oxford* had been the foundation stone of a generation of spin-off dictionaries, including the *Pocket* (bigger than the average pocket), the *Little* (okay, that was little), and later, when everything had to be offered in miniature, a *Mini*. In the mix, too, was the large, two-volume, and enticingly named *Shorter*, which every self-respecting student had been given by their doting parents on their eighteenth birthday.

> The first records in English of the word *juggernaut* date from the early years of the seventeenth century. It goes without saying that not everybody knew about the word then, but those who were alert to language change did. This was a time when the British Empire was expanding. Britons were travelling and trading far away from London, and they were bringing strange words back from their journeys, many of which eventually found a place in the English language.
>
> Early travellers to the Indian Subcontinent were amazed by the enormous processions they witnessed at Puri in Odhisa, on the Bay of Bengal. An idol of Lord Vishnu was led through the city on an enormous "car" (a ramshackle vehicle maybe four storeys high, according to one account), followed by thousands of adherents. This great crush of people made the procession a potentially dangerous event, at which over the years many people were said to have met their death. Stories like this were lapped up by the travellers and their subsequent readers.
>
> European visitors came to hear of this "Jagannath" festival: they adapted the spelling to the way they heard the word pronounced in India (the *OED* explains our spelling of the first vowel by saying that the short *a* in Hindi is pronounced like the English *u* in *cut, mutt*, etc.). What they may not have known was that "Jagannath" (lord of the world) was a Hindi name for the Lord Vishnu. Travellers used the word as if it applied specifically to the glorious car (or "Juggernaut") on which the idol of Lord Vishnu was carried. By the early nineteenth century we were happily using the word of any large cart—and later lorry or truck—that rumbled along our road systems.

The cabinet of Oxford's lexicographical delights was completed by the *Compact*—the two-volume version of the big dictionary sold *with a magnifying glass!* What a fantastic idea that was. The whole dictionary had originally been published in this format in 1971, with nine pages to a compact page. You wouldn't think it would be popular, but it certainly was—especially amongst people who loved the idea that they were still sharp-eyed enough to read the tiny print *without the need for* the magnifying glass. It had found its way on to the shelves of many English academics in the early 1970s, especially through rock-bottom book offers in the Sunday newspaper supplements. In retrospect, this was old technology used to revivify old text: but there weren't any other options at the time. The little Oxford dictionaries were being updated rapidly, and the bigger ones were being updated at longer intervals. The *Compact* was eventually just provided with a stronger magnifying glass. And sadly, this meant that the big, multi-volume *OED* was not being properly updated at all, but was just being given a big add-on addendum (its "supplement"), because it was too much of a task to update it properly all the way from *A* to *Z*.

My interview at the dictionary was in June, at the beginning of the long hot summer of 1976, and Hilary and I took the train up from the earnest red brick of Reading to the medieval grandeur of Oxford to see if I could be settled into steady employment and the salary-earning classes. We arrived at the railway station and made our way to the Oxford University Press offices in Walton Street—to what I later came to regard as the **epicentre** of dictionary-making in the Western world. From here I was on my own. Hilary decided to look around the local shops, confidently but naively expecting me to reappear—elated or dejected—about thirty minutes later.

You and I would think *epicentre* was a good classical word, maybe arising in English around 1660, with the birth of the new, empirical sciences and the Renaissance affection for ancient words. But it's not; we know it entered into the English language considerably later than that (1880). Scientists typically reach for classical words—or just broken twigs of classical words—when creating a new term, in a tradition of pan-European scientific enquiry that reaches up to the present day. The immediate predecessor of *epicentre* in English was *epicentrum* (1874), used in the same sense ("the point above the centre," especially in seismology). Maybe *epicentrum* looks barbaric to us, but that's the word the German scientist Karl von Seebach invented in 1873, in German but from Greek elements, for his new word in the new science of seismology (itself from Greek elements: the study of earthquakes). We just made the new word look English, by changing *epicentrum* to *epicentre*. Try not to make assumptions about the origin and usage of words; there may be more of a story to it, especially when it is in the hands of white-coated scientists.

The front of the Oxford University Press was imposing, especially to someone whose only experience of Oxford until then derived from regular trips over the county border from where I lived in Gloucestershire, as part of a school sports team. The massive black wrought-iron gates set between thick stone columns were designed to exclude and yet—by offering a passing glimpse on to a college-style lawn and quadrangle, with a towering copper beech tree leaning over an idle pond—to incite wonder and fascination. The building itself looked classically eighteenth century, as was intended when it was built in the early nineteenth century to house under one collective roof the University Press's editorial staff and print workers, who were previously scattered elsewhere in Oxford. I was, needless to say, suitably impressed.

The University Press porter let me into the grand quadrangle, or "quad." Before I had a chance to reach the sumptuous lawn, I was directed off to one side—you didn't get to experience the full splendour of the place unless you deserved it—where I found the Personnel Department and my recent correspondent, the Colonel.

The Colonel was the human face of the Personnel Department at OUP in those days: he was a delightful military chap—"(ret'd)" of course—and something of a leftover from the days when old soldiers ruled Personnel. He was almost certainly modelled closely on the character actor Wilfrid Hyde-White, Colonel Pickering of *My Fair Lady*: quite short, dapper, balding, chatty, and charmingly military in tenor. We shook hands, and then he sank into his seat behind a substantial desk while I was directed towards an easy chair designed principally to make you feel that you weren't the most important person in the room. We talked about the magnificent history of the University Press, as seen through the eyes of the Personnel Department, and we wondered jointly how easy I might find it moving from Reading to Oxford, should I be fortunate enough to be offered the opportunity. The distance between the two places is about twenty-five miles, but I discovered much later that there were people in Oxford who thought civilisation ended just a few hundred feet outside the old city walls, where the barbarian hordes were dug in for the foreseeable future. Others are said to believe that "the sun rises over Wadham [College] and sets over Worcester." Worcester College, that is: there wouldn't be much point in referring to the City of Worcester here.

Once we had exhausted all possible areas of conversation, he took me on a little walk round to the dictionary department. In those days most of the University Press operated out of a single large block of buildings tucked away amongst the terraces of Jericho—an area of Oxford by the canal, made famous as Beersheba in *Jude the Obscure*. The dictionary occupied two small terraced houses, No. 40 and No. 41 Walton Crescent, on the edge of the main site. Its offices were very close to the centre of the University Press's publishing control rooms, and so the Colonel and I did not have far to walk. I was taken through the corridor-snaking interior of the University Press and **debouched** at No. 40 Walton Crescent.

> According to its entry in the *OED*, the verb *to debouch* entered English in the mid-eighteenth century from French. It's not a particularly common word these days, but this again illustrates how we pluck out and make use of words from different layers of the contemporary language—archaic, historical, geographically distant,

upper-class, or whatever. French words had been storming into English since at least the days of the Norman Conquest in 1066, but *debouch* apparently had seen no need to seek asylum here until quite late in the day, around the year 1740. It derives directly from the French word *déboucher*, "to unblock, uncork—let run out freely." It's quite unrelated to the word *debauch* (which originally meant "to lead from the straight and narrow, or from the path of virtue"), also borrowed from French, but several centuries earlier. A river can debouch into the sea, after having been pent up by its banks; a military force can debouch into open country after marching under cover of a forest; I was debouched unceremoniously by my guide in front of the dictionary department.

No. 40 Walton Crescent was the nerve centre of the *OED* in those days. The Colonel chattered away as he led me up to a room on the first floor, where he introduced me to the departmental secretary, and then left me to await my interview with the *OED*'s chief. I was told that my waiting room was the departmental library. There was a central table around which editors would sit while consulting the weighty books arrayed on shelves throughout the room; and right in the centre of the table was a book-rest displaying the latest texts that had been voraciously consumed (it was carefully explained to me by my guide) by the dictionary's stable of "readers"—that is, the people who volunteered to make their way steadily through countless works of literature, hunting down words and expressions which they wrote out on index cards and sent to Oxford for possible inclusion in the dictionary. The *Collected Letters* of George Bernard Shaw had made its appearance there that week, along with several other books and magazines whose titles I forget.

The possibility of a group of *OED* readers scattered around the world, whose sole objective in life was to collect extracts from books such as Shaw's *Letters*, exclusively for the files of the dictionary, was an entrancing prospect. I envisaged these troops of readers being asked to read the latest prize-winning novels, or a run of racy tabloid newspapers, just looking out for new words. Who were these people? How did they land a job like that? Did anyone ever meet them? But this was just something to mull over. I didn't need to think out all the implications just yet.

Though I did not realise it at the time, I was at that very moment the object of all-consuming attention to numerous dictionary editors, keen to spot what their potential new colleague might look like. I affected nonchalance as I investigated the contents of the library, but I was left to await my fate.

I was nervous about the interview—there were so many questions I could be asked to which I would not want to commit an answer. I think I'm quite a slow learner. At least I don't like to commit myself until I know what I'm talking about. Given time I can usually work things out, but not necessarily right away. Hilary would have had no problem in the same situation, because even if she did not know how to respond correctly to any particular question, she would have answered at length and convincingly on what was the nearest thing she knew a bit about. I would just dry up, not wanting to commit myself and be wrong. I'm fine after a while—after I've had a chance to absorb things. But for those first crucial ten seconds of an interview I wouldn't put my money on me.

My anxious wait was soon at an end as a door across the landing opened and an elderly, academic-looking gentleman peeked out and beckoned me into his office. This was Robert Burchfield, the chief editor of the *Oxford English Dictionary*. I tried to remember what little I knew about him from my cursory pre-interview research: (*a*) he had been appointed back in 1957, and (*b*) his job was to produce a scholarly addendum or supplement to the big dictionary.

I knew that this plan for producing one long single-volume supplement had soon crashed. There was just far too much new twentieth-century language that needed to be crammed into the dictionary. Had no one ever heard of the rise of the film and music business, the

Depression, the Second World War, radar, the mini-skirt, psychedelia, and everything else that had acted as a crucible for the appearance of new words throughout the twentieth century? By now it had been generally accepted that the *Supplement* would eventually fill four volumes. Volume One had already been published (1972), and Volume Two was all set up in type, bound, and ready to be released almost as soon as my interview was over.

As I edged uncertainly into the editor's lair, I think I imagined I'd find him lying languidly on a chaise longue with a pipe in one hand and an ancient Sumerian text in the other, mulling desultorily over a definition. But my romantic preconceptions were quickly quashed. The chief editor had a small, long office demonstrating a determined absence of design and decoration. Clearly location was its best quality: easy access to the books, the departmental secretary, and the editorial staff. There wasn't room for a chaise longue in there. There *was* room, however, for an armchair, in which the editor was reclining, doubtless ready to roast me with impossible questions about the English language. I regarded myself as being reasonably well-informed about language and the dictionary, but in this extreme, hot-house context I was concerned that the level of my knowledge was likely to prove quite unserviceable.

At the time, I had only a hazy conception of the work of a "lexicographer." On the one hand, I had read about the physically imposing, socially assertive, and convivial wordmonger Dr Samuel Johnson, whose mould-breaking dictionary was published in 1755, and on the other hand I knew a very small amount about the painstakingly sinewy Scottish erudition of the *OED*'s founder editor, Sir James Murray, which I had gained from reading up on the subject for my interview. The current chief editor, Bob Burchfield, matched neither Johnson's nor Murray's stereotype. At this stage of his career he was just over fifty, with an approachably kind smile and full but greying hair; he was very amiable but had a quietly insistent and penetrating voice which seemed to me excessively prissy—as if he were weighing every word and didn't want to waste time with redundant ones. There was a beaky, pecky air to him—the air of a scholar searching austerely for wheat amongst chaff. He'd say something and wait for a response, rather than giving you much of a lead as to what was expected of you. He wasn't a proponent of pullovers or open-necked shirts. There was a properness about him that stemmed from years of Oxford life, rather different from the casual informality I'd been used to at York.

I chose a seat in his office—slightly better than the one I'd occupied in the Personnel Department, but, truth to tell, the only one available that he wasn't already sitting on—and said my hellos. I had had little experience of discussing the time of day with Oxford academics, but I knew I was ready to chat about medieval Latin poetry or St Anselm, should that prove to be absolutely necessary.

As luck would have it, there was no need for St Anselm, John of Salisbury, Walter Map, the Arch-Poet, or any other old friends from my recent medieval studies to make an appearance. In fact, after the statutory preliminaries (name, rank, and serial number), we settled down to a quarter of an hour in which he told me all about the dictionary, himself, and life in Oxford generally. He made it sound like a fairy-tale town, and despite his (to me) unnatural precision in all things, he was a charming host. He had himself come over to Oxford on a Rhodes Scholarship following his university studies in New Zealand, and he had lapped up Oxford and its close-knit scholarly community. He had never returned to New Zealand to live, but had plunged himself into Oxford academic life. In those days he was best known for his exacting work on a difficult medieval text called the *Ormulum*, written by a monk called Orm. I, in my turn, dredged up the name of the long-dead editor of a medieval Swedish dictionary I had encountered along the shelves of the university library at York— Knut Fredrik Soderwall—and we chatted about him for a while. It couldn't have been long, as the amount of information I possessed about Soderwall extended just beyond his name and was clearly less comprehensive than that of the chief editor, who displayed an alarmingly sharp overall appreciation of Swedish medieval studies.

As the interview with the chief editor progressed, we suddenly encountered a topic of mutual interest. For the previous few months, I'd been working day and night on my MA dissertation, which, by the sort of chance that changes your life, had a crucial link with the *OED*.

When I was studying for my first degree, and had been struggling manfully through the poetry and prose of our forefathers and mothers, it had occurred to me that the earliest period of English, Old English, might be more exciting if I could understand the more colourful (and linguistically related) Icelandic sagas: tales of families torn apart, countries ravaged, and helmets adorned with pointy horns (though it turned out that the pointy horns were a later invention). Most surviving Old English is historical or ecclesiastical, not creative and narrative, and therefore on the surface less appealing.

The problem with this approach (as I had immediately appreciated) was that the Icelandic sagas were not written in Old English, but in medieval Icelandic. And by dint of switching classes, I had (surprisingly) mastered enough of this language to read the sagas, or at least some of them—which led to my master's work analysing the medieval Icelandic words which had filtered through into *Sir Gawain and the Green Knight*.

This led to my tenuous link with the *OED*: J. R. R. Tolkien. It happened that a modern edition of *Gawain* had been edited by Tolkien—at the time a young professor at the University of Leeds, and before that an assistant on the *OED*—in his academic guise as a medievalist rather than as a Hobbit-weaver.

I explained to the chief editor that I had scoured the glossary that Tolkien and others had put together at the end of his edition, looking for the words that Tolkien had thought were of Icelandic origin. I had made a list of these words, proceeded to subject each of them to my own razor-sharp intellect, and usually came up with exactly the same conclusion as Tolkien (especially if I'd peeked to see what he had said first). From time to time my opinion differed from his—or my professor's did—and I accordingly wrote a little note to put the academic world back on its axis. (Several years later, after I'd started to work on the *OED*, a very few of these learned interventions would be published in the medieval periodical *Medium Ævum*, to my personal joy and to the combined and everlasting silence of the academic community, who were obviously off at a conference somewhere else when the issue was published.)

When I mentioned Tolkien, I noticed a flicker of additional interest on the brow of the chief editor. Little was I to know, given the only modest amount of preparation I had done, that the chief editor and J. R. R. Tolkien had been well acquainted with each other in Oxford, and indeed that the chief editor had been Tolkien's student and then colleague in the English faculty for many years.

Coincidence piled on top of coincidence. Although Tolkien had died three years earlier, he was clearly much in the mind of the chief editor at the time of my interview, and he started speaking about his old friend. As chance would have it, it appeared, at this very moment the entry for "hobbit" was about to make its appearance in the soon-to-be released second volume of the *Supplement to the OED* (containing words starting with the letters *H* to *N*)—the imminent publication of which I had been, until recently, so blissfully unaware. A hobbit, as any reader of Tolkien's fantasy writings will know, is "one of an imaginary people, a small variety of the human race, that gave themselves this name (meaning 'hole-dweller') but were called by others *halflings*, since they were half the height of normal men" (*OED*). The chief editor was well aware that this was one of the most publicity-worthy items in the forthcoming supplementary volume. It was also a popular favourite, as it lacked the out-and-out naughtiness of the four-letter taboo words that had been crammed unceremoniously into the early letters of the alphabet, and had been published, to academics' delight and purists' despair, in the first volume of the *Supplement* (*A–G*).

The *OED*, the chief editor told me, had asked Tolkien to advise on the draft definition and etymology of *hobbit*. The editor reached into his cabinet and took out a dusty file entitled "Men of Letters." This was the thin cache, he explained, into which he placed a copy of any letter to the *OED* from anyone with a claim to literary merit. He pulled out a piece of paper, clearly one of his most prized. It was Tolkien's response to a polite enquiry from him several years earlier. On closer inspection it transpired that Tolkien did not have much to add to the *OED*'s effort to define the word *hobbit*, but that he said so beautifully over several pages, in true Oxford style.

With this passing flicker of interest we arrived at a critical moment in the interview, marked by a slight and quite clearly prearranged knock at the door. In strode John Sykes, the tall, thin embodiment of scientific—as opposed to historical—lexicography, the editor of the *Concise Oxford Dictionary*. He was the polar opposite to the gentleman with whom I had been happily conversing for the previous half hour: sparing of words to the point of disappearance, but with sharp, narrow eyes which focused you in their penetrating and relentless stare. I felt unravelled by his attention. At this point I realised that it was *this* man, the editor of the *Concise*, who would have the final say on every applicant for the post on his tributary dictionary, the *Pocket Oxford*.

The downward trajectory to the interview that followed his appearance was all my fault. I'd never had much time for people who didn't show any interest in me, and the editor of the *Concise* was just such a man. A colossus in his field, able to complete *The Times* crossword (as I later discovered) in less time than it took me to open the newspaper, he nevertheless regarded medieval poetry in general as a whimsical and illogical flight of fancy. He was a scientist through and through, and I had been in the wrong queue on the day they handed out scientific brains. He enthused (in very few words) on areas of the language that seemed to me dry, insipid, flat, and irrelevant (how many pages his new edition could have; ideas about making definitions even more compact and crossword-like cryptic); and I'm sure that the same feelings about me flitted through his brain. I was interested in the history of English (or so I thought), and he was interested in concise definition as an art form in itself.

Somehow I had survived those first ten seconds with the amiable chief editor, but his deputy saw through me immediately—or, as I like to remember, he formed the wrong and worst opinion of me from the moment he walked through the door. Furthermore, I suspect that he didn't like playing second fiddle to the chief editor in an interview for a post reporting to him.

My protector, the chief editor, sat on one side as I was subjected to a barrage of silence interspersed by short, piercing, staccato enquiries. How would I characterise the *Pocket Oxford Dictionary* in comparison with the *Concise*? Smaller, I ventured? Silence. What audience did I think the *Pocket* was designed to reach? Younger, I guessed? Silence, followed by more silence. How would I differentiate between *continuous* and *continual*? A very fair question this time, but not one I had ever contemplated before. Silence and embarrassed shuffling on all sides. Had I been aware that the Fowler brothers (founder editors of the *Concise*) had published their dictionary well before its supposed source, the full *OED*, was finished? Yes, that one I definitely knew the answer to. Was I in the least interested in working with him? Of course he didn't actually ask that.

As the minutes passed I slowly realised that the *Pocket* had to be even more concise than the *Concise*. But where was the fun in that? Words have meanings, and even then I had a suspicion that the meanings interlocked or overlapped or at least impinged on each other; that their etymologies took you down curious paths, through societies you could only mistily imagine, back to cultures that had ceased to exist many years before you were even thought of. The *Pocket Oxford* wasn't, I realised, a project on which I wanted to work: it didn't involve the same luxuriant historical spread as the big, multi-volumed *OED*. The editor of the *Concise* and I held diametrically opposed views on what made language interesting. The editor of the *Concise* and I were on the reverse of a collision course, and we were likely to leave the observable atmosphere through opposite doors.

That didn't matter to him. He was the man in post. I was the junior upstart with no hope of pulling this conversation back on track. After a while it was clear that my forty-five minutes were up. In fact, they had been up about an hour and a quarter earlier. My interview had extended to around two hours, owing to the tendency of good-cop Chief Editor No. 1 to talk at length about language and life, from which I profited immeasurably, mainly by not having to speak and therefore say anything that would have precluded me from success in my application. My nemesis, bad-cop Editor No. 2, had continued to say little, but he let his withering eyes settle on me for, say, half an hour. There came a tide in the affairs of the interview when I knew the game was up, and I was ushered back out of the office, leaving both editors to discuss my prospective candidacy.

As I left the dictionary offices after my interview I was aware that I had encountered a piece of "old Oxford," the Oxford of Tolkien, Lewis Carroll, Benjamin Jowett, and C. S. Lewis. This was the Oxford of careful scholarship—often creative, but hard for an outsider to penetrate and understand. It was an environment to which you had to earn entry, and one which showed no signs to me of wanting to relax its powers. The *OED* had been moulded inside this old Oxford environment, and yet it reached outside it, out to the real language and the real world that everyone knew. It would be far too early in my involvement with the dictionary for me to have formulated any plans, but what if the dictionary, instead of sliding into the past, could instead redirect itself towards the future? Could there be a "new Oxford" in which this might happen, or would the old Oxford just engulf you if you tried?

I left the dictionary house under no misapprehensions that I might have sneaked the job. I sauntered casually and somewhat sadly up the road to meet Hilary, who was exhausted by hours of window-shopping, and we took the train back to Reading and our quiet life. A few days later I heard from the Colonel that unfortunately I would not be offered the post.

TWO

Lexicography 101

For a few weeks after receiving OUP's letter of rejection, I carried on with my dissertation and left those around me to contemplate how I might best be employed in the years to come. I didn't think badly of OUP and the dictionary for their decision. I was convinced that there were lots of potential candidates who were more egg-headed and therefore more suitable than I was. So that was that—time to look around quietly to see if anyone else out there wanted my services. I buried myself deeper and deeper into my dissertation and applied optimistically for one or two research grants. I'm naturally optimistic: something would turn up. Hilary didn't go into overdrive either; I think secretly she considered that she'd found me the perfect job, and that if I'd messed up, then that was my problem.

I was shaken out of my contemplative complacency a month or so later, when a further letter from Oxford University Press arrived unannounced in my letterbox. This one was altogether sunnier than the last. It informed me in the usual scholarly code that another job had arisen out of the ashes of Job No. 1 (which they were by now almost devastated that I had not been offered), and would I be interested in accepting this alternative post? The position involved working on the full *Supplement to the Oxford English Dictionary* instead of just the little *Pocket*. To me, this felt like a remarkable challenge: one that offered the chance to explore the language—how it had changed and how it might change in the future—rather than one which boiled this information down (as I loftily thought) into a reduced-size and derivative dictionary.

The new job would become available later in the summer of 1976. I'd discover in due course that this opening had arisen because one of the spirited young editors on the dictionary had taken the unlikely step of leaving the learned ranks of the *OED* and setting sail for another dictionary job in America. When I met him several years later, he'd left the world of dictionaries and was teaching Middle English **101** to EngLit students.

Some people wonder what numbers are doing in a dictionary, and indeed who can say? But don't overthink. There it is in the *OED*—an entry for "101," defined along the lines of "a postmodifying adjective designating an introductory course at American colleges and universities in the subject specified." The number 101 is used with a specific meaning in regular English sentences, so there is no reason to exclude it from the dictionary. There are two questions that are important to ask about *101*, but it's the third that's actually fascinating.

Firstly, when were the first 101 courses set up? The answer, according to the *OED*, is in 1929, in Buffalo, New York. In that year, the New York educators devised a course called General Science 101, which, as far as we know, is the starting point for the modern expression. When they put their minds to dreaming up another scientific course, they rapidly decided that it was to be called General Science 102, but that didn't take off.

Secondly, why the number 101 rather than 1 or 001? We at Oxford don't seem to know the answer to that, but maybe someone can tell us. (Perhaps it's like American hotel rooms, which all start with a

1 for the ground floor, even though everyone knows this should be called level zero.)

Thirdly, and most interestingly, why do we pronounce "101" the way we do? Why—when we pronounce numbers—do we pronounce the "nought" or "zero" as if it were the letter O? One-oh-one; one-zero-one. That's a big question, but maybe a step too far for the historical lexicographer. My guess is that there are several factors. Firstly, "Oh" is easier to say at speed than "one" (which starts with a phonetically challenging "w" sound). Secondly, I would not be at all surprised to find that it was popularised by "double-oh seven," James Bond, and then fed back into single occurrences of "oh." But lexicographers don't guess. The OED simply alerts any person who wishes to say "101" out loud that they must pronounce the zero as if it were "Oh."

Once this new letter had arrived from Oxford University Press, Hilary and I had to decide whether to pack up our things lock, stock, and barrel and relocate almost immediately to Oxford. We talked about it. Hilary was happy to shift her research to Oxford, with instant access to the gargantuan holdings of the Bodleian Library, so she needed little convincing. I still toyed with the possibility of further medieval research, but the idea of becoming involved in a major international language project based in Oxford was starting to sink its teeth into me. I'd always liked approaching things from odd angles: maybe dictionary work would be an intriguing outlet for my interest in language, literature, and historical research. Also, there were no other job offers available on our kitchen table that day. So, arguments in favour: more or less everything. Arguments against: we would have to move.

Soon another letter was on its way back to OUP informing the powers that be that, even before I had my MA in medieval studies tucked under my belt, I would be "delighted" to launch myself on the sea of historical lexicography.

Once we'd made the decision, we needed a base in Oxford: preferably somewhere near the University Press but also within striking distance of the Bodleian Library, for Hilary's thesis. As luck, or diligence, would have it, she was passing a newsagent's near the University Press one day when she spotted a card in the window advertising accommodation in a shared house nearby. I didn't have the necessary level of clearance at home to make this sort of decision myself, but within days we were moving into rooms in the smallest house in one of the smallest streets ready to begin our life in Oxford.

Victor Street consisted of a series of terraced houses that started off reasonably large at each end of the street and became gradually smaller until they reached our house. Our front door opened on to a corridor on the left-hand side of the house. There is no simple way to describe how you found the stairs to the first floor. And then once you did get up the stairs, there wasn't all that much to write home about. Mind you, this was not an uncommon set-up in small terraced houses. Our succession of house-sharers—who occupied (serially) the downstairs front room of the house—used the communal stairway for their occasional forays into the bathroom. I can't remember speaking with any of them, except for a summer visitor from America who informed me that it was a well-known fact that coffee cooled faster if milk had not been added, a piece of advice by which I was momentarily tempted to live for the rest of my life.

Almost before I knew it, it was time to venture into my first day at the *OED*. So in early August 1976, I arrived back at the dictionary offices in Walton Crescent to present myself for work. I climbed tentatively up the stone steps of No. 40 and then further up, to the first floor, to present myself to my new friend, the chief editor, in the heart of the dictionary's sanctum.

He was too busy to see me this time, and I could see his point. It was doubtless going to take several years to get me up to editorial operating speed, and why should he involve himself in that when there were plenty of other experienced editors to act as buffers to shield him from me? So instead I was met once again by the departmental secretary, both alphabetically and actually named Beta, and escorted to my handler.

Needless to say, I had no idea what to expect from my first day on the job. This was, after all, my first job, and my application for a job with the Oxford dictionaries had been my first-ever job application. The dictionary offices felt like a university department, with a focus on research but without the responsibility for students. I was led into a long room at the rear of the first floor of Dictionary Terrace and introduced to Lesley Brown, who was—I soon discovered—as sharp as an icicle when it came to editing the dictionary. She was my handler, though they preferred the word "trainer." As a senior editor she was ranked considerably higher than me, and I came to look up to her as a dog looks up to its master. She'd only been at the dictionary for a few years, but had risen into the lexicographical stratosphere. Give her a handful of sentences containing examples of a word, and she would craft you a fully-fledged dictionary entry in the time it takes to make a pot of tea.

After the preliminaries, I was shown to my office. The nearest thing I had previously experienced to an office was a carrel in a university library. But within minutes of arriving, I was marched downstairs and taken into a real, live room where I could stack my pencils and arrange my family photographs, just like I'd seen on American cop shows.

I could not help but notice that the office was already occupied by two editorial ladies scribbling furiously on pieces of card. (This was well before computer screens invaded the dictionary offices.) *Good morning. Good morning. This is John. This is Edith. Here's Deborah.* Lovely old names. The dictionary maintained a roughly fifty-fifty male-to-female staff ratio (to his credit, the chief editor promoted all sorts equally), but based on my experience up to then, it seemed that most of the offices were occupied by women. In this case, they both had desks parked nonchalantly at angles to the wall; the sunlight played across them as the day advanced. I was shown a desk facing the wall. This was where I would start my long **apprenticeship**.

> *Apprentice* wasn't one of the old Germanic words which formed the original bedrock of English, after the Angles and Saxons arrived in Britain in the sixth century or so AD. It came along years later, from French, after the Norman Conquest. In fact, *apprentice* is first re- corded in English in the Middle Ages, in the fourteenth century (the *OED* offers William Langland's *Piers Plowman* as the first reference). The word derives ultimately from Latin's *apprehendere*, "to learn."
>
> Words typically arise at a particular time for a particular reason, and *apprentice* is no exception. Back in the Middle Ages, when an ap- prentice signed up with a trade master, he or his minders signed a legal agreement—which was likely to have been drawn up in French—establishing the terms of the training. The French language (and particularly that version spoken in England, Anglo-French) was the language of law in fourteenth-century England, so inevitably a new word in this subject area would come from Anglo-French.

I had assumed that, on my first day, my handler would give me a relatively easy word to work on. That would seem fair. I'd heard that the department was at the time engaged on a thorough review of the letter Q. There was little chance of overstraining myself here, I thought to myself. Perhaps it was a good time to sneak into the department without being noticed, and gain some experience by editing up some quiet, out-of-the-way words in the byways of language. I thought maybe *quack* (you can't go far wrong defining that, surely), or *quadren- nial* ("once every four years": surely no problems there for me), or maybe *Quakeress*, if such a word existed.

But no, things didn't work like that. There was a training scheme of sorts, and it meant not rolling up your sleeves and tackling real editing until you'd been around the track with all sorts of ancillary tasks de- signed to ensure that you were passingly confident with alphabetical order, the parts of speech, and the general content and shape of the *OED*. In retrospect that sounds sensible, but at the time I struggled to see the logic. I imagined that I already had majestic command of the parts of speech and the job each one performed; in truth, I was doubtless as casual about these as some of the young editors I've encountered since, who are initially equally foxed by participial adjectives, and absolute uses of nouns, and *quasi*-adverbs, and all the rest of the **paraphernalia** of slightly off-centre and old-fashioned grammatical categories that the original editors of the *OED* were happy to work with. Because, don't forget, we weren't writing a dictionary from scratch, we were labouring on a supplement, or long addendum. We were taking as read the venerable words written by Sir James Murray and his fellow editors back in the late nineteenth and early twentieth centuries and adding the new words and senses of recent days.

I have a predilection for words that entered English in the seventeenth century. Well, we all have our preferences. *Paraphernalia* looks Latin, but like no Latin you are likely to have encountered. Not all words from Latin date from the days of the Roman Empire; many come from later versions of the language—religious Latin, scientific Latin, and by definition the languages into which Latin developed in the first millennium AD (for example, Italian, French, and Spanish—known nowadays as Romance languages not because of their suitability as the language of love, but because of their derivation from the language of Rome). *Paraphernalia* entered legal English, according to the *OED*, around 1650, directly from the legal Latin of the contemporary courtroom, though the word elements hark back to Greek. *Para-* means "besides" or "alongside"; *-phernalia* derives from the Greek word for a dowry. To the seventeenth-century lawyer, *paraphernalia* were those articles of a woman's personal property (typically clothing and ornaments) which didn't—like everything else—pass by law into her husband's possession on marriage. By the eighteenth century we were using the term in a wider context—of any of the trappings or accoutrements belonging to a person. The lexicographers amongst you will be interested to hear that it could take either a singular or a plural verb ("paraphernalia is" or "paraphernalia are"). Its onwards trajectory does not stop there. By the 1920s we associated the word with the apparatus of drug-taking, and then—more recently—in South-East Asia and the Philippines, it is used in the plural (*paraphernalias*) to mean any of the bits and pieces associated with any activity.

To my disappointment, instead of setting me loose on the dictionary, my handler introduced me to the simpler aspects of the job. Instead of writing (which I thought I'd been recruited for), I was given some reading (which I thought I'd already spent years perfecting at university). And my chosen reading—that's "chosen" by someone else, not chosen by me—was not even written by an English-language author. I immediately gained the sympathy of the two delightful women with whom I had the honour of sharing my first office when I was presented with the task of reading a translation of *Film Language*, an esoteric French text on the semiotics of film by Monsieur Christian Metz. Neither of my new friends could imagine curling up with such a dry text for a quiet bedtime read. What I should have realised was that the dictionary's editor and his senior team had selected this modernist text as part of the project to modernise the dictionary. The dictionary was starting to move with the times, even though its Victorian and Edwardian scholarship harked back to earlier ages.

Unsurprisingly, I had not previously read anything by Metz. According to the jacket copy, he was something of an expert in his field, but as the semiotics of film wasn't a field into which I had ever stepped, that didn't really help. Fortunately the book had been translated from French into English before I was asked to read it.

The purpose of the read, I was informed, was to find words, meanings, and expressions that might prove useful to the *OED*, and then to write them out on index cards called, I'd soon learn, "slips." These cards would be filed in the dictionary's word dungeons, awaiting that future day when an editor needed them to help compile an entry. The task wouldn't improve my knowledge of the semiotics of film: I wasn't expected to retain any information after the book was read. English obtains many *termes cinématographiques* from French, so reading a translated French text was adjudged an excellent way of catching them at the moment they passed into English.

There are people who argue that extracting example sentences from books is a poor way to collect information about words. They contend that when people are set to read a book for significant words, all they find are significant words (and they miss a lot of those, too), and so the result is skewed data: too much of what you don't need—words towards the rarer end of the spectrum—and not enough of what you do—everyday but easily missable nuances of language. But at the time, (*a*) no one could really prove that the method was problematic, and (*b*) the Victorian editors had worked their fingers to the bone finding examples of everyday words to conceal the problem.

So I continued with the task I had been set. I had my book, my slips, my ballpoint pen, and my desk facing the wall. The multiple volumes of the First Edition of the *OED* (1933 reprint) were ranged on the shelves in front of me. I needed to consult those fairly often, to check whether a word I'd found in my semiotically charged text was already suitably covered in the dictionary. There was no point in inundating the card files with slips containing words already perfectly well evidenced.

It took me a long time to reach the end of *Film Language*, for reasons that will be obvious to many people. I excerpted about two hundred slips from the book over the following three weeks, which I'd later learn is about average for a medium-sized academic text.

More than forty years on, you can miraculously still find evidence of my reading of Christian Metz's *Film Language* in the *OED*. The dictionary documents everything, so when it defines a word, it presents a selection of example sentences containing the word from its card files (such as the ones from Metz's book that I had culled). You will see a sentence from *Film Language*—collected by me—illustrating the entry for *diegesis*, meaning "the narrative presented by a cinematographic film or literary work," and also another one transcribed by me illustrating *non-chronological*. There's nothing particularly filmic about the latter word; it's just a (nineteenth-century) alternative for the older (eighteenth-century) *unchronological*. Metz's example was just available as a useful filler (doubtless not a role to which Metz would have aspired)—it wasn't presented as the earliest example ever found of the term in English. In fact, in the OED Online today there are fifteen quotations from Metz's *Film Language*, and you can bet your bottom dollar that they all came from my pen.

The process of reading Christian Metz proved to me one central plank of the *OED*'s philosophy: that anyone who takes the time to read a text carefully can uncover information that is useful to the dictionary. It's just that, normally, people keep this information to themselves, or don't even bother to check whether they have made a discovery. You need to separate the collection of information from its analysis: not everyone can manage the second activity, but anyone can contribute to the information-gathering. That was one of the great discoveries that the dictionary made when it was starting up, back in the 1860s and 1870s. So much new information about the language had to be collected that the early editors asked the reading public to help by noting down interesting words and usages they encountered in their reading, just as I had done when reading Metz. And it turned out that many people in those days had some leisure time and wanted to help. Right at the beginning, the *OED* discovered a hidden army of potential contributors.

You will want to hear about my biggest Metzian successes: the words I found and carefully transcribed on to index cards which are currently printed as the first-ever known use of the terms in the English language. There are two of them: *prefilmic* and *screening room*. When I encountered these terms in *Film Language*, I didn't know they were first usages. There were no entries in the dictionary back then for either *prefilmic* or *screening room*, so as a reader I was working blind. Word-collection relies almost exclusively on the intuition and experience of the reader. You often just card a word in the hope that it will prove to be useful, but you aren't always right. It's not an exact science, and you have to accept a certain amount of redundant data in the file. Some people develop the right historical radar and others don't.

But since we can research more efficiently these days—thanks to computers and enormous online historical databases—it may be worth checking whether either of those celebrated first uses would pass muster today. Let's look at *prefilmic* first. A single search on Google Books rapidly brings up an example from 1967 (Sheldon Renan's *Introduction to the American Underground Film*). So in the *OED*'s next pass-through, my brilliant first use will disappear. And what about *screening room*? That seems an odd English compound to be first encountered in a translation of a French text on semiotics. A moment's search on the online historical databases, and we're back to 1936 and the American magazine *Popular Mechanics*: "In the quiet of the screening room our little band of silent adventurers watched the film that had been automatically ground off by Jim's motor-driven cameras." *Popular Mechanics* was clearly not a source combed by the *OED*'s cerebral editors.

So my two little first dates are destined for the scrapheap of history. They twinkled for a few years before new ways of researching caused them to be brushed aside.

By this simple act of reading a book for the dictionary, I was joining a group of thousands of people who, over the previous hundred years or so, had contributed in smaller or larger ways to the dictionary's word-store. These crowdsourcing "readers" have never been predominantly academics—they were typically just ordinary people who wanted to share with Oxford in the exploration of the English language. Old ledgers of these readers still exist: their names are mostly forgotten nowadays, but there you find reverend gentlemen and their wives, well-educated people concerned that knowledge of the language should be respected and treasured; members of London clubs with moments to spare before dinner or billiards; elderly spinsters from the Victorian leisured classes with afternoons stretching ahead of them; and sometimes literary figures—the novelist Charlotte Yonge, extremely popular in her day, would send the results of her reading to the editors in Oxford.

Many of these readers had been attracted by short "Appeals Lists" of words "wanted" for the dictionary: lists of common and abstruse terms for which earlier, better, later, explanatory, or defining examples from printed texts or manuscripts were badly needed before the dictionary could make proper progress. These lists were drawn up by the dictionary's editors and distributed by OUP throughout the world by means of the Press's network of booksellers and other contacts. They were also published in OUP's own in-house magazine, *The Periodical*, from where they might find their way into the national papers. Many readers lived in Britain, but concerted efforts were made to involve American readers as well as others from around the English-speaking world. The Philological Society had, very early in the life of the dictionary, invited American politician and man of letters George Perkins Marsh to drum up support across the Atlantic. He was not entirely successful, but later efforts produced a steady influx of American English material, and as the dictionary grew in size and acclaim, more and more readers became attracted to the work.

"Reading" for the dictionary was all very well, and it helped to gather together a mass of material that might be useful in future years to the dictionary's editors, but it didn't do any good at all for my own ability to read. The process of reading text word by word, and then weighing up whether each word was worth carding for future reference, played havoc with my appreciation of literature. My estimate is that it would take the average person about five years of working on the dictionary and "reading" texts of all sorts before he or she came through the barrier and was able to read properly again.

Put yourself in the reader's shoes: You are reading *Jane Eyre*, perhaps not for the first time, but you're enjoying it all over again. You've followed the narrative through its twists and turns, past the fire, towards the very end. You find yourself at the start of the last, cathartic chapter. What happens next? The chapter title is "Conclusion," followed by "Reader, I married him. A quiet wedding we had; he and I, the parson and the clerk, were alone present." What are the man-traps here for the budding lexicographer?

Your growing lexicographical intuition stops you dead in your tracks. Firstly, there's the word *conclusion*. You probably know that Charlotte Brontë didn't invent it, and you probably have some inkling that it had been in English for many years. You would be quite right, as we borrowed the word from French towards the end of the Middle Ages. But would the *OED* be interested in this particular use of "conclusion" (dating from 1847) with reference to the conclusion of a story? How old is that use? Should you spend two minutes jotting all the information down on an index card for the dictionary's files? You check in the big dictionary and find that even Geoffrey Chaucer used *conclusion* in roughly that sense. It takes a long time for new editors to develop a confident feel for the age of words, and that's something which (though hard-fought) separates historical lexicographers from most other people.

"Reader, I married him." Your eye, closely followed by your brain, halts at "reader." Again you know full well that *reader* has been around in English since the dawn of time (in this case from way back in the Anglo-Saxon period). But when did authors start addressing their readers directly as "reader," or maybe "gentle reader," in the text itself? Was that Victorian? Was Charlotte Brontë in the forefront? You reach up again for the relevant volume of the dictionary, and once again you sit down abashed. Any author might have addressed his (or her) reader in this way ever since the Middle Ages. William Cowper, in 1785, talks politely to "my gentle reader." Charlotte Brontë is deep in the following pack and you don't need to bother yourself with carding this use.

You get the idea. For the new lexicographer, reading a historical text *in search of material for the dictionary* for the first time is an uncomfortable ride, full of pitches and tosses and jolts as you stop and start to check a reference which, as often as not, proves irrelevant to the job in hand. We can proceed a little further, if you like, and then I shall have to leave you to read the rest of *Jane Eyre* yourself.

The next sentence reads: "A quiet wedding we had; he and I, the parson and the clerk, were alone present." People can be quiet, dogs can be quiet, and even rooms can be quiet, but when did we start to think that weddings might be quiet, and what precisely does it mean? Is it a new sense, applied to something that wouldn't normally speak or make a commotion? Again we consult the dictionary. Again we find we might have spent our time better: the *OED* already knows about this sense of "free from excess; moderate, modest; restrained" from the sixteenth century. Where have your lexicographical antennae gone? Will you ever get one right? You will, and you do, but not this time.

It turns out, as we have just seen, that you don't need to stop and consider *any* of those words. The *OED* had already taken care of them, but *you don't know that.* So you check. And you spoil your reading of one of the classic passages of English literature because you are too worried about the language. Well, good for you. You can read *Jane Eyre* again later, but you may not have the chance to think so carefully about the language of the early nineteenth century as you do now. And once you've checked those facts, you'll stand in much better stead when you meet the same expressions next time round in another text from that period.

There was more to lexicography than writing definitions: that much I'd discovered by now. But in my first weeks on the dictionary I found out that large-scale historical dictionaries such as the *OED* weren't compiled by editors thinking deep thoughts at their desks and perusing scholarly books on language, but by editors grabbing hold of the evidence of the language that was racing past them, in the form of whatever text they could lay their hands on. Information had to be collected before it was analysed, and the scope of this collection influenced the scope of the dictionary. My first job had not involved learning how to write definitions, as I had expected that it would, but reading a book on the semiotics of film, in search of background material that might be useful to the dictionary at some unscheduled time in the future. And I learnt that we had to read a wide range of texts to hope to capture a representative sample of the language. If we only "read" novels, then we would be missing out on a stream of language swarming through newspapers; if we avoided poetry, we'd miss other types of language; and so it went on.

The example quotations in the First Edition of the *OED* are often and (I think) rather ungenerously said to be drawn too much from famous, classic authors (Shakespeare, Milton, Swift, Pope, and—surprisingly high up on its ranking list—Sir Walter Scott). I don't think the editors intended to privilege "highbrow" literature; it was just that these were the texts to which readers had easiest access, and which the publishing world of the day made most readily available. But I've always had the greatest respect for those early editors: they did a remarkable job with the resources at their command. At the same time they had left us ample scope to add new evidence from less formal sources (earlier evidence, informal idioms, technologies not popular with the original Victorian readers) and to show that language is never the exclusive preserve of the literary giants of the age. I had also found out that it wasn't only editors who were competent to collect important dictionary information; anyone with an ear for language and history could make discoveries.

I realised that the dictionary was, even then, more enlightened than I had expected. The editors were kindly, for the most part, and keen to show me the ropes—though some appeared rather remote and obsessed with words rather than people. Would I make friends here? Would I fit in? Would I be good enough to do the job? I had arrived with preconceptions about Oxford, but the edges of these preconceptions were gradually being knocked off as I engaged more and more closely with the workings of the dictionary and its staff, and, in turn, with the workings of the language. I enjoyed the steady methodology by which you gradually built up information for words. This was a system that had worked in the past, and it still seemed appropriate for the work we were carrying out in the mid-1970s.

At this stage I was really only concerned with what *I* was given to edit. I hadn't seen enough of the department to worry about the speed at which the project as a whole was moving (too slowly, I soon learned, for the peace of mind of the University Press), or whether we were editing the right words, in the right way. These were matters that would mean more to me in the future. The more I learnt, the more rapidly I was able to make decisions about the words I had been entrusted with. Could I cope? With the brashness of youth it hardly occurred to me that I could not.

THREE

Marshallers of Words

I didn't have to wait long, as it turned out, before I was invited to try my hand at defining words. Within a month of my arrival at the *OED* I was given my first batch of words to edit. It began with *queen*: a very British and rather formal word with which to start, and one which—you might think—hasn't changed very much in recent years. Was there a roll of patriotic drums somewhere as the monarch's personal word was revised by the *OED*? If so, I wasn't aware of it. I had been looking forward to this momentous day with some trepidation for several weeks, and was excited when it had at last arrived and I could get down to some solid work.

The First Edition of the *Oxford English Dictionary* had been completed, after forty-four gruelling years of editing, and in ten dense volumes, in 1928. It was a dictionary, so—of course—it did already contain an entry for the word *queen*. My job now was to *update* this entry in the *OED* with new material, which might consist of entirely new meanings, new expressions involving the word *queen*, new historical information about the word, and anything else that was relevant to a comprehensive modern description of *queen* in the English language of 1976.

For reasons that had been decided long before my arrival, we were mainly dealing with linguistic changes that had happened in the present (and that meant mainly the twentieth) century: just the recent past. We were not to tinker with the hundreds of thousands of words and meanings which were already in the dictionary, and for which the old definitions could still be regarded as valid. Perhaps there would be time for that later. Much later. The University Press acutely remembered those forty-four years of editing from *A* to *Z* over the turn of the nineteenth century, and it had no wish to allocate funds to a lengthy and comprehensive overhaul of the text quite yet. The *Supplement to the OED* had already grown from its projected single volume to four large volumes, and I soon appreciated that the University Press was watching the chief editor very carefully to ensure he didn't argue for additional time and even more resources to complete the task.

So one of the first things I learned was that editing an entry for the *Supplement to the OED* did not usually involve creating it from scratch. Although we had to do this for modern words that were completely new to the language (such as *quadraphonic* or *rehab*), when we addressed old stagers like **queen**, we left the old meanings as they were, and the etymology unchanged—even though they were becoming increasingly antique by then. Antique? Take *quay*, just nearby in the alphabet: the original *OED*'s definition for *quay* was "an artificial bank or landing-place, built of stone or other solid material, lying along or projecting into a navigable water for convenience of loading and unloading ships." It's not wrong, but it's slightly antiquated, with a whiff of the nineteenth century. It could be left as it was. It wasn't our job to update everything; we would never finish if we started along that route.

We wouldn't spell the word *queen* Q-U-E-E-N if we hadn't experienced the Norman Conquest. Before that, we were quite happy to use the old Anglo-Saxon spelling: *cwen* or thereabouts. We'd been doing that for hundreds of years, without knowing any better. But along came the Normans, and their newfangled ways of doing things.

They brought their scribes with them to write down what happened in legal courts and anywhere else the language needed recording. These scribes heard the word *cwen* and couldn't bring themselves to write the letter sequence <cw>, because <cw> was a consonant cluster that didn't occur in French. The members of the Anglo-French scribal union put their heads together and decided to use what they *were* familiar with—the cluster <qu>, which makes the same sound. (Okay, fair enough—there wasn't actually a National Union of Scribes back then, but you get the idea.) Over time writers unilaterally eradicated the sequence <cw> and replaced it with <qu>, and we found ourselves continuing to say /cwen/, but spelling it <queen>. This shift didn't only affect *queen*: we have the same process to thank for the modern spelling of *quick* (in Anglo-Saxon times *cwic*), *quench*, *quoth*, *quern*, and a handful of other words.

And so began my first years at the dictionary, learning its ethos, its style, what it was trying to say, and how it tried to say it. There was a routine to my days as a trainee lexicographer back in the 1970s. And the routine wasn't just mine, as there were about ten of us, young and old, who were following this same editorial path. We'd meet up in the various dictionary offices as we worked our lonely way round the building checking facts in the shelves of reference works or along the cabinets of card files.

On my first day of real editing, my trainer handed me a batch of index cards containing *queen* words which she had selected as likely candidates for addition to the dictionary. She had chosen these by searching diligently through the *OED*'s main sequence of index cards that had accumulated in the dictionary file store since—in some cases—the mid-nineteenth century.

She had passed over all of those older meanings that were already in the dictionary: *queen* in the sense of "a female monarch"—perhaps the oldest one of all; then the rather similar meaning, "the wife of a king" (please note: this is not always the same thing); instances of *queen* applied to fabulous or mythological beings—the *queen* of the fairies, and (as a title) *Queen* Diana the Huntress; *queen* meaning any woman of pre-eminence, or applied to the moon as the *queen* of heaven, or to the monarch of a bee-hive; verbs, nouns, adjectives, and adverbs using it (*to queen it, queenship, queenly,* etc.); well-worn compounds (*queen cake, Queen Mother*).

I did not need to do anything to these old meanings already in the *OED*, but instead she had found me female cats, sizes of bed, girl-friends, homosexuals, Cunard liners (all *queens*), and many more. As this was my first range of editing, I was not in any position to argue with her selection, and doubtless would not have needed to.

Once I had assessed the words I had been asked to work on, I had three stages to work through: collecting more index cards for my words from other, older card files (downstairs, in the basement), gathering more information from books in the department's reference library (first floor), and then finally writing my definition and crafting the whole entry (in my office on the ground floor).

I always found the basement sweep through the card files full of magical possibility. At any moment I might make a small discovery that had eluded earlier linguists and lexicographers. There have been many accounts of the dictionary's history, but very few (if any) have managed to capture the excitement of the job—the fact that each day you are uncovering small but significant facts that have been almost entirely forgotten, often for centuries, and you have the opportunity to bring them back to the surface. That thrill of discovery, like the elation of a well-rounded definition, is almost like creating a poem. Maybe I'm romancing, but there is a point here which is usually overlooked. You had to ensure that you didn't miss anything—that was considered, by the department's old hands, almost a **court-martial** offence.

Court martial: one of the few remaining terms from French—outside the areas of food and cookery (*chicken chasseur, moules marinière*)— where the noun precedes the adjective: we'd say *military court* if we were inventing it now instead of in around 1600—the era from which the *OED* dates it. As *martial* is the adjective, the plural, as you will recall, is *courts martial*. But if you inadvertently slip into the solecism of saying "court martials," then you're not the first. Records of this go back to 1750 and earlier.

Courts martial are not usually associated with lexicographers, but there is one exception. The rotund Francis Grose, best known to hardline lexicographers for his *Classical Dictionary of the Vulgar Tongue* of 1785, spent much of his time as a paymaster in the British Army. While he travelled around the country with his regiment, he made sketches for his *Antiquities of England and Wales* (1772–1787) and collected words for his dictionaries. It is a fact known to almost no one today that one of his duties as military paymaster was to sit on courts martial, deciding the fate of his fellow soldiers and (I like to think) using many of the same skills in balancing evidence and pronouncing his decision that he employed as a lexicographer.

Queen of puddings was in my first batch of words. I didn't remember ever having eaten—let alone cooked—the queen of puddings, so this was my first encounter with the dessert (which everyone in Oxford but me seemed to know was a trifle-like concoction of breadcrumbs, jam, and meringue). My job was to hunt out more examples of this expression (and of my other words) in the historical card sequences. The first example already contained in my little bundle came from the year 1917, on a card transcribed hastily and slantingly from bottom left to top right. It came from May Byron's *Pudding Book*, and had been written out in the characteristically diagonal script of Marghanita Laski. You could instantly identify many of these long-gone contributors from their handwriting on the slips. You could even tell, sometimes, if they were having a difficult day; if they didn't really want to be writing out cards at that particular time; if they liked or disliked a word—just from their handwriting. Or at least I liked to think that you could. Later—with computers—we largely lost this intuitive association with the raw material, unless you could be bothered to decipher tiny sets of initials hidden away somewhere on the screen.

Marghanita Laski, the producer of my current *queen of puddings* slip, was by this time quite an elderly lady. She had been born into a prominent Jewish intellectual family in Manchester quite soon after the outbreak of the First World War, and she was the modern *OED*'s most prolific supplier of quotation material. Nowadays, she is regarded with the same hushed reverence accorded to one of the original *OED*'s most obsessive readers, Dr William Chester Minor. Minor was the co-hero (with James Murray) of Simon Winchester's first book about the *OED*—*The Surgeon of Crowthorne*; quite unlike Marghanita, Minor had been busily and lucidly active for the dictionary in the nineteenth century from his rooms in Broadmoor mental hospital, to which he had been confined for murder (not guilty through insanity), fifty miles from the dictionary's offices in Oxford.

Marghanita's influence on the content of the *OED* in those days was significant. Her personal contribution amounted to a total of some 250,000 index cards. She had been involved with the *OED* since the 1960s, having been ensnared by one of the chief editor's regular appeal lists of wanted words. She sent in her findings to us, and soon discovered that there was precious little else she liked doing more than contributing illustrative quotations to the dictionary.

The reading habits of a little, elderly lady would not normally be of interest to us today, but Marghanita's idiosyncratic interests permeated the quotations she provided for the dictionary, and in that way had a minor effect on the representation of the English language offered by the *OED*. Any editor from those days will tell you that she had a preference for detective fiction, and particularly for lady writers of the 1920s to 1950s. As a result, our files were weighed down with the vocabulary of Ngaio Marsh, Margery Allingham, and Dorothy L. Sayers's Lord Peter Wimsey. She read voraciously. She admired Rudyard Kipling and P. G. Wodehouse. In addition, she followed the chief editor's instructions and dutifully read the once-famous First World War poet Edmund Blunden (*Undertones of War*) and several other writers who were even then heading pell-mell towards oblivion. She mixed socially in pleasantly refined and elegant circles, and this, too, affected her contributions, which inclined towards words from writers who spent most of their summers in the south of France sipping the local wines and sampling the regional delicacies (including the Trollopes, cookery writer and social historian Dorothy Hartley, journalists working on *House and Garden* and *Country Life*, and many others).

When I did eventually meet her, many years later when I was running the *OED*'s reading programme myself, she seemed to like the idea that I was English, which struck me as odd. The *OED* had been in the hands of a Lowland Scot and a New Zealander for most of its recorded history, and hadn't done too badly. In fact, it seemed to have brought a vitality to the *OED* that might otherwise have been missing in the academic cloisters of Oxford. I think she thought of me as more "Oxford" than I was—or at least more "Oxford" than I thought of myself as being. Others invariably see you through Oxford-tinted glasses, however different you think you are yourself.

As far as her reading for the *OED* was concerned, I don't remember having the nerve to suggest she change her reading habits; what she had provided us over the previous twenty and more years had served us very well. Her reading verged towards the popular, but still had an air of refinement and of high literature which I didn't regard as mainstream, as far as collecting real-language information for the *OED* was concerned. As time went on, I wanted more and more to move away from what I regarded as this slightly elitist view of English. She belonged to a literary coterie but—like me—wanted to bring the dictionary up to date. For her, "contemporary" meant including the new vocabulary of the 1950s and early 1960s, before the new freedoms of the mid-1960s and later broke through. Her culture wasn't mine—but it was equally valid. She collected mounds of evidence for terms such as *cappuccino, Latino, Nabokovian,* and *tabbouleh*: all expressions which the dictionary needed and which had informed her life. They were important, but to me they were indicative of her generation. I had my own cultural perspective, and it was more technology-driven, more based on popular culture, more emerging than emerged. That was what excited me at the time: *Afrocentric, demo tape, ombudsperson, weaponising*—not just street talk, but the new vocabulary of sexism, multiculturalism, exploratory music, and the environmental and military threats to the world. I felt it was our duty to be in at ground zero as this new vocabulary was arriving.

Stage two of my work on this batch of *queen* words involved further research in the departmental library. The library had been built up over many years to be of crucial importance to dictionary-makers, but of little consequence to anyone else. So it contained hundreds of dictionaries covering the major languages of the world, and a good share of the less major ones; it held concordances of particular writers, as finding aids and short-cuts into their vocabulary; it encompassed poetry and novels, in which editors could check the spelling and meaning of extracts others had previously copied out on to slips. Generally, it housed books that most people don't need, but which are absolutely essential to the lexicographer. A stand-out title—and one of my all-time favourites—was the *Dictionary of Occupational Terms: Based on the Classification of Occupations in the Census of Population, 1921*, published by the Ministry of Labour, after six years of analysis and compilation, in 1927. If you wanted to know what sort of work the ordinary person did in Britain in 1921, this was the place to look. You'll find *batchers, beaders, beastman, beatsters, bevellers,* and the *big tenter* (in a cotton mill)—with explanations of what they used to spend their time doing. I'd take it to a desert island with me.

It was absolutely necessary to be *very quiet* in the departmental library, as (*a*) it was a library, (*b*) other editors were working, and (*c*) the chief editor was somewhere across the corridor, and the last thing I wanted to do was to encounter him, in case I'd be given some inconsequential secondary task, which would deflect me from the main purpose of my day. The following year he would send me to the nearby sweet shop to buy a Chocolate Orange as a birthday present for one of his daughters. So keeping a low profile on one's trips to the departmental library was of the utmost importance.

Some of the library's books were obviously more useful than others—you knew them because they had been well-thumbed by generations of dictionary editors. Many of the books dated back a hundred years to *OED* chief editor Sir James Murray's time and the compilation of the First Edition of the dictionary. One or two still contained labels saying that they had been lent to Dr Murray. By some oversight they had never been sent back to their original owners, whose descendants had by now presumably given up the books as lost.

I wrote lots of notes at this stage, but also carried a mass of information around in my head. I would need all of this later when it came to writing up my definitions. For a few moments while working in the natural history section, I was the world expert on one of my terms: the *queen excluder*, "a metal screen with holes large enough for worker honeybees to pass through but too small to allow the passage of the queen." Over on the nautical shelves I would investigate the *queen staysail*, "a triangular maintopmast staysail in a schooner yacht," apparently first designed by Captain Nat Herreshoff (born 1848; died 1938) for his 1906 racing schooner *Queen*.

My favourite reference text amongst the many I had to investigate systematically at this stage of the research was Eric Partridge's *Dictionary of the Underworld* (*PDU*). The *PDU* was a knuckle-bruising, rapid-fire, brief-citation-after-brief-citation tour through the terrifying vocabulary of the thieves and murderers of London, Sydney, and New York. Eric Partridge had compiled this dark book some years after his more popular *Dictionary of Slang and Unconventional English* (1937), but this time round he was writing from aggravated and heartfelt and macabre interest. It was a lexicographical triumph.

Partridge, as I soon discovered, was an expert on the lesser-known aspects of queens. He had read books about the ghettoes of London and the underworld of New York that the average reader would happily bypass, and so his references to early uses of *queen* and *quean* (especially in homosexual contexts) were vital. The *Dictionary of the Underworld* is a dictionary that lexicographers knowingly discuss amongst themselves, in the certain knowledge that hardly anyone else has ever heard of it. Several years later the chief editor was asked to write the life story of his fellow New Zealander Eric Partridge for the *Dictionary of National Biography*. I was walking past his office one day, minding my own and the dictionary's business, and the next day found myself on a train to London commissioned to hunt out Partridge's birth and death certificates at Somerset House. Still, it was for a better cause than the Chocolate Orange.

Once I'd exhausted the departmental library, by which time my clutch of index cards had normally doubled in size, I reverted (stage three) to my office to set about the final task of **marshalling** the facts and defining the words.

The word *marshal* is something of an oddity, because English found it in French, but it started off life on the other side of the great Romance/Germanic divide. I've always liked the word *marshal*, even though, as a neutral lexicographer, I have absolutely no right to take sides with words. Perhaps I just like it because, like Chinese boxes, it contains inside it a sequence of other words: the letter *M*; and then incrementally *ma*, the shortening of *mama*; then *mar*, to spoil or ruin; *Mars*, the red planet; *marsh*, the swampy ground; *Marsha*, the personal name; *marshal* (itself); and even *marshall*, its spelling variant, and another personal name.

Marshal is an important word in the *OED* department, because it's the word my chief editor was soon to use, in the preface to one of the volumes of the *Supplement to the OED*, to describe his role. He was a "marshaller" of the language, documenting the twists and turns of its progression. In some ways this was a good word for him to use, because it avoided the sense of "guardianship" that people too easily associate with lexicography. Historical lexicographers don't "guard" the language from change or decay, but they observe, monitor, and report back on change (or lack of change) as it occurs.

Marshal is another of those words that entered English because of the Normans. (The Normans, as you will have worked out, have been heavily involved in providing work for lexicographers.) *Marshal* entered English from Norman French quite soon after the Norman Conquest, in what was effectively still the "late Old English" period, before the French influence really took hold of the language. It's one of those words you can look at and look at and still fail to appreciate its derivation. Well, that's where dictionaries help. *Marshal* is made up of two older words that started life in the Germanic languages, but were assimilated into French and Late Latin, and so looked French by the time *marshal* came to be handed over to the English. That's not too unusual. Although the story runs that French is purely a Romance language, it contains numerous examples of Germanic words integrated at an early date.

The French word *maréchal* ultimately comes from the Germanic root that gives us *mare* (a horse) and from another Germanic root, *shalk*, which existed in English from the Old English period until just into the sixteenth century, when it was swept away for good by numerous alternative terms. Word death happens all along the way. *Shalk* meant a servant, or (in early poetry) just "a man." (Did the related word *seneschal* just float into your head? That must be worth a few marks: a *seneschal* is the chief steward of an aristocratic household, though sadly chief stewards are not so common these days as they used to be.) So a *marshal* was a farrier, someone who shoed, or shod, or more generally looked after, horses. But even in the days before the word entered English, the horse was such an important animal in medieval warfare that the job of the chief farrier became invested with strategic importance, and the word shifted imperceptibly into other areas of army life. The French—and other Europeans who had the word—started to call a military or even a royal officer a *marshal*.

Its use spread in English from the royal court to the legal circuits, and even to the names of specific officers at the universities of Oxford and Cambridge, and then, by the early twentieth century, to car-racing meets, where the *marshals* are responsible for supervising the arrangements of competitors. In fact, in the seventeenth century, the word rather overshot itself, and people sometimes referred (incorrectly) to a *court martial* as a *marshal's court*. So, when the chief editor of the dictionary regarded himself as the "marshaller" of the language, he was making use of a meaning applied to anyone (not necessarily military or royal) who put things in good order. John Dryden, the *OED* tells us (at *marshaller*), was "the great Refiner of our English Poetry, and the best Marshaller of words." So our chief editor had competition.

All the time that I had been collecting information about my words, I had been building up in my head little phrases which might help me towards the definitions I now had to write, once the background research was done. I rarely attempted to leap straight into an authoritative definition, but amassed a list of the important attributes of a term as a sort of mood board from which to select the key ingredients. Some of these verbal hints and clues might work later in the more formal context of the definitions. The *Queen of the Gypsies*, I mused, was clearly a "high-status Roma woman," and *Queen City of the West* turned out to be "Cincinnati, Ohio," a place which had previously possessed no cultural references for me—but I had yet to puzzle out why it might be called the "Queen City." I played with phrases to describe my compounds: *queen-pin* (a crime boss king-pin, but one who was relentlessly female), *queen substance* (a pheromone or sex attractant produced by a queen bee), *queen's head* (the image of a queen's head on a postage stamp), *Queen's Scout* (not a loyal personal retainer of the Queen, but a

Boy Scout who had reached the top of the tree in the movement), *queen's ware* (porcelain), etc., etc. As I worked through this world of *queen* phrases—many of which I had never heard of before, and most of which I had at first little idea how to describe—I would be looking for signposts, little expressions that gave me a sense of their meaning, which I might pass on to readers as I composed the definitions.

That's—for me—one of the charms of lexicography. You have to be the sort of person who can turn your hand to most subjects—know a little about everything, but not enough to dig yourself in too deep. And with these *queen* words I was often in virgin territory: I wasn't a great one for sailing; I hadn't thrown a pot in my life, or lived with the gypsies; I'd never made it from the Wolf Cubs into the real Boy Scouts and had had no hope of becoming a Queen's Scout; and I'm fairly certain that a degree in English literature had not prepared me to know what a pheromone was or why it would bother a queen bee.

Perhaps the most arresting cluster of examples I found for *queen* was in the sense of "a homosexual person." We had what amounted at the time to a reasonable amount of documentary evidence for the usage— say, around thirty index cards. In modern terms that is absolutely nothing, but it was a gold-mine back then. The earliest reference we possessed came from a glossary of slang published in the Australian newspaper *Truth*, from 1924. Slang terms often surfaced in glossaries, so this was a good sign that we might already be back in the early period of the term's history. But how significant was it that the first reference came from Australia?

From 1924 onwards my little collection of evidence contained a mixture of literary references. Exhibit A was Evelyn Waugh in *Vile Bodies* (published in 1930): "'Now what may *you* want, my Italian queen?' said Lottie as the waiter came in with a tray"; then New Zealand writer Ngaio Marsh in *Artists in Crime*: "We met the chap that runs the place. One of those die-away queens" (1938). After that there were later quotations from newspapers and novels, which brought the picture up to the present day. On my scout around the department library there had not been a substantial amount of new evidence to find. Eric Partridge's *Dictionary of Slang* thought the word was a corruption of the older *quean*, meaning "a harlot." Really? In 1920s Australia? We had a 1929 reference from the New York writer Max Lief. What did that say about the possibility of Australian origin only five years earlier? Anyway, if it was Australian, wouldn't the New Zealander Eric Partridge have picked up on that?

After collecting as much information from as broad a range of sources as I could, and after reading all the evidence through several times, and after thinking about how the term *queen* fitted generally into the language—jostling with parallel terms—I (or in this case probably my trainer) came up with the definition, assembled from the evidence: "A male homosexual, esp. the effeminate partner in a homosexual relationship. *slang*." We weren't prepared to hazard a guess as to whether it was originally Australian English, despite the first reference, as it was followed too closely by that American and then English evidence. We gave a general definition, and then narrowed it down to a particular observable nuance.

When we came, in due course, to revise *queen* = "homosexual" for the Third Edition of the *OED* in December 2007, we did find new, earlier evidence which helped to set the term in better context. A secondary text from 1988 (*Perverts by Official Order: The Campaign Against Homosexuals by the United States Navy*) pointed to a reference dated from 1919 which contained our term. It seems we were right not to leap in and label the term "Australian." But even today we don't feel confident enough to ascribe its origin to any particular variety of English. If you are not certain, it's better to say nothing.

That 1988 title is an indication that the *OED* of the future would feel able to cite from a wider range of non-literary texts. A groundswell of change had been working through society since the First Edition of the dictionary was published around the turn of the nineteenth century and into the early twentieth. The original dictionary exemplified words from many types of sources, but particularly from those read by the educated gentleman or the refined spinster of the English capital and shires. It was curious, it seemed to me, that the collection of information about the language was conducted by "readers" who belonged to the old world of literary, educated English. Language was an extension of empire for many of them. This is an oversimplification, but it flags up the general tenor of the texts cited (classic literature, formal newspapers, accessible—but not too esoteric—technical manuals and periodicals). Even when I started working on the *Supplement* to the dictionary in the 1970s, the chief editor was most proud of those words from modern literary texts that he and his staff were adding to the dictionary (D. H. Lawrence: *dool-owl*, "dull person," and *momentaneity*; James Joyce: *codology*, "hoaxing," and *dishybilly*, "state of undress"). But the groundswell was too powerful. Society had changed; the dictionary's readers and staff had changed; and a broader—and in my view more enlightened—selection of sources was even then providing us with a new stream of vocabulary: more global English, more slang, more popular or regional magazines, more everyday, informal jargon.

There was plenty of opportunity, as we approached the end of the twentieth century, to expand the scope of sources plundered for words by the dictionary's readers. As time went on, I came to feel that I should become more and more involved in seeking out the sort of language the ordinary person might use in Britain, America, Australia, and so on, and to let a breath of fresh air into the new *OED* in this way. The chief editor had made a considered decision before my arrival to avoid contact with computers in the collection of data, reasoning that becoming familiar with new technology so close to the completion of his big project would only slow things down. There was a lot in that. But there would come a time when we would need to reverse this decision if we wanted to keep up.

J ust a few weeks into my dictionary career, and even before my first pay cheque came through, Hilary and I decided to get married. We gave our parents about a month's notice and told them we would plan everything ourselves, in a quiet way, without fuss, but that we would be very happy if they were to come along to celebrate with us.

The wedding day itself had a couple of hiccups. We were marrying in the Oxford register office, which, in those days, was marooned above a supermarket in the middle of the city's one-way traffic system, which made parking difficult. Despite my father's supposed prowess at un-locking secret codes, the business of finding somewhere to park the car in Oxford that day proved too much for him, and he missed the wedding ceremony. He dropped the family outside the register office and found himself swept up into the traffic. We saw him later for lunch.

After the ceremony, we ate at a hotel restaurant in Oxford: parents on both sides, my brother and sister (Hilary is an only child), my remaining aged grandmother, and my father's elderly archaeological cousin, "Aunt" Grace, who was invited because she lived in Oxford and therefore couldn't be avoided. The lunch was fine. No speeches: I was far too self-conscious in those days to want to break up the quiet of the dessert course with a few poorly chosen words. The main problem, as I found out in later years, came at the end. Instead of running off on honeymoon, which we couldn't afford to do on the first month of a lexicographer's salary and a PhD student's grant, I had agreed to turn out for the local hockey team in a crunch league match. Hilary had given her okay in advance, but it seems that sometimes people agree to things in advance that they are going to hold against you for years to come. On my side, I had absolutely no excuse and can only offer in mitigation that my team, the City of Oxford Hockey Club 2nd XI, won that afternoon. (In years to come, I played regularly for the first team, but this was only my third week at the club, so they were taking the opportunity to observe me. I realise that this isn't making things any better . . .)

Like language, attitudes to **marriage** have changed, even since those days of the 1970s. Nowadays, leaving before the wedding lunch was over would probably put me beyond the pale. In those days it was per-haps unusual, but just within the bounds of acceptability. The wedding itself was low-key: Hilary wore a long purple Indian print dress, and I had a prickly pullover made from goat's hair (or so it felt) over my cheesecloth shirt. No friends, no newspaper notice: we just got on with things in those days.

In 1976, *marriage* was not a controversial word, but nowadays it is just the sort of word that can get a lexicographer into deep trouble. Traditionally, *marriage* has concerned the union of a man and a woman. We've used the word in English since around 1300, from French, and for almost all of that time this has been the major meaning. More recently, dictionaries have noted same-sex marriage—a lexical pulse that started flickering several years ago, as we took note that various American states were reviewing how they understood the boundaries of the word *marriage*.

The definition of marriage remains a hotly contested issue, and the lexicographer needs to remain absolutely neutral when crafting a definition: weighing up the evidence and deciding on the factors of the term that are significant. The definition should not include every single attribute of *marriage* that can be found in the observable documentation. It's not significant, for example, at what time of the year the marriage takes place, or whether one spouse is older or of a higher social standing than the other (we might refer to a *morganatic* marriage, in the latter case). It doesn't matter, nowadays, whether the person who marries a couple is male or female, or whether it takes place in a church or other approved location. The lexicographer normally has to select only the universal aspects or attributes of the term. In lexicographical theory, that applies to every word, of course, not just to *marriage*.

The issue of how to handle same-sex marriage introduced a new attribute, which gradually gained in social importance, and gradually demanded to be noted. But the means of dealing with this change is different for smaller, desk-sized dictionaries and for their large-scale historical counterparts. If a dictionary alters the basic definition of marriage to accommodate this new feature, then it falsely creates the impression that this broader meaning has coexisted since the early days: this is the technique that smaller dictionaries are often forced to follow, through lack of space. Alternatively, the historical dictionary can add a sheepish clause or a note saying that this nuance was introduced into the language at a particular time, say in the later years of the twentieth century. Both sorts of dictionaries can also take the bold option (and this would be a significant change) of deciding that the same-sex sense of *marriage* is established enough to have its very own subsense. At present we've elected the second option—the historical lexicographer's natural choice.

As it happens, this isn't the first time that *marriage* has been hotly contested in lexicographical circles. In 1791, the *Monthly Review* took a look at Charles Coote's *Elements of the Grammar of the English Language* (published in 1788). The reviewer was unhappy with Coote's observations on the way *marriage* was being pronounced in some quarters:

> In many instances, [Coote's] *pronunciation* is inelegant and vulgar;
> as when he gives sanction to dropping the sound of *a* in the last
> syllable of *marriage, carriage,* &c—thus, *marrige, carrige.*

We didn't like that back then. But time moves on, and we've forgotten that was ever an issue now.

O ver the course of my first year at the *OED*, I gradually moved along the alphabet from *queen* to *quid* to *rap*, and all the way up to *Rastafarian* and beyond. There is a freedom about the alphabet: it's democratic—if you follow the words that arrive on your desk alphabetically, then you meet candidate words from all walks of life, not ones chosen with marketing strategies or any political intent in mind. I remember being puzzled by *rannygazoo* ("nonsense; foolishness; a prank"). We never did discover who invented the term. It appeared in the works of P. G. Wodehouse, surprisingly a bellwether for informal Americanisms of his day, and we tracked it back to the *Washington Post* of 1896. With the help of the *OED*'s researchers I found piano *rags* in the late 1890s, first played by African American bands in Kansas (according to the evidence, at least). We tracked the first occurrence of *quisling* (a wartime collaborator with the enemy), named in 1940 after the Norwegian officer Major Vidkun *Quisling*. Every discovery excited me and helped us to plot the stages through which the English language had progressed in recent decades around the world.

As we made our way through the alphabet, there was, naturally, increasing pressure on us from the University Press to bring this nineteen-year project to an end. We had published two volumes of the *Supplement*, and we knew that there would be another two volumes to come. At, say, four years per volume, we would not be finished until the mid-1980s, or maybe even later. Oddly, none of us gave much thought to what we might do when the work ran out. Maybe Oxford University Press would contemplate a further supplement to the dictionary, updating yet again what we had just spent years trying to complete. In our lucid moments I think we doubted that. Maybe the academic world would be so impressed by what we had achieved that it would offer us jobs in whatever English department we wanted when we hit *Z*. That was unlikely, but I didn't mind—it was all too far ahead, and at the moment it was all too much fun. Although I had only been at the *OED* for a year, time seemed to move so slowly. I was absorbing all of the rules and secrets of the process and coming to terms with the magnificence of the language spreading back from our day to its very first appearance 1,500 years earlier.

The *OED* has a reputation for taking a very long time to complete anything. This perspective is, needless to say, a travesty. But whenever we tried to tell people that we were working at top speed, they would eye us with indulgent disbelief. I was recently asked by a mid-European historical dictionary project to supply some data on how fast the original *OED* travelled on its journey towards the letter *Z* between 1884 and 1928 (44 years). It was, in fact, a very lean machine for its day. Its main counterpart in Europe was the *Deutsches Wörterbuch*, the so-called Grimm dictionary (launched by the fairy-tale brothers Grimm). That great dictionary started on its lengthy publication history in 1854 and was not completed—many instalments later—until 1961 (that's 107 years later, for those of you without a degree in numbers). So the *OED* deserves a small pat on the head for knocking 63 years off the German world-record schedule. It's a similar picture with the great Dutch dictionary, the multi-multi-volume *Woordenboek der Nederlandse Taal* (*WNT*). The first volume of the *WNT* was published in 1864, and the final one rolled off the printing presses in 1998 (I was there at the ceremony in the cathedral in Leiden). That's 134 years. The former German record fades into insignificance. But length of time isn't necessarily a bad thing. The hard-pressed editors in Germany and in the Netherlands were doing a thorough job. A very thorough job. The long gestation period does make their dictionaries hard to update, though, as the editorial style changes over generations of editors. The *OED* came in at a sprint by comparison and maintained a fairly regular style throughout, which (as we'll see) made it feasible to consider revising and updating when the time came.

But at the moment, the possibility of doing that didn't even exist in our heads. We were driven by **deadlines** to complete the final two volumes of the *Supplement to the OED*. I didn't mind deadlines, as I'd always been a pretty quick worker. Each month the dictionary's managers would compile progress lists, and I was usually at the top of them. Progress was important. Deadlines were not targets I liked to miss.

Times of crisis are times when new words are generated. In mid-nineteenth-century America the dangerous and yet thrilling push into the Wild West, and then the California Gold Rush, followed by the Civil War, brought a jumble of new words into the emerging variety called American English. (At the moment, Charlotte Brontë is accredited with the first recorded use of "Wild West": I don't think that will last.) Much of this new vocabulary is self-confidently adventurous, like the new country: *badlands, bloviate, bodacious, bo-nanza, braggadocious, buckaroo* (sorry: that's enough of a list).

The earliest recorded use of the term *dead line* comes from angling (1860). It's not a new creation in the world of words, but it takes another approach—it's a creative metaphor. A *dead line* is one that doesn't move or run while it's lying in wait for fish to bite. To get into the stream of the modern meanings of the term we need to travel over to America around the end of the Civil War, where the same pairing of words produced a new and unrelated meaning. It seems that mid-nineteenth-century Americans did not hold enlightened views on prison management: they apparently used to draw lines around military prisons, and if a prisoner went beyond that line, he would be shot. The dead line. Here's what the prolific American writer Benson John Lossing said, in his *Pictorial History of the Civil War in the United States of America* (vol. 3, 1868): "Seventeen feet from the inner stockade was the 'dead-line', over which no man could pass and live." Deadlines became less lethal in early twentieth-century America, when the newspapers picked up the expression to describe their time-limit for receiving copy. Make the deadline or else. Then it drifted into numerous other areas of life, including the *OED*'s own schedule.

In the days before the Internet, I came to see that one of the characteristics that really distinguished *OED* entries was the quality of the historical research that went into their compilation. Later, we had help from all manner of digital resources to discover earlier references to the words or phrases we were working on. Back then, it was just the researcher against a shelf full of books and library catalogues, and no one gave you any hints about where to start looking. A classic example of this is illustrated by the work we conducted to research the history of the expression *the thin red line*.

The thin red line was an expression that the original *OED* compilers had utterly forgotten to include. Arguably, this was rather casual of them. The expression was well established when they reached *red*, and even if it hadn't been, there would have been another chance to include it several years later when they reached *thin*. I presume they thought that, since it consisted of three words, it was more of a phrase than a word, and so its natural right of entry into the dictionary was compromised. We had to be practical: two-word compounds could easily be included if they had gained a firm foothold in the language; three-word compounds were more questionable, and it was sometimes hard to determine whether they were fixed expressions or chance collocations of the three elements; four-word compounds were even less likely to be included.

By the late 1970s, when we were working on *red* for the *Supplement to the OED*, we concluded that *thin red line* was admissible. Almost all of the work on *red* had been edited by my old trainer, Lesley, and she was not one to leave any stone unturned. Her bundle of *red* words included *thin red line*. Everyone knew, in those days, that this was a historical expression that referred to the British Army in line of battle, in its role as protector—thin and stretched out in its redcoat uniform trying desperately to save the British Empire from the forces of darkness. The more of these forces that came along, the thinner the line became.

Suggestions in our card file indicated that the phrase was redolent of the Battle of Balaclava, in the Crimean War. But Lesley had a serious problem here. She had an armful of documentary evidence for *thin red line* collected over a hundred years or so by the dictionary's "readers," but none of this predated 1935 and a jingoistic occurrence in a novel by George Orwell. The Battle of Balaclava took place on 25 October 1854. So either the expression *thin red line* had nothing to do with the battle, or our documentary evidence started almost a hundred years too late.

For the everyday dictionary editor, there were precious few resources on the Crimean War in the language-flavoured *OED* library. But all was not lost. In researching the expression in the dictionary's reference library, Lesley had followed protocol and inspected quotations dictionaries, just on the off-chance. As well as the standard *Oxford Dictionary of Quotations*, we also checked through various editions of John Bartlett's *Familiar Quotations*, published in America since the mid-nineteenth century and a powerhouse of recondite information on sayings familiar and less so. My personal favourite in this corner of the library was Burton Stevenson's *Home Book of Quotations*, a massive red brick of a book published posthumously in New York in 1967, and amalgamating much of Stevenson's early work on phrases.

But this time it was John Bartlett who nearly came up trumps, with a reference to *The Times* report of 25 October 1854 on the Battle of Balaclava, which provided a reference to the "thin red streak tipped with a line of steel" at the battle, and attributed the reference to the paper's Irish war correspondent (later Sir) William Howard Russell (1820–1907). Problem No. 1: this wasn't actually the expression we were looking for. It was close, but not close enough.

Lesley called in the help of our researchers in London and Oxford. At the British Library's newspaper library in Colindale, out in the north-west suburbs of London, long-time *OED* word researcher George Chowdharay-Best looked for the 25 October *Times* report and found that it didn't exist. That was Problem No. 2. Facts were dissolving like butter in a pan. At this point, the research was transferred back to Oxford, where it was taken up by my colleague Yvonne Warburton. She hunted through issues of *The Times*, looking for the report, and eventually found it on 14 November—but still it read "thin red streak," not "thin red line." We had to put that lead on hold.

The bloodhounds now picked up another trail. Although John Bartlett hadn't come up with the goods, a later reference from 1877, in the *Oxford Dictionary of Quotations*, offered a fall-back position. This was to another William Russell source, his *Expedition to the Crimea* (1877 edition). Sure enough, this did contain the "thin red line tipped with steel," but only twenty-three years after the battle. There was still hope. There always is. Russell's *Expedition to the Crimea* (1877) was a later edition of his book *The War: From the Landing at Gallipoli* (1855), so it would be no trouble to convert *thin red line* to 1855. No, back then he had still used "thin red streak." How about his 1858 edition? Back to our London researcher to check this, as the book wasn't in Oxford. But no, it was still "thin red streak" there.

We were flummoxed at 1877. We had *red line*, but not *thin red line*, from 1855. It was frustrating, but in the absence of any other leads, we had no option but to publish the entry with 1877 as the earliest reference to the precise phrase *thin red line*.

There is naturally a postscript to this everyday tale of lexical folk. Several years later Yvonne published a brief article about her research and asked readers to see if they could find earlier evidence for *thin red line*. Sure enough, the challenge was taken up, with quotations supplied to the dictionary back to 1859, including a commemorative verse contained in Sebastian Evans's *Rhymes Read in the Queens Drawing Room at Aston Hall*, which linked the expression directly to the Battle of Balaclava: "How too, on Balaclava's hills, / Two miles of deadly riding, / That 'thin red line' charged,—and returned, / How thin! to tell the tiding!"

The icing on the cake came a year or two later. More and more historical publications were steadily becoming accessible on the Internet, and the possibilities for lexicographical research were changing dramatically once again. By this time, *The Times* archives had become searchable online. There was a dash for the keyboards around the world, and one of the *OED*'s back-room contributors found what we wanted—"The services of that 'thin red line' which had met and routed the Russian cavalry"—from an edition of the newspaper published on 24 January 1855. Maybe the quotation marks imply that it was a misremembering of Russell. The text places it all in context, as the British government debated which soldiers should receive medals for their service in the Crimea:

Where in history was a parallel to be found to the glorious charge of Balaklava? Nor were the services performed by the gallant 93d

Regiment, under General Sir Colin Campbell, to be forgotten—the services of that "thin red line" which had met and routed the Russian cavalry.

Folk-memory and documentary evidence had finally come together to clinch the deal.

L earning how to edit for the *OED* wasn't something that was achieved overnight, or with that very first bundle of work containing the word *queen*. There were many larger lexicographical issues that I became aware of as I became more experienced. But when, a couple of months after receiving the assignment, I'd finished with the word *queen*, I'd followed the cycle from beginning to end for the very first time: the laborious and yet exciting collection of material, the solid research in the departmental library, the frustrating struggle with meaning and how to express it succinctly—all parts of a complex procedure that I would conduct hundreds of times in the future, and pass on to those who entered the ranks of the *OED* staff after me. Many of the details of those early procedures are redundant nowadays, but at the time I felt a thrill of connection with the earlier editors in the nineteenth century, who used precisely those procedures in their own work. I had the best job in Oxford.

I was also learning a new rigour. The English student in the mid-1970s was not necessarily encouraged to be a rigorous literary analyst. On a spectrum of rigour, I would have proudly put myself towards the more impressionistic, soft-edged end. But I soon learnt, from my trainer, that those were not qualities that marked out the lexicographer. Much as I had the academic background and the natural curiosity, I needed to sharpen up if I was to write curt yet informative definitions based on a careful examination of the evidence. Fortunately, I had the patience to learn, though there were times when it seemed I was going through a tough initiation.

The future was unknown and we gave it little thought, happy in our little bubble. All we could do in those days was to research and edit with the tools available to us at the time. Subsequent technological developments, which allowed us to discover so much more significant new information (the *thin red line* at Balaclava, for instance), lay way ahead of us: different from what we knew then, and quite unprecedented. In due course we had to understand how to retain the rigour of old-style lexicography, and yet how to harness the power of the new information networks which were then just hidden from us below the horizon.

FOUR

The Longest Way Round

I f my first year at the *OED* had seemed to last for ages, as I concentrated on learning how to become an editor, the next few years—as we steered the *Supplement* project to a conclusion and finally brought the curtain down on old-style Oxford lexicography—seemed, in contrast, to rush by. Once I knew how to edit, I found myself working my way up the dictionary ranks, being given new projects, and supervising newer editors in their efforts to achieve editorial competence.

There was no doubt that the language was changing, too, as it always does, as we entered the Thatcher and the Reagan years. As a contrast to the freedoms of the previous two decades, we were starting to appreciate the benefits and disbenefits of what became known as political correctness: I spent some time working on the entry for *-person* as a gender-neutral suffix, we reviewed our entries for *racism* and *sexism*, and we kept an eye on new *-isms*, such as *ablism* and *lookism*, both soon to find a place in the dictionary. Lexicographers joined the rest of society in wondering how best to describe peoples that earlier generations were happy to refer to as "tribes." New technology was seeping through into popular parlance (*microcomputer, EFTPOS, data protection, electronic music*): sometimes these terms were older in technical use, but they were becoming part of the regular vocabulary of everyone. A new affluence in the West, backed by a new politics of individualism (*big bang*, *debt counsellor*, *enterprise culture*), contrasted with consciousness-raising regarding the environment (*biofuel*, *ecofeminism*). In Britain, *Estuary English*, the mix of standard English and Cockney which seemed to spread out from London from the 1970s and 1980s, identified a new generation of would-be entrepreneurs, and in America *ebonics* gave a new validity to African American speech. We were entering a new domain, and cutting ourselves off both from the austerity of postwar years and the colourful eccentricities of psychedelia.

O ver the years I worked in several offices in the University Press. Each time, a sense of place was important. Each office seemed to characterise the type of work that I and my fellow editors were doing and somehow epitomised the language changes we were describing. When I joined the editorial staff of the dictionary in 1976, we were working in a quiet Victorian semi-detached house on a residential side-street in Oxford. And the work itself was quiet and gentle—gradually adding new words and meanings to a massive Victorian dictionary. The building fitted the sort of work we were carrying out.

We didn't know it in 1976, but our time in those offices was drawing to a close. The dictionary had shifted for itself in Walton Crescent since the chief editor's appointment back in 1957, but now—in 1977—there were plans to ship us and all of our files up the road to a grand Georgian building on St Giles', one of the main streets in central Oxford and the former home of the Press's world-famous cartographic department. We had become cramped in Walton Crescent. To me, the new offices symbolised the palatial old-world dignity that people expected of the *OED*, where an elegant entrance hall led on to rooms crowded with words. We were very much on public display here, pointed out by the tourist **buses** that edged slowly past as they plied along the road throughout the working day.

New technology was not a new concept in the 1970s. Every generation considers its defining technology to be new, whether it is the
printing machine, the railway, or the computer. On the streets of
France in the early nineteenth century, the *omnibus* (or the *bus*) was
part of a new wave of technology which helped to manage the shift in
society from horses to horsepower towards the end of the Industrial
Revolution. It nicely illustrates how the vocabulary of the horse-
drawn carriage was "repurposed" for the new technology of the motor engine. And the analogy extends into our modern vocabulary: if
the invention of the horse-drawn *bus* hadn't occurred in the early
nineteenth century, then we wouldn't have *data buses*, or *busboys* and
busgirls to clear tables in American restaurants (the original busboys
collected fares on buses).

Back in the 1820s, the French, exhausted by the Napoleonic
Wars, turned their attention to mechanics and the machine that became the *bus*. The older word is *omnibus*, and at the relevant entry,
the *OED* reports carefully that "the earliest use [of the word *omnibus*] in French was in 1825, reportedly to denote vehicles run by a
M. Baudry for the purpose of transporting passengers between
Nantes and a nearby bathing place." In Britain we heard about this
alarming French invention around 1828, and by 1829 Mr George Shil-
libeer had introduced omnibuses to the streets of London "upon the
Parisian mode" (*The British Traveller*: 4 July). We reshaped *omnibus* to
the shortened *bus* rapidly, by 1832. Although the name *omnibus* derives formally from the dative plural of Latin *omnes*, "all"—and so
means, literally, a public-transport vehicle "for everyone"—there is a
sneaking suspicion that there may be more to it than this. The *OED*
neutrally observes: "The idea for the name is said further to have
come from a tradesman with the surname *Omnès* who had the legend
Omnès omnibus written on the nameplate of his firm."

From a lexicographical point of view, there was one aspect of the
dictionary's move to St Giles' that dominated all others. For some

reason, our chief editor was determined to discover whether the street name "St Giles" should end in an apostrophe or not. The English are temperamentally obsessed with the presence or absence of apostrophes. It remains for many people a divide between civilisation and chaos. If the *OED* was found, on its grand letterhead, to have added an apostrophe where no apostrophe was necessary, or to have omitted that most crucial of English punctuation marks when its presence was regarded as *de rigueur*, then the bedrock of our society would be in jeopardy.

If the *OED* could do anything, it could research just such an issue, and one of our most experienced editors, Alan Hughes, was charged with discovering the truth about "the apostrophe of St Giles." Local records were read, newspapers were consulted, etymologists dug up for opinions, and the actual evidence of the living language (one of the *OED*'s specialities) was quietly analysed. After weeks of debate and drama, the gavel came down on the side of the apostrophe. St Giles' was adjudged the one true form in which our address could be written. It appeared that no one else was particularly bothered, including (*a*) the Post Office, which had long ago abandoned apostrophes as a bad idea except in street names involving the names of kings and queens, and (*b*) any of our neighbours further along in the street, who continued to display a variety of options in their shop windows and nameplates.

Once all lexicographical objections to the move were resolved, we settled down to work, observing—by our traditional methods—where the language was heading in the late 1970s. I was still the youngest member of the department, and so naturally I regarded myself as the *OED*'s eyes and ears on the street, as far as language was concerned. In order to promote this image I occasionally came to work in a pink kaftan-style tunic, in what I regarded as the manner of the day, even though suit and tie was said to be the order of the day elsewhere in the University Press. Of course, the *OED* didn't need a streetwise editor, as we already had numerous perfectly adequate, tried-and-tested systems to ensure that we captured for our files both the language of the street and any other form of language emerging or surviving out in the wild. But it suited me to consider myself the standard-bearer of the new, and it reinforced a growing feeling I had that the dictionary had been looking for so long towards the past that it now needed to spend a little more time responding to the present and the future.

If my pink tunic signalled that I was searching for a way to mark myself out as a harbinger of the new, so, too, did the lively interest that I took at the time in two cultural tides that were washing through the language in the late 1970s: punk and Rastafarianism. I don't think I'd regard myself as a devotee of punk music (and I'm almost certain I wasn't a Rastafarian), but I imagined that punk was a cultural phenomenon that needed to be covered in its entirety by the *OED*. To this end, I amassed as many underground, cyclostyled, and badly reproduced punk magazines as I could lay my hands on. As soon as I'd begun to assemble this library of lowbrow musical ephemera, I started reading it, panning for lexical gold. I extended my reading to *Rolling Stone*, to catch an early glimpse of modern American vocabulary which, I suspected, would be making its way over to Britain in a few years' time.

My efforts had little effect on how the powerful *OED* captured and recorded this transient cult, but they were successful in showing the senior members of the department that I had the sort of interest and stamina which might be relevant to the dictionary in the future, if my efforts could be redirected to more productive ends.

At the same time, I bought an old set of eighteenth-century novels from a secondhand bookshop that I visited that year while on holiday, and I "read" them painstakingly against the *OED*—and with more enjoyment than I had experienced reading Metz's *Film Language*. I found countless references for words and meanings earlier than those already included in the dictionary, which I then showed to the chief editor before directing them off to the card files. Without realising it, I was bringing myself into the spotlight, and starting to etch out a future for myself.

W hile I was beginning to make a faint appearance on the chief editor's radar as a prospect for the future, changes within the University Press meant that the dictionary offices in St Giles' were witnessing the end of an era. These were the final years of the flowering of hand-drawn Oxford lexicography, with its profusion of pens, index cards, books, and brains. The *OED* was the last major reference work to employ hot-metal typesetting (superseded by phototypesetting and more recently by digital typesetting), whereby the individual metal letters or types were cast—literally from hot, molten metal—and then built up in metallic rows of words in the typesetting machine, ready for the next stage of the process, when the relevant page would be printed. When one of the last remaining firms finally closed down its hot-metal department, we even supervised the transfer of heavy printing plates of the *Supplement* by train halfway round the country to another printer.

The new technology of printing was matched by new technology elsewhere, but the *OED Supplement* remained intent on reaching *Z* by way of its old-fashioned, index-card-based methods. If they were good enough for the Victorians, then they were apparently good enough for us. We employed our traditional techniques to explore the new language of the times; readers all around the world, and the general public, too, provided us with their linguistic findings on slips, and we hurried to include as much as we could in the *OED*. This was the **crowdsourcing** that the *OED* had always done, before the term was invented. We found *Reaganomics*, but we missed *Thatcher's Britain*, and had to leave that for a later editorial phase. We tried to second-guess where the language was going, but we weren't right about every trend. After a visit to the United States in the mid-1970s, our chief editor became captivated by the idea that the vocabulary of American truckers' Citizens' Band radio was going to dominate the world of slang: the *ten-code* (the code of signals, all starting with the number ten, used first by America's police and then by CB radio truckers), *breaker* (a trucker who breaks in on the conversation of other truckers), *handle* (a trucker's identifying nickname). There were some eyebrows raised in the dictionary office (Oxford's own code for utter disbelief, and right up there with the imperceptibly flaring nostrils), and although we were instructed to file evidence of this glittering new-word hoard, many of us correctly expected that its traces would be swept away by the next tide.

In the end, a handful of the better-known CB slang expressions did find their way into the *OED*. That validates the dictionary's selection process rather well. The files were filled with countless "amusing" and forgotten terms, but they didn't generally stand the test of time. The ruthless selection criteria by which we worked—looking for a good spread of evidence over a range of years—saw most of these parvenus fall at the first fence, though they still languish in the card files in the unlikely event that they should experience a revival. The system also makes it impossible (we strenuously maintain) for word pirates to smuggle invented words into the dictionary. It surprises some visitors to the department that the files contain so much that didn't make it into the dictionary. The *OED* doesn't just include the tip of the iceberg of language, but there are levels beneath the water that will be hard-pressed ever to make their way into the editing process.

Crowdsourcing is a word that later on broke the dictionary's inclusion rules. When we came to add it to the *OED*, we accepted it even though we had only collected evidence of its existence over seven years. The rule was that we didn't add a word to the dictionary until we had records for it spanning over ten years, to give it a chance to settle down in the language (this was in the days before the Internet). Our first notice of *crowdsourcing* was in *Wired* magazine as recently as 2006, and it crept into the dictionary in June 2013. Actually we had a second rule, deeply hidden most of the time, which said that if a new term came to extraordinary prominence, then we bent the first rule. We did that in the old days for *perestroika* and *glasnost*. I'm not sure *crowdsourcing* is quite as significant socially or politically as those terms, but we do make the rules. *Crowdsourcing* developed from the older word *outsourcing* (source materials or products), so it's not a new-word-out-of-nowhere, but a welding together of *crowd* (a sixteenth-century noun from an Old English verb) and *sourcing* (*source* comes from Old French, but *outsourcing* is 1980s business jargon). It's worth following the sequence of linguistic changes, as it shows that they happen in a logical order.

As the *Supplement to the OED* was tracking doggedly towards its conclusion, we became more and more aware of the chilling public perception that the dictionary overall (not the newer sections which we were adding) was slipping further and further, and irretrievably, out of date. We could gauge this perception by a number of criteria. Firstly, fewer and fewer people were sending information to us about old words. They knew, from observing the dictionary over previous decades, that those older meanings of the central vocabulary of English were not receiving an editorial overhaul. That wasn't our remit, and even we didn't know if there would ever be resources to accomplish it. Secondly, references to *OED* definitions cited in newspapers and journals in those days were kindly, but resigned to the fact that the very text they were citing was obsolescent. It was as if the journalists knew they were handling a dinosaur's bones.

But most of all, we could judge our own antiquatedness against the changes we saw elsewhere: the *Encyclopaedia Britannica*, for instance, had apparently reinvented itself and continued to publish new editions in which the content was, to all intents and purposes, up to date. We fared badly against that.

Worse, there were innovations in linguistics that appeared to make the *OED*'s handling of language old-fashioned. In the 1960s, linguistics had undergone a revolution under the supervision of Noam Chomsky and transformational grammar. Transformational grammar described the rules for transforming or converting the deep, unseen, fundamental grammar of an utterance into the "surface" grammar that we recognise—and vice versa. If we had decided to incorporate this, then all of our grammatical terminology and descriptions would have taken on a new, mathematical flavour. How did the *OED* respond to this new, structural, grammatical perspective? It didn't. We didn't change anything. Gradually linguistics developed new ideologies, and still the *OED* plugged on with its old, Victorian grammatical framework. Sociolinguistics? The study of language in relation to its social factors (such as gender, dialect, class). We watched the discipline develop from a distance, but we continued to address these social issues in our own way. These were aspects we would need to address, it seemed, if we ever wanted to bring the *OED* back into the scholarly limelight.

Worse still, other dictionaries were trying out new ways of working. Larry Urdang and Patrick Hanks had invented the all-new *Collins English Dictionary*: not a historical dictionary, but a modern dictionary of contemporary English, which defined words in ways which the ordinary person could easily understand.

Worst of all, the Collins COBUILD project (short for the Collins Birmingham University International Language Database) was reinventing the theory of how definitions should be written: in coherent sentences rather than lexicographical fragments.

Worse than worst of all, the new science of computational linguistics was starting to offer computational analysis of regular language, automatically identifying the most significant language patterns in huge corpora or databases of text. This was one area where new technology could really help the *OED*, it seemed, and yet assimilating it had not fitted into the *Supplement's* timetable.

How could the *OED* ever keep up with these changes? Well, at the time we couldn't. We just had to press on to the end of the *Supplement*, and see how the land lay after that.

But the strange and very dangerous thing was that hardly anybody appeared to mind. It was as if there was an acceptance that the dictionary was and would remain a leftover folly from the Age of Empire. Commentators made excuses for its decrepitude without ever expecting the situation to get better. There was a counterbalancing sense of urgency about the dictionary offices: the editors knew that the dictionary was falling out of date, and wanted to fix it before too many people noticed. Everyone was trying to drag the dictionary slowly into the twentieth century just as the twentieth century was starting to turn into the twenty-first. And this faint shadow over our work gradually darkened as we approached nearer and nearer to the end of the alphabet.

A curious adjunct to the fading glory of the dictionary took place most days in the dictionary offices, and had done since I had first arrived on the *OED* staff. It took place in the twilight realm of the dictionary's large grey metal filing cabinets in which index cards by the million, contributed by our readers, were stored. Throughout the 1970s and 1980s, these cabinets played host to a strange piece of Japanese theatre—the dictionary tea-time. The dictionary tea was symptomatic of the sedate environment in which the dictionary had grown up in the nineteenth century. It illustrated an old university common-room attitude to scholarship, and this was capped by the appearance here from time to time of the chief editor and his deputy. To some of us, the dictionary tea resonated with the sense of genteel editorial refinement and cocktails on the *Titanic* that a modern dictionary should have shunned.

By a quirk of fortune, building structure, and architectural common sense, the dictionary's quotation cabinets had been located in the basement of our previous offices in Walton Crescent, with a convenient and yet dismal tea room adjoining. Now in St Giles', with its stronger floors, the quotation cabinets were on the ground floor, and the room in which they were contained was itself deemed suitable for the imbibing of afternoon tea.

Every afternoon, the dictionary editors (or those of them who still wanted to meet regularly with their colleagues) descended to the tea room. At every other office where I'd worked (on summer jobs, etc., before university), the stock topic of conversation when any two members of staff happened to meet was either (*a*) football, (*b*) what was on television the previous evening, or possibly (*c*) work colleagues. I *never* heard any of those topics raised at the dictionary tea.

There were sometimes days of great excitement, when the chief editor condescended to attend the dictionary tea and draw conversation from his many acolytes. On particularly good days, he would launch into a (largely one-sided) conversation with our great and silent deputy chief editor, John Sykes—whom I had hardly met since the days of my interview. As the two of them did not really share any interests, and came at language from different angles, it was hard to see where these conversations would go, but they made for good listening. Their exchanges resembled casual chats between Captain Kirk and Mr Spock. In the absence of John Sykes, Captain Kirk would sometimes reminisce about the early days of the dictionary in the 1950s—which none of the staff by then could remember, for a number of reasons, but mainly because they weren't there. He might be encouraged to relate how he had arrived at work on his first day, back in 1957, sat in his office, and wondered how he should go about editing a dictionary. After much deliberation and doubtless many lonely cups of tea, he decided (to the alarm of modern editors) that the best way to establish how the language was moving was to read the copy of *The Times*—at the time a bastion of conservatism—that he had brought to work that day, in order to discover evidence for new words and other barbaric additions to the language.

One of the dangers of the dictionary tea was that an editor might be induced to take some expression too literally and then start publicly deconstructing it. This is a trap into which it is too easy for the lexicographical mind to fall. The subject of the plural of *referendum* came up once. Was it *referendums* (as any self-respecting English speaker under the age of twenty at the time would have said), or was it *referenda*, as Cicero and his circle (and any English speaker over twenty) would have preferred? Lexicographers have to present linguistic or lexical reasons for their choices, and a voice of authority, in the form of my colleague Bob Allen, raised the excellent point that, in Latin, *referenda* would mean "*things* to be referred to a vote of the people," whereas in English two *referendums* might each be about individual points on which popular opinion was sought—so *referenda* would be "wrong." By the time arguments had been exhausted and the white smoke had risen from the chimneys on the dictionary's roof, you can be assured that almost all arguments had been exhausted in the most literal sense possible.

Amidst the fading glory of the *OED*, there were gleams of hope. New staff members were only occasionally appointed these days, but each one was optimistically viewed—at least by the senior editors—as the first of a new generation rather than the last of the old one. A year or so after I joined the editorial staff, there was a new arrival, Ed Weiner, with whom I would find myself working very closely on the modernisation of the *OED* in years to come. Although I was a year Ed's senior in length of service on the dictionary, I was several years younger than him in real life, as he had been busy for the previous few years on a doctorate on the so-called Wycliffite Psalter commentary, which had more or less passed me by while I was at university, to my shame. After a while we shared a room on the ground floor of the St Giles' offices, a room which I had earlier shared with a Latinist, David Howlett, before he landed the top job on the *Dictionary of Medieval Latin from British Sources*, also in slow progress elsewhere in Oxford.

It was an office I had also shared for a while with another classicist, Philip Hardie. It was a pity that Phil didn't stick with the dictionary, as he was probably the most accomplished lexicographer I have ever encountered. He had a facility for knowing which entry in the *OED* was the exact counterpart to the entry you were struggling with, and which would therefore help in your attempt to dig yourself out of whatever lexicographical hole you were in. He also spoke very softly, as I do. When people came into our office it would take them a while to realise that we were in fact conducting a conversation below the level of their hearing. "Susurration" was what Philip called it. The more prosaic tended to refer to bats. It's hardly surprising that Philip picked on "susurration," as soon afterwards he left the dictionary to become a junior research fellow in classics at Corpus Christi College in Oxford, leading to a glittering subsequent career as a classics professor at Oxford and then Cambridge. *Verb sap*, etc.

Until Ed's arrival I had been the youngest member of the dictionary staff, and I soon learned that I still was. In fact, because of the vagaries of our recruitment procedure, I remained the youngest member of the department for what seemed to me decades. Ed came with some background—he'd been teaching Old and Middle English at Christ Church—and the chief editor was clearly relieved to have found someone who might shape up as his successor. Ed and I had very different characters, but as time went on we found that we worked together very well on a complementary basis. Anything I didn't know Ed would know, and I'd tell him the time of day when he needed it. Well, it was a bit more even than that, but that's how I felt sometimes. And it was gratifying to see, at first hand, someone else going through the same gruelling editorial initiation that I had undergone over the previous year. Gradually, we forged a solid friendship as we contemplated the dictionary's present and future.

B y the late 1970s I had started to become interested in how the chief editor managed his editorial team. It was generally felt that, for all his editorial strengths, he didn't get everything right. For instance, there are three things you should never say to historical lexicographers. The first is that directing a dictionary project is like commanding a regiment. There is nothing lexicographers like less than feeling that they are part of a unit being ordered to carry out impersonal routine tasks as part of someone else's grand design. You can see why. Each entry they work on is personal, and all of the research and analysis they conduct is (in their own minds) of the most vital importance to the history of the language. If they are likened to foot soldiers marching to someone else's beat, then their work is somehow diminished. The second metaphor you should steer well clear of is that of the production line. Historical dictionaries are massive, and involve an enormous amount of work, but the regular editor likes to think that he or she is one of a band of independent researchers who consent to work together for the greater good. There's a third term I've heard more recently that you should never use in reference to the dictionary text that editors struggle to create, and that is *content*. *Content* is publisher's jargon that reduces text to the level of filler, to be manipulated by a higher power. For lexicographers, the opposite of *content* is *discontent*. I've heard the editorial offices referred to as the "Content Area," as if it were filled by comatose cats contentedly purring.

Now, our chief editor had seen active service in the Second World War with the New Zealand Army in Italy. He'd played rugby in the forces, and tended to regard projects as military undertakings. He liked to imagine the editorial staff as troops committed to the larger goal of servicing the dictionary. This isn't unreasonable, and you need to take an overview to develop the vision necessary to manage a **project** such as the *OED*. But, as I learned, it's best to keep the metaphors to yourself.

Project is a word that entered English in the late Middle Ages (around 1450). Lexicographers, it seems, don't know everything: sometimes it is impossible to say whether a word like *project* entered English from French or from medieval Latin. Both were languages actively used at the time, and the medieval mind didn't necessarily try to separate language sources to the same elaborate extent that we do today. Formally, the English word *project* derives from Latin *proiectum*, "a projecting structure," "a projection," but the Romans didn't use the word in a business-management sense. Our meaning, "a plan," seems more indebted—as the *OED* tells us—to the related medieval French word *projet*, which did carry the meaning "a plan." The two sides of the prospective etymology don't quite meet: Latin gives us the form/spelling, and French gives us the meaning, but at present we can't explain the cross-over point.

This meaning also seeped through Europe into Italian and Spanish in the sixteenth century. If we think that we borrow a word from one language, we should remember that other languages might find it convenient and borrow it too. Networks spread; language development isn't linear.

But the modern association of the term with business and research (like much comparable management terminology) dates from the emergence of management studies and business planning in the early twentieth century. The first evidence that the *OED* has found for this meaning of the word dates from 1916, suggesting, aptly, that some of the terminology of business practice could have arisen out of new organisational theories pioneered by the military in the First World War. The *OED* cheekily cites W. H. Auden: "Thou shalt not worship projects nor / Shalt thou or thine bow down before / Administration" (*Nones*, 1952: 61).

There was one aspect of the chief editor's management style which was far-sighted. Even though he cherished his ablest editors, and desperately wanted to make use of them to complete his pet project, the *Supplement to the OED*, he knew that the only way to help them develop was to offer them small projects of their own. Other colleagues in the department had been offered small dictionaries to edit themselves. A *Junior Dictionary* had been prepared, and an *Oxford Dictionary for Scientific Writers and Editors* had been edited by one of my scientific colleagues. People seemed to enjoy the chance to work independently that these dictionary projects brought. The thought of editing my own dictionary had not really occurred to me at this point. I was too engrossed in tracking the histories and definitions of all the words I had found in my latest batches of *OED* work.

But one day, while I was busy researching and writing up dictionary entries somewhere in the letter *R*, I received another of those occasional calls to the chief editor's office. This time (mercifully) he didn't need any help buying birthday presents, but wanted to float an idea about a future project that I might like to be involved in. "Float" suggests I had some choice, and "involved in" suggests there might be someone else involved too. As it happened, neither was the case. I like to think that my reticence over the previous few years had endeared me to him, since I appeared to possess a copybook as yet unblotted. As a result of this unusual circumstance I was seated in the second most comfortable chair in his large new office, which I had only glimpsed previously and which contrasted starkly with the functional seating arrangement I had in my office downstairs.

As I continued to sit in comfort in the chief editor's second-best chair, I realised that I had naively walked into some publishing politics. Oxford had an *Oxford Dictionary of English Proverbs*. However, in those days you shouldn't *just* have a full Oxford dictionary of any subject; it was also advantageous to have a *Concise Oxford Dictionary* on the same topic, and possibly even a *Little* one, too, if you thought the market wouldn't object. There is an element of publishing-by-numbers here, but it made sense: you might not want to buy the full weighty and complex version, but you might want its little sidekick. "Little side-kick" was, as usual, where I came in. It had been suggested, in one of Oxford's grand publishing meetings, or perhaps in one of the narrow but unending corridors of the main University Press site on Walton Street, that our chief editor might find an underling to run up a con-cise version of the late Professor F. P. Wilson's magisterial *Oxford Dic-tionary of English Proverbs*. This large volume had been all but completed when Professor Wilson died in 1960, and had been brought through to publication by his wife in 1970.

While working on the *Supplement to the OED* I had had little to do with proverbs, as we were predominantly dealing with the emergent vocabulary of the nineteenth and twentieth centuries, and most proverbs were well and truly set in stone by then. Modern proverbs tend to have a long gestation period, beginning as quotations from known authors, and only gradually assuming the status of universal proverbs or maxims many years later, when the identity of the original author has been largely or completely forgotten. It's a moot point whether we should still call *If it ain't broke, don't fix it* (Bert Lance, US President Jimmy Carter's director of the Office of Management and Budget: 1977), or *Work expands to fill the time available* (Parkinson's Law—British naval historian C. Northcote Parkinson: 1955), quotations, or whether they have moved into the more abstract world of proverbs. Proverbs are pithy sayings that offer some general truth, by and large. Also, I had expressed no interest in proverbs over my time at the dictionary.

None of this mattered, of course, and so after a while I was allowed to leave the hallowed office to consider whether, for the next year, I would abandon my work on the *Supplement to the OED* and devote myself to the unknown realm of "old said saws" and proverbs.

I discussed the possibility with Hilary (now officially a Doctor of Philosophy, and therefore authorised to dispense literary advice). She, too, was surprised that I had been singled out for my knowledge of English proverbs. It came with no financial inducement, such things being considered as below regard in the leisurely world of Oxford scholarship.

Nevertheless, I could see how my cards were marked, and several days later I informed the chief editor that I would be delighted to take on this unusual project, and what should I do next?

Although I received no immediate reward for the shift of work towards proverbs, my colleague Ed Weiner and I were now informed that if things went to plan we would both be promoted to senior editor in 1980 or thereabouts, when our immediate bosses moved to new projects (the *Concise Oxford Dictionary* and the major revision of the *Shorter OED*). So I needed to make sure things went well on the proverb dictionary, or I would be sliding down a long snake rather than climbing up a short ladder. The prospect of working closely with Ed was good, though, as we had developed quite a friendship amongst the cobwebs and must of the dictionary's files.

And so I spent the next year, which expanded to eighteen months, writing out by hand—as you did in those days—the entire text of a *Concise Oxford Dictionary of Proverbs*. By the end I could speak fluently in "old said saws" and offer trite truisms on demand to anyone who approached me with a problem. One man may steal a horse, while another may not look over a hedge; a stern chase is a long chase; near is my shirt, but nearer is my skin; the best thing for the inside of a man is the outside of a horse (i.e., take some exercise); little pitchers (i.e., children) have large ears; bairns and fools should not see half-done work; if you lie down with dogs, you will rise up with fleas (a saying translated from the Roman sage Seneca); the looker-on sees more of the game. Proverbs were universal truths (or what passed as these), normally presented in sentence form. Some were abstract (of the "Hope springs eternal" variety), but many evolved from the home and hearth of the medieval peasant, and so their subjects were often homely subjects—cats, dogs, friends, the weather, churchgoing, food and drink. They were extraordinary, colourful, reassuring adjuncts to everyday conversation.

I soon realised that one of the reasons I had been given this task was to familiarise myself with editing a whole dictionary. Work on the *OED* was episodic, and editors needed the experience of a full *A-to-Z* run to appreciate all the aspects of dictionary life. Ed was soon to be handed a similar project, which would familiarise him with this whole-world view, when he was invited to take time off from the *Supplement* to prepare an *Oxford Miniguide to English Usage*. Without realising it at the time, we were being slowly groomed to see how we'd manage on a larger stage.

Professor Wilson's big Oxford dictionary of proverbs followed roughly the same format as the *OED*, illustrating each proverb with quotations of its use in texts from the earliest known occurrence to the present day. But he had had no collection mechanism, so his entries trailed off far too early in the twentieth century. Fortunately, the *OED*'s stalwart reader Marghanita Laski had taken a shine to me, and she came on board, redirecting her own word collection for a period to proverb collection. Together, she and I and a handful of other readers managed to plug the documentary gaps.

Like the Victorian *OED*, each quotation in Professor Wilson's proverb dictionary had been provided with information about the work from which it was taken (the author's name, the title of the work, the edition used, and the page reference on which it might be found). But, as with the old *OED*, much of this information had been presented in a very abbreviated and cryptic manner, and sometimes—in the light of modern scholarship—it was plain wrong. Not everyone nowadays would recognise the title *L.L.L.* as a shortening of Shakespeare's *Love's Labour's Lost*, or *P.R.* as Milton's *Paradise Regain'd*. It was necessary to bring the text of the dictionary closer to the modern reader, but to retain the historical principles. Also, quotations themselves were typically extracted from modern editions, and so—following the principles of modern historical lexicography—I had to recheck these in original editions. I had to convert historical quotations from, say, Sir Thomas More, collected from weaselly nineteenth-century editions (which modernised the spelling of words for the convenience of contemporary readers), back to the original forms of the words as presented in the first editions of the sixteenth century. It was a fascinating experience, seeing the text as it fragmented before my eyes from the cosmetic versions using modernised spellings back to what people would actually have seen and read when the texts were freshly published. Not everyone cares, but in order to recreate an image of what the language originally looked like, and to experience it as it was experienced back then, I became convinced that I had to ensure I was looking at the original historical text and not a later editorial refashioning. You could not analyse historical data if you were observing modified evidence.

Here, for the first time, I was immersed in the early history of the language, which my work on the big *OED* had not yet involved. The proverb dictionary was not such a complete challenge as the *OED*, but it took me through aspects of work at a much deeper level than I had previously had an **inkling** existed.

> *Inkling* is too good a word to pass over in complete silence. It's an example of a noun which we still use that is derived from a verb which has drifted deep into obsolescence. Not a lot of people know that *inkling* derives from the good old English verb *to inkle*. This was not in fact a good "Old English" word, as it wasn't around in the Old English period (up to around AD 1150). But *to inkle* does at least date back—like *project*—to the late Middle Ages, when it meant "to utter or communicate in an undertone or whisper, to hint." If you "inkled the truth," you hinted at it.
>
> It should by now come as no surprise that there was also at the time a noun derived from the verb: *inkling*, or hinting through whisper. The evidence seems to show that the meaning of the verb and the noun developed in the sixteenth century towards our modern meaning of "having an inkling" about something. The word *inkling* was of course commandeered by the Oxford writers and scholars C. S. Lewis, J. R. R. Tolkien, and others, who formed the literary discussion group called the "Inklings" in the 1930s, meeting just down the road from the *OED*'s St Giles' offices at the Eagle and Child public house. In their case, the name was a pun on *ink* and *-ling*.

There is one question that is always asked of lexicographers: What is your favourite word? We are plagued by this seemingly innocent request. I always say I haven't got one—the historical lexicographer needs to remain neutral, and not show any favouritism. Each word has its own type of significance. This response has proved a frustrating stance for journalists, who are keen to establish some humanising factor in their stereotypical lexicographer.

But with proverbs, I did not feel that I had to subject myself to such a rule. And I discovered that my favourite, the old and now almost-forgotten saw "The longest way round is the shortest way home," dated from the early sixteenth century, to "The road to resolution lies by Doubt; The next way home's the farther way about" (where *next* is used in its etymological meaning of "nearest"). It is a thought that applies to historical lexicography in spades, where you need constantly to remind people that the shortest way of doing something isn't necessarily the best way, and that there are advantages in being a little more considered.

There was one final thing about proverbs that served me in good stead in later *OED* revision. I knew, from the full proverb dictionary I was abridging, that many proverbs had their origin in expressions from the classics, both Latin and Greek. The big dictionary was very keen to point out, in an Oxford sort of way, if a particular thought had been previously expressed by Pliny, Horace, or Herodotus. Well and good. But if a saying was originally Latin, the chances were good that it took a path into English that was similar to the path that other *words* from Latin took. I gradually recognised that I should be looking not just for classical prototypes for English proverbs, but for the trail of development from Latin, say, into French or Italian, and then into English. As with words, the situation was much more complex than first meets the eye, but the final resolution is far more satisfying. The longest way round is the shortest way home.

A good example of an expression that illustrates the mixed international heritage of proverbs would be *When the cat's away, the mice will play*. It's a typical old proverb, with imagery from the domestic environment, which is a hallmark of many old sayings. We know it in English from the early seventeenth century (Thomas Heywood's *Woman Killed with Kindness*). Even here it is offered as an "old proverb." In the absence of earlier English evidence, we can see, however, that the proverb existed in French from the early fourteenth century: *Ou chat na rat regne* ("Where there is no cat the rat is king"). Maybe we are more squeamish than the French, and prefer mice to rats.

Before the proverb dictionary could be published, it had to survive an internal review. This turned out to be crucial to me and my prospects of promotion on the main *OED*. I was nervous about how my draft dictionary would be received. Oxford likes to criticise—on the principle that it is the making of good scholarship—but a bad review would be catastrophic. After a few months of anxious waiting, the review came in. The review was read first, naturally, by my chief editor, who called me in again for a debrief. The internal reviewer was Peter Opie (who with his wife, Iona, had edited the excellent *Oxford Dictionary of Nursery Rhymes*). After some character-building introductory remarks by the chief editor, I was fortunately informed that I had got the thumbs-up, and the next thing I knew I was joining Ed in a more senior role on the *OED*. As a footnote, it's curious that the first major printed notice of the proverb dictionary appeared in the *Times Literary Supplement*, in the same issue as its (equally positive) review of Hilary's book *D. H. Lawrence and Feminism*. Things were looking up.

In the same year in which the proverb dictionary was published (1982), things took an altogether different track at home: we had our first baby, Katharine Jane (Kate). Despite my rather curious job, we did all the usual, ordinary things: bringing the baby home very cautiously the first time, photographing her in her carry-cot, etc. Over time Kate hit all the right percentiles, fitted the right-sized clothes, and developed her eating habits just the way the books said she would. Later, Kate would come to argue with me about words, not appreciating that I was in fact the ultimate arbiter. Sometimes kids just don't realise.

True to his word, in 1982 the chief editor moved Ed and me into the grandiose role of senior editor on the *OED*. Ed and I had until then been proceeding on parallel tracks, each editing our own ranges of words, or our own dictionaries, and discussing knotty issues when we encountered them.

Our new jobs as senior editors on the *Supplement to the OED* meant that we were reporting directly to the chief editor, and had overall supervision of the ten or so assistant editors preparing first drafts of entries for the dictionary. Although I no longer had to do the basic research and defining work on dictionary entries, I had to review and improve the drafts produced by junior editors, for final approval by the chief editor; I had to appoint and train new staff, send completed ranges of work to the printers, and handle all the stages of proof prior to publication.

There was an inherent problem with deadlines on the dictionary. Earlier, my colleague Phil and I had established that there were always more words begging for inclusion in the final phases of the *OED* than we had room for. We had decided that Zeno's paradox applied to the *OED*: however fast the editors worked, in the end the words always moved a little bit further ahead, so there was—philosophically—a danger that the *Supplement* would never be completed. So, Ed's and my first job was to refocus the scope of the dictionary project, with only the chief editor in the know. We had to restrain the *Supplement* to its four volumes, and we had around four or five years to complete the task for publication before the 1980s ran out of steam. Dispensing with slide rules and measuring tape (the traditional lexicographers' planning tools), we upscaled to pen and paper, and calculated how many words and meanings we could realistically ask the editors to complete before our deadline arrived and the University Press's exasperation boiled over. Anything else would have to catch the next bus.

We soon concluded that we couldn't afford to let our progress be determined by the vast quantity of data in our word files. We calculated that each editor should be able to complete around twenty-five entries each week. We would then have to revise that material, both of us dealing with some 125 draft entries a week, and leave them in such a state that the chief editor would be able to review them all rapidly, so that they could be dispatched on time for printing. It was simply a case of training, encouraging, and cajoling the junior editors to get through the requisite amount of work each week, and the *Supplement*'s final trajectory would be more or less in the bag.

I was always confident that Ed and I would be able to keep up with our own targets—you just made time. Almost all of the work was problem-solving: the easy parts of the job took no time, and you were always wrestling with the problems, the hard parts, the bits for which there were no obvious rules. You had to resolve each issue, however, in line with the dictionary's own rules, or as near to them as you could. I think that helps to explain why many lexicographers have a strong logical and mathematical background, even though they spend much of their time writing elegant definitions for everyday words. The issues didn't simply concern definitions. Editors needed to be able to analyse data fast, finding patterns that might appear hidden to the readers (what were the typical types of nouns to which the adjective *rustic* attached itself? did this change over the centuries? could you identify any semantic progression?). It helped, too, that Ed and I both seemed to have the knack of making the right decisions, rapidly.

What Ed and I now found was that the main part of the job, the "real" part of being a senior editor on the *OED*, was that you had to work extremely rapidly and accurately, reviewing all of the work of your junior colleagues—rewriting definitions, initiating further research work from our group of dedicated researchers in all of the main research libraries around the world, and deciding quickly how to handle each of the lexical problems that inevitably arose.

The secret was to acknowledge that there are always at least two ways of doing something, and that if the junior editors had already written good definitions, then you shouldn't change them just because they weren't written in precisely the way you'd write them. The job required understanding that someone else could be equally right (not a very "Oxford" attitude back then). The junior editor wasn't always right, so there were often times when we'd need to cut off the tail of a rambling definition, refocus it by introducing new words, or (occasionally) rewrite it from scratch. And that applied to all of the other elements of the dictionary entry. We had to review all of the selected quotations to see if they'd been chosen according to our (largely unwritten) guidelines—covering as broad a range of sources, years, spellings, contexts, and so on as one reasonably could. We had to check that the etymology presented the most likely explanation of the term's emergence. And there was a fair amount of correcting of punctuation and style. Sadly, I quite liked doing that, but it's not something all editors appreciate at first.

The other part of the job was dealing with proofs as they came back from the printer for checking and correction. These were so-called galley proofs, single-column strips of text maybe twice as long as the printed page, produced before the columns were formatted into pages. These galleys gave us scope to make even quite significant alterations without having to find concomitant savings within a single page.

Galley-work was close work—difficult but extremely satisfying, though galleys themselves are now long gone from the publishing process. We'd cut up one set, and send specialist sections off to academic experts for review. Other sets we'd send out to pairs of "critical readers." These critical readers were typically senior academics or experienced non-Oxford lexicographers who knew the *OED* inside-out, who would take an educated view of a whole stream of entries, and whose critical comments were likely to represent the most searching level of critique to which the entries might ever be subject. Their comments, written in the margins of the galleys, were sometimes characteristically explosive ("WHAT???" "Surely Tennyson was referring to love???," "NO!! Recheck"), but often they were more reflective than that. After a few weeks, when all of these comments had been returned, Ed and I would revise the entries in the light of these learned critical (and, to be fair, often complimentary) responses. At the time, I couldn't imagine anything that was as much fun as doing this: working fast, assimilating insightful but sometimes mistimed comments, taking a good entry and making it as perfect as possible.

Experience came, it would seem, in large doses. I was by now reasonably familiar with the inside of the chief editor's office, as he insisted on meeting with Ed and myself every morning at nine o'clock to review our previous day's work, and to make sure the editors were all on track. So this time, when I received yet another summons to the chief editor's office upstairs, I was almost expecting the outcome. But again I was surprised. It turned out that the chief editor had further plans to expand my vocabulary. Unknown to me—as I found was often the case—the previous few months had been a time of turmoil in the Australian dictionary market. Plans were afoot to create and publish a national dictionary of Australian English in 1988, two hundred years after the First Fleet arrived in Australia from England to found a colony. The excitement in Oxford was that, somewhat against the odds, OUP had won the right to publish the historical *Australian National Dictionary*—a sort of *OED* of Australian words—against homegrown opposition. A group of Australian editors, led by New Zealander Bill Ramson, was beavering away at the Australian National University in Canberra and had produced their first range of edited text.

This had been kept a secret from me until then. Our chief editor in Oxford was a New Zealander by birth and inclination, and so might be expected to take enormous interest in the lexicographical pickings of his Australasian fellows. Whilst I'm sure he did, he also considered that he was too busy at the time with his work on the *OED Supplement* to worry about something new, and had decided that it was a project I would be able to manage between my other activities.

The proposal put to me was the normal one: that I should continue doing more or less everything I was already doing—i.e., a full-time editing job in Oxford—and that I should also do more. This "more" meant reading the stream of proofs that was about to descend upon us from Canberra, as well as advising the project in Australia generally on lexicographical practice and procedure, on the basis of my detailed knowledge of Oxford lexicography.

It wasn't a dream job, as far as I could see. That was also as far as the chief editor had got in his thinking, but the difference was that he had the power to delegate the work to an underling. So I crept out of his office and back downstairs to consider my "choice." A day or so later I was, predictably, climbing the stairs again about to announce how delighted I would be to take on this extra work.

In no time at all I was handed the first instalment of yet another book with no plot. It began at *A* and seemed to continue over many pages a little further into *A*. So I settled down to read and annotate the Australian dictionary. The format was very familiar to me, as the new text was based in all essentials upon the tried-and-tested structure of the *OED*.

I was well aware of the old misconceptions about Australian vocabulary—which had enjoyed around a one-hundred-year history even then. I knew about the early settlers who had asked the locals the name of that strange animal bounding along in the distant bush, only to be told "kangaroo," or "I don't know," in the native language. Sadly, the story is nonsense: *kangaroo* was just the name for the animal in one of the native Aboriginal languages.

I didn't know the editor, Bill Ramson. Lexicographers from that side of the world didn't normally make their way over to European lexicographical conferences back then. I was worried about how he'd take my comments. People have a habit of thinking Oxford is trying to belittle them even if you just say hello, and I was keen not to do that. We pussyfooted along, exchanging courteous comments and responses, for a few instalments into the letter *B* before I started to understand the code. Bill, it turned out, was delighted that my chief editor wasn't the person he had to deal with on a day-to-day basis over his dictionary, and he found a few of my comments helpful. As intended, I ought to add.

There was plenty for me to learn, too, from the experience. In particular, I learnt how Australian English came to be formed, from the time the continent was opened up to Europeans by Captain Cook in the 1770s right up to the present day. At first there was no Australian English, obviously. The first distinctively Australian words the *Australian National Dictionary* recorded were either regular English words reinvented in a new context, or words borrowed from Aboriginal languages. The new English expressions were typically for the flora and fauna encountered by the sailors and scientists on the first ships to explore around the coast. New words are needed for things that are unfamiliar, but a new thing is often similar to something already known: Captain Cook knew the fantail pigeon from back home, so when—in 1773—he encountered a type of Australian flycatcher that habitually spread its tail-feathers, he naturally called it *a fantail*. When the early settlers wanted a term to describe their action in allowing a transported convict to become a free man, they re-employed the word *emancipation*, which they knew from British legal usage. Language doesn't usually invent, but it recycles and welds together what it needs from existing materials.

When the new visitors came across Aboriginal weapons for the first time, they could create their own word from words they already knew (the boomerang was called the *throwing-stick* in the 1790s), but they might also use the Aboriginal word for the same thing: *boomerang*. *Boomerang* is a Dharuk (or Darug) word, from an Aboriginal language spoken near Sydney in New South Wales—a region colonised by the new settlers (notice that the borrowing implies verbal communication between the white settlers and Aboriginals). Bill and his editors were fortunately able to make use of new research by Aboriginal language experts, who had been active for many years identifying the specific languages in which Aboriginal words are used: another word for a boomerang, a *kylie*, derives from Nyungar and other western Australian languages; the Aboriginal weapon the *wirri* derives from Gaurna, around Adelaide in South Australia.

New geographical features were named after what the first visitors and settlers already knew, as were the new institutions they developed: a piece of Crown land granted to a settler was called an *allotment*. New

Australian uses sprang up for many old words: *house* (the principal residence on a rural property, distinguished from a *hut*, and probably maintaining an old penal-colony distinction), *public* (provided by the government for the benefit of a penal colony), *settlement* (a small town, inhabited by non-Aboriginal settlers). The prevalence of sheep-farming and mining as characteristically Australian occupations brought more creative twists of language into Australian English: a *gun* was a fast shearer; an *out-station* was a secondary station on a sheep farm; a *cradle*, for prospectors, was a box-like structure used to separate particles of gold from sand. Language wasn't led by literary gods in those early years, but by ordinary people striving to gain a living in a hostile environment.

But there was fun and creativity in their coinages too. Although we might think of rhyming slang as the Cockney's preserve, it became a common, and humorous, pattern of word-formation in Australia, especially in the twentieth century: *Aristotle* was a bottle (of drink); a *Jack Shay* (a characteristic Irish name) was a large vessel for brewing *tay* (= tea); *steak and kidney* was rhyming slang for the city of Sydney.

You could even find words which were not well known in Britain except in regional dialect, but which enjoyed a new lease of life on a national scale in Australia. *To fossick* (to search or rummage for something—originally for gold) is perhaps one of the best known of these. It has been detected in Australia from around 1850, but it derives from the English dialect *fossick*, "to obtain by asking, or to ferret out," recorded by the *English Dialect Dictionary* only from Cornwall. It would be fascinating to see a computer model of this process of language birth.

By the late twentieth century, the Australian variety of English had grown to appreciate itself as an independent language, and not just as a derivative outcrop of British English. Nowadays it revels in its own creativity; it has gained its self-confidence—following a cycle similar to that which British English had followed five hundred years earlier.

I commented on Bill's entries right through to the end of editing work, in the mid-1980s, and the dictionary was eventually published right on schedule for the 1788 bicentenary. Much of the new research Bill and his team had conducted on Australian words was very relevant to the *OED*. **Pom** was one of the best examples. It is an affectionate term of abuse used by Australians to describe a Briton. I say "affectionate term of abuse" as a sort of shorthand for what it actually is: we naive Britons think it's affectionate (even when concealed in the friendly expression *Pommie bastard*), and for every Australian it is knowingly ambiguous—on the one hand it can be interpreted as an out-and-out term of abuse, and on the other as a creative, humorous example of the new informal Australian language. It intentionally puzzles us.

Australia has a tradition of playful word creation. Take yourself back to the year 1845. Britain had been transporting convicts to Australia for decades, in a desperate policy which continued into the 1870s. But well before it ended, the British government and the state authorities themselves were keen to encourage civilian emigration to Canada and Australia—to accommodate the perceived "surplus" population in mainland Britain, caused not least by the famines in Ireland. By 1845 immigration was a major cultural reality in Australia and New Zealand. So much so, in fact, that people started playing with the word *immigrant* (as well as *emigrant*). They invented the name for a typical incoming settler, playing on the word *immigrant*, and called him *Jimmy Grant*. Soon enough, the jokey name *Jimmy Grant* (or just *jimmy*) was common enough as a slang alternative for *immigrant*.

By the early twentieth century, with immigration still a hot topic, Australians started tinkering with their word again. The closest word they could find in English to *jimmygrant* (except for the words it was derived from) was *pomegranate*. Now a pomegranate isn't a typical English fruit, but it amused the Australian wordsters of the day and they decided to make use of it. So the *jimmygrant* became the *pomegranate* (1912), both meaning an "immigrant." In the same year the cumbersome *pomegranate* morphed to the ubiquitous *Pom*, and by 1913 it had become the "affectionate" *Pommy* or *Pommie*.

Each time I thought I'd finally learnt how to be a lexicographer, I found that there was more to learn and new problems to solve. But I had found that I enjoyed working at the forefront of a discipline, and on an international stage—even though to date I had only watched other departmental members play their parts on that stage. All of the editors, researchers, and "readers" felt a sense of the significance of what they were doing in producing the "official" record of the English language. Even though the full dictionary was becoming antiquated, it was still our dictionary of record, and adding new material to it was a privilege.

When I had turned up for my first day at work, I had been uncertain whether I'd be competent to do the work, and whether I would fit into the rather rarefied atmosphere of the *OED*. The work, I discovered, was fascinating, and presented problems of the sort I liked solving (finding the right word for a definition; researching historical usage so that the evidence made sense; collaborating with fellow editors and specialists way beyond the dictionary's borders in Oxford). But this excitement came at a price. I had to experience the rites of passage: to eradicate the sense of hopeful imprecision that had dogged me until then, and gradually replace it with hard-edged analysis. Not everyone could make this change. Sometimes editors were appointed who had the right academic background, but rebelled against the rigour: they didn't last long. I was accommodating to it, and I was proud of the new weapons in my editorial armoury.

There was a fly in the ointment. Despite the complexity of our work on the *Supplement to the OED*, I and others found ourselves becoming dissatisfied with the concept of supplementing—of adding lights and tinsel to the dictionary, rather than addressing the whole of the language all the way from the Anglo-Saxon period to the present day. You couldn't form a whole-world picture of the language in the way we

were working, and we knew that much of the language had been neglected by the *Supplement*. When the *Supplement* was complete, would
there ever be scope for a full, proper revision of the big dictionary?
Would Oxford (the University and the Press), not always known for
forward thinking, ever be prepared to countenance this adventure? Was
such an undertaking even feasible?

By now, I had been a member of the *OED* department for almost
ten years. From those first tentative footsteps into editing, I'd become
involved in training and planning, running my own dictionary projects, and generally obtaining an overview of the language. I'd come to
appreciate that studying and describing the history of the English language involved looking at it across the world, across time, and in the
full spectrum of registers from formal to slang. And I'd been doing this
in the traditional way, with index cards and pens. It was only as the
curtain fell on the final years of our work on the *Supplement* that we
began to wonder more seriously about the future and how that future
could include the *Oxford English Dictionary.*

FIVE

Uneasy Skanking

W hen the fourth and final volume of the *Supplement to the OED* was eventually published in 1986, almost thirty years after the start of a project marked by the appointment of the chief editor, Bob Burchfield, in 1957, it was justly seen as a stupendous achievement. The *Supplement* had successfully registered the changing language of the twentieth century from the sun-filled summers before the First World War through to the technological inventions and global uncertainties of the mid-1980s.

But in the final years of any large dictionary project, after the basic editorial work has all been completed, there is no room left for the full complement of editorial staff, and as the early 1980s progressed, some editors had left and others had gradually been transferred to other dictionary projects, eventually leaving the chief editor as the lonely general seeing his dictionary through to publication. Ed Weiner was one of those who had agreed to help out on the revision of the *New Shorter OED* (which, like the *OED*, had not been revised since its original publication—in this case in 1933). The *Shorter* was a big project: a two-volume historical dictionary scaled down from the full *OED*, containing half a million definitions (about two-thirds of the big dictionary's definition count), but only a trifling 80,000 quotations (against the *OED*'s 1.8 million). It restricted itself largely to English after 1700.

But the prospect of working on the revised *Shorter* just didn't appeal to me. I was much more interested in what I selfishly regarded as the real thing, not the cut-down version. And then, remarkably, there arose at much the same time the dim prospect of an olive branch offered for the eventual revival of the full *OED*, if the cards fell in the right way. This, it goes without saying, became a matter of great interest to Ed and myself. Everything overlapped in the early 1980s as we navigated ourselves through this period of uncertain transition, and so for the moment I will concentrate on traditional editorial matters, so as not to overcomplicate things. But we will return soon to pick up the possible future for the *OED* in the next chapter.

Fortunately, chief editor was looking out for me at this moment of transition. In the turmoil of restructuring in the last years of the *Supplement*, I found myself handed my own project to work on. The University Press knew that new words kept arriving in the language, and it was decided that the most appropriate option for the dictionary department was that it should maintain a rapid-response force of editors who would mould them into dictionary entries whenever the opportunity arose. And I was put in charge of the "New Words" group, comprising a handful of editors no longer needed to produce text for the *Supplement*, but charged with continuing its mission of preparing entries for new words and meanings for whichever Oxford dictionary might require them (which was all of them, of course), and in the longer term, for the *OED* itself, should the old warhorse ever survive. Notice that the end of the *Supplement* had immediately heralded a new community spirit in the halls of the *OED*.

Running the New Words group didn't represent the future, but it gave us a breathing-space while we, and the University Press generally, thought about how we might work in the years to come. The group gave me my first opportunity to organise an area of the *OED*'s work from the ground up, and over the next few years my New Words colleagues and I lived very close at hand with the lexical changes to which the language was subject in the early to mid-1980s. I don't think I'd heard of a steep learning curve in those days, but I would have appreciated its meaning.

Leading the New Words group also gave us the opportunity to test out how we might go about demystifying the dictionary for the ordinary user. One of my key roles as head of the group was to set the tone for the areas of vocabulary on which we might particularly concentrate. My preference was for less "literary" and more "popular" vocabulary—more "world" English. Whatever I'd managed to achieve in this area in the past had been introduced almost by stealth: now I had the authority to develop my own policy.

At first I attacked the type of data that entered the dictionary's files. By adjusting the texts read, I could begin to influence the scope of the dictionary's coverage. I developed a plan that involved ensuring that more fields of popular interest were addressed by our loyal "readers." We read "serious" books on most subjects (Metz's *Film Language* yet again being—as so often—a case in point), but we had often missed the more populist edge. So for every serious book on a subject that we read (in education theory, politics, fashion—even do-it-yourself and car mechanics, etc.), I'd now have the readers go to their local bookshop and find high-street magazines covering roughly the same topic. When they read these for the dictionary, I hoped that we would find different levels of formality in the material entering our card files. And it worked. Reading popular motorcycling magazines, for instance, helped to draw the expression *dirt bike* to our attention, and to secure its inclusion. So as not to miss a trick, we engaged in a correspondence with a dirt-bike magazine about the finer points of the term. There were dirtbikers out there who wanted to help. Reassuringly, there are always people who want to help the *OED*.

Along the same lines, if you bought food in a supermarket in Britain in the 1970s, you'd see—each week—that new and strange foodstuffs with unfamiliar names were regularly making their appearance on the shelves: *aloo gobi, arrabbiata, carpaccio*, etc. If you stood still and thought for a moment, you could see that there was a parallel here with the way new words were brought to Britain from far-flung places by traders in the sixteenth century.

The normal person confronting these delicacies in a modern-day supermarket would just buy them to try them out. But that is not necessarily the lexicographical way. I decided it would be beneficial to the dictionary to card for our files selected items from the entire stock list of the supermarket, so I wrote to one of the directors asking politely if he would be happy to post me a full printout of all the foodstuffs that his supermarkets carried. Sometimes you have to do foolish things—as a detective lexicographer—for the greater good. I hoped that he would take the same view. There was silence for a few weeks. My in-tray did not bulge with reams of computer printout containing lists of exotic fruits for the dictionary. I had almost given up hope, when finally a package arrived with a tentative note from the director, begging me not to divulge the secrets of his company's success, but offering his wordlist for the good of society. We ransacked that list for months looking for new material to draft for the dictionary—and words like *semifreddo* and *halloumi* and *teppan-yaki* found their way into the editorial stream and eventual publication.

As well as updating the scope of words entering the dictionary, I started to adjust the style of these new entries, trying to edge them away from the academic complexity sometimes sought by my forebears. This was a slow process, and it's still going on even now. We would tend to introduce slightly longer illustrative examples, so that the reader could appreciate more easily the context of the word they were investigating; we updated subject labels, for example changing *Cinematography* to *Film*; and we tried to make definitions more flowing. *Intro*, for example, was defined in the *Supplement to the OED* as "colloq. abbrev. of INTRODUCTION n."—using crabbed abbreviations and diversionary cross-references which might confuse some readers. When we confronted the more informal *outro* (recorded since

1971), we preferred a less cryptic model, with "a concluding section, *esp.* one which closes a broadcast programme or musical work." We didn't get everything right, because we were inching towards a new style, but it felt good that change was possible.

The New Words group quickly developed a plan for hunting down the significant words we should be working on. We knew that the early parts of the dictionary were the most out of date, as those were the areas that had languished the longest. So we decided to concentrate our initial efforts on the letters *A* to *G*. In those days we still had no computer files to take the place of our primary resource, the card file. So for several months I worked with colleagues through words in the card file from *A* to *G*, looking out for batches of evidence for high-profile new words and meanings that we ought to define. It had been about twenty years since anyone had properly sifted through this material, so it wasn't hard to find them.

Aerobics was one of our first finds. The original *OED* had not included the term, nor had it included *aerobe, aerobian, aerobic*, or any of the other related terms (some of which were in existence in the late nineteenth century but had not been deemed sufficiently common for inclusion in the original dictionary). We rushed in at *aerobics*, but it was important to portray the full picture, and for this we needed to research and include the related words. Everything is a network. You can't edit terms in isolation. At the time, the passion for jogging was entering the mainstream, and its associated vocabulary knocked on dictionary editors' doors for attention.

Our investigations of *aerobics* immediately took us into the chamber of nineteenth-century science, where we have previously met the German creation *epicentrum* and English *epicentre*. This time we were in debt to Louis Pasteur (1822–1895), French chemist and microbiologist extraordinaire. In 1863 Pasteur published an article in a French scientific journal in which he coined the term *aerobie*, as an adjective and noun. You might correctly guess that *aero-* relates to "air." You might be harder pressed to uncover the origin of the final -*bie*. And yet the steady hand of the *OED* tells us that Pasteur took these letters from the end of the word *amphibie* (as in *amphibian*, a creature able to live both in water and on land: the -*bie* derives ultimately from Greek *bios*, "life"). *Aerobie* meant "(of an organism) able to live in the presence of oxygen"; the opposite, *anaerobie*, meant "able to live in the absence of oxygen."

As English doesn't as a rule use words like *aerobie* as adjectives, when English scientists reported Pasteur's work in the *Lancet* in 1865 they generously gave it an English colouring, as *aerobian*. But even that didn't sound scientific enough as the word settled down in the language. After the scientists had tried to get used to *aerobian* for several years, they decided that they would prefer *aerobic* (and *anaerobic*), both of which are found in English from 1878, again in the context of Pasteur's work.

The terms were largely the preserve of microbiologists for a century, until the late 1960s, when scientists began to investigate how the body efficiently processes oxygen in physical exercise. As *aerobic* entered a more popular theatre of action, in the mouths of trainers and exercisers, we observed that they found it convenient to develop a new noun, *aerobics*—at first in America (1968), and later in Britain and elsewhere. New joggers found that *aerobics*—in keeping with its lexical origins—referred to physical exercise that "increases the body's oxygen consumption in a sustainable manner" and "is aimed at improving cardiovascular fitness." It is noteworthy, given the centrality of British and American English on the world stage at the time, that these linguistic developments—begun when French science was perhaps the prestige language of scientific investigation in Europe—were concluded (to date) in the melting pot of English. I doubt if there are any early photographs of Louis Pasteur demonstrating his discoveries, but it is Pasteur whom we have to thank for our word today.

Not unconnected with *aerobics*, we noted a new, vociferous, popular interest in environmental concerns and the caring society—again reflected in the vocabulary we encountered. We found *animal rights* in the card files and tracked it back to 1875: and again this arrived as part of a package (*animal rightist* came attached to it: 1979). Computer technology was moving mainstream, too, as microcomputers found their way into homes rather than offices for the first time (*home computers*, as struggling neologists named them at the time). People were beginning to realise that computers *booted up* (1980), and so that brought a new set of terms (its origin in *bootstrap*—1953, in computing, and then *bootable*—1982, and so on). We discovered *disinformation* (1955), and followed up Russian leads to find that it may have derived from a Soviet term in the early Cold War. Soviet Russian words were always a possible source of words from the realm of espionage, and we had previously followed the same route with John le Carré's word **mole** (an agent deeply infiltrated in an enemy organisation).

The *mole* is a small, burrowing animal of the family Talpinae. And yet features of the word have consistently caused it to be used in the context of espionage. *Mole* apparently first entered English around 1400, and all of its word-relations are Germanic (Old Frisian *moll*, Middle Dutch *mol*, etc.). The animal's attributes do not seem to fit it for spying. The dictionary notes that the mole has very poor (or no) vision, and has short, strong forearms adapted for digging. It fetchingly describes its velvety fur "that can be brushed in any direction."

English availed itself of the mole's burrowing propensities when, around 1600, it employed the word to mean anyone who works underground (such as a miner). Hamlet says to the Ghost: "Well said old Mole; can'st worke in the earth? so fast, a worthy Pioner" (a *pioneer* was a soldier who specialised in digging mines during a siege). Working underground could involve working in the darkness, in secret, surreptitiously. Francis Bacon was perhaps the first to employ *mole* in the context of espionage, saying that King Henry VII needed to have spies working for him, because in return "Hee had such Moles perpetually working and casting to undermine him" (1622).

The mole could burrow deep, and the mole could work in secret. These attributes of the word encouraged English-speaking spymasters in the twentieth century to readopt the word in the context of espionage, meaning what was later also called a "sleeper": an undercover agent, and especially someone who was embedded in an enemy organisation and who might be activated years later, when still trusted and yet unsuspected, to catastrophic effect. The use apparently arose in the context of the Russian Revolution, but it was popularised later in the twentieth century in John le Carré's *Smiley* books.

I had final say on what we selected for our work, but word-selection wasn't really an issue, as we had drawn up rules and guidelines based on hard evidence of currency, which took any guesswork out of the whole process. We applied a rule of thumb that demanded that any term had to have existed over several years (we said five in the early days, and later modified that to ten); had to be documented in various genres (formal, technical, everyday, slang—not all of these for every word, of course); and had to be evidenced by at least five documentary examples in our card files. If a term passed these tests, then it might find its way on to the editorial conveyor belt.

This was the mid-1980s, the period of my dictionary career when— as leader of the New Words group—I carried around a small flip-top notebook in the back pocket of my trousers, ready to pull it out (like a policeman's notebook) as an "incident" arose—i.e., when I heard a new word or meaning we might want to add to the *OED*. Words were only admitted into the *OED* if we had printed evidence for their existence. When I heard a new word on the radio, on a record, or in conversation, this clearly didn't represent printed evidence. But it was a hint that we might need to dive into our word files to see if other evidence had accrued for it which we had so far overlooked. Did my system have any effect on the dictionary? Well, this time—yes. Soon enough, we were researching Bob Marley's "natty dread" and investigating "knotty" dreadlocks (*natty* being a regional variant of *knotty*). My notebook prompted us to work on *bubblewrap* and *clingfilm*, which my predecessors had missed up till then. Obviously this procedure went completely against our established policy of letting the collection of data in our word files determine what we edited, but I made sure that any findings were validated against our word files.

My informal method of word collection worked well for a couple of years. I could imagine I was a street-level lexicographer stealthily collecting terms no one else would ever come across. The problem was that one day I left the notebook in my trousers when they went into the washing machine, where it was categorically destroyed. I never did buy another one—our new-word-detection methods were getting better, and I was happy enough that they were starting to produce reliable results without my extra help.

The 1970s and 1980s were a time of steadily increasing affluence backed by the new computerised technology which was seeping into everyone's lives. It was always important to recognise that the new words on which we found ourselves working reflected these trends, and that they were entering into the language at an astonishing rate. It's not hard—in retrospect—to spot examples. *Affluenza* (ultimately traced to 1973), for instance, was just the sort of blend (of *affluence* and *influenza*) that language purists hated. Advances in robotics brought us *animatronics* (1971); research promoted by new social issues brought us *antiretroviral* (1979) drugs and *biodegrading* (1970); and heaven knows what little pixies brought us *AOR* (= album-oriented rock: 1977). More money in our purses and wallets in society generally (though not, sadly, on the dictionary) paved the way for the *booze cruise*, and more leisure time provoked travel firms to offer *awayday* tickets (1972 onwards), which later (1976) morphed, along with reshaped business practices, into a seminar away from the office, and (in the eyes of anyone not attending) an opportunity for favoured employees to enjoy a luxury lifestyle for a day or two. *Business-speak* (1973) dates from this time, too. (When business awaydays finally filtered down to the editors of the *OED* in the 1980s, they consisted of a training session with a mug of coffee, a Danish pastry, a free stubby pencil, and an orange juice in an office off-site but well within sight of work.)

We found that computational vocabulary had seeped through from first-level, professional computing into a second tier of business such as finance, film, and the music industry. Ordinary people started to encounter this second-level computing in their daily lives: at banks, at checkout tills, and around their Walkman. They began using terms like *EFTPOS* (electronic funds transfer at the point of sale—another fine piece of gobbledegook crafted on the workbench of financial computing), *ATM*, *paperless office*, and *cashless society*, and were told to admire *synergies* and to respect *fusion*.

The words that streamed into our card files had always been an index to changes in our culture. When I first came across quotations for *debit card* in the early 1980s, I wondered how on earth it might work. It was characteristic of this wave of vocabulary that it had often been fully operational in America for some years before it reached our shores, though it seemed that I had not been concentrating enough on the global economy to take notice.

We needed to prepare definitions for these lifestyle accessories—a *debit card* became:

> a card issued by an organization, giving the holder access to an account, via an appropriate computer terminal, esp. in order to authorize the transfer of funds to the account of another party when making a purchase, etc., without incurring revolving finance charges for credit.

That's not a definition I am—in retrospect—proud of, but it was a child of its time. Its interminable length shows how lexicographers struggled with these emerging concepts and technologies. At the same time we had to write definitions in a style that would help readers understand both concept and meaning. As a result, we provided them with what amounts to a short manual in place of a definition.

Selecting and defining words, as you can see, can have many pitfalls. It is easy to be too precipitate in selecting a word for inclusion in the dictionary. But if we'd held off defining *debit card* until the British public had become familiar with it, then we would have disappointed other audiences, especially in America, where the expression was becoming commonplace. In general, we learnt to shy away from trying to define any new word—wherever possible—until it had a chance to settle down in the language. We adopted this cautious approach for two main reasons. Firstly, we know that the meaning of a word, and the perception of its meaning by users, can drift subtly while it becomes acclimatised to the language. Secondly, it is helpful for us to see whether others publish preliminary accounts of the word from their own impressions or research. That's not cheating; it's just good research sense. The *OED* is a historical dictionary, taking a long view. It doesn't need to leap in at the first breath: better to present a considered picture. Smaller dictionaries of contemporary English don't have such qualms, and offer an indication of meaning from the off. We give things a few years first.

Channel-surfing soon attracted our attention (1988). I have never felt happy with the application of *surfing* to this television context, as it smacks of the forced welding of new technology waterborne prowess more appropriate to California beaches. I could appreciate *downloadable* (1982 onwards), once I understood the process it was attempting to describe, but still baulk at *cyberspace* and all of those other lazy *cyber*-expressions, mainly because closer acquaintance with them seemed to involve putting on 3D specs. I did find that in the late 1980s some new words—such as these—were starting to annoy me. I shouldn't have let it happen, as a neutral observer. The new wealth and the new technology of the Thatcher and Reagan years were creating a new decadence and a new polarisation in society, where redundancy and excess could fester. That's a bit harsh on *channel-surfing*, but, as a thesis, I still think it's tenable.

At this time, other words, outside this narrow, restricted *A–G* range, came within our editorial purview—such as the Caribbean term *skanking*. The 1970s and 1980s were an era of growing multiculturalism in British society, and hence in language. The major multicultural linguistic influences in Britain were the Asian languages and the Caribbean variety of English, mirroring the increasing number of immigrants from these areas in our major cities. Music, food, and fashion found themselves in the forefront of our editing activity, and one of the successes of integration was *chicken tikka masala*, which rapidly rose to become one of our national dishes, despite never having been cooked previously in India. The *OED* dates the dish from 1975, but it was during the following decade that it achieved its stranglehold on the British palate as a bland and safe alternative to the hot and spicy Indian curry. Northern Pakistani cookery introduced us to *balti* in 1982 (it was first spotted in Birmingham): a more highly spiced dish "accompanied by naan bread," according to the *OED*'s gastronomical aside.

I didn't read much in the way of cookery books back then, but I did read a biography of Bob Marley, to add credibility to my expertise in Rastafarianism. It was from this multicultural background that the *OED* decided to address *skanking*.

I remember one day we were hard at work on this new non-technological musical term. Even I could work out from the evidence of our word-files that it was a Caribbean dance (or at least some sort of Caribbean movement to music). Despite my earlier transient interest in Rastafarianism, I had failed to develop any awareness of skanking, so things were looking rather desperate for us on the definition front. Predictably, our academic advisers were predominantly not skankers, so we could expect little help there.

Around that time, I appeared on a TV programme discussing language in a multicultural society with the performance poet Benjamin

Zephaniah. Lexicographers are always asking people irregular questions, so I thought I'd try one of these on Benjamin. I enquired politely if he could explain to me the secrets of skanking. After one or two deep, old-fashioned looks—of the kind lexicographers are quite used to receiving—he told me that he was fully aware of the meaning of *skanking* but was also entirely unable to describe it to me in words. I even wondered if this was his polite way of secretly retaining the necessary information within the Caribbean community, and not letting it spill out into the popular forum represented by the *OED*.

Plan A had fallen flat on its face, but as a lexicographer I was bound to persist to the point of annoyance. In due course, Benjamin realised that he might as well give in, but instead of providing me with a written or spoken definition of *skanking*, he cunningly said that the next time he was in Oxford he'd drop into my office and perform a *skank*. This event would allow me to scribble down the particulars I needed for the definition.

True to his word, a month or so later I received a phone call from Benjamin to say that he was pointing his car in the Oxford direction and he'd see me soon. I don't think I told any of my colleagues about the festival performance that would soon take place in my office on the ground floor overlooking the street in St Giles', so none of them were privileged to witness it. When Benjamin arrived, we cleared an area in front of my desk and he danced, rather embarrassedly to start with, but with a growing sense of performance, his hands grasping the air in front of him in time to a silent beat. I wrote notes as the dance continued—the only time I have ever done such a thing. When it was over I had enough material to construct a definition, and Benjamin had to move on to his next (scheduled) performance that evening. If you look at the *OED* now you'll see how to *skank*:

> A style of West Indian dancing to reggae music, in which the body bends forward at the waist, and the knees are raised and the hands claw the air in time to the beat; dancing in this style.

We know the word arose in the mid-1970s. We have records of *skanking* from 1976 (the *New Musical Express*—probably one of the issues read by Tony Augarde, my predecessor as the eyes and ears of the street on the *OED* in the early 1970s). But we did find an earlier, 1974, example for the noun *skank* in the same sense, in the second of Charlie Gillett's *Rock File* series. Charlie (1942–2010), an English radio presenter and rock-music specialist, probably best known for his influential *Sound of the City*, later assisted the *OED* on and off as a popular-culture consultant. I think he, too, wondered whether he was selling out by advising "Oxford" about popular culture. The verb *to skank* we took back even further, to 1973, with sources from the Caribbean itself, such as the Kingston, Jamaica, *Gleaner* newspaper. It was good and right and proper to have it recorded from real texts back in the home of reggae.

We scratched our collective heads, though, over the etymology of *skanking*, and after hours of deep and collective thought we eventually fell back on our old favourite, "of unknown origin." New Jamaican sources now suggest that *to skank* could have other meanings at that time as well: one is "to throw a person over your shoulder." Another involved cheating and deceit. From an etymologist's point of view we still cannot decide—on the available evidence—which of these or other meanings were primary. This isn't that unusual. Etymology isn't an absolute science. We can trace some words back through the languages— say from English to French, and then on to Latin (lots of words: *advantage, benefit, chance, opportunity, seasonableness,* but not *timeliness*), but somewhere the trail ends. If that happens before written records, then the etymologist has to rely on conjecture (which is sometimes a scholarly term for "guesswork").

Words from predominantly oral cultures (such as Caribbean English) hit this point of etymological invisibility in the much more recent past: *reggae, ska* (music), *samfie* (a trickster). If *skank* is unrecorded before the late twentieth century, and there are no obvious hints as to where it derives from, then the lexicographer is forced back to

"Etymology unknown." But this is a worthy and valid position, and doesn't upset lexicographers. Better information may turn up at some time in the future, and waiting for it to arrive is preferable to guessing now and being wrong. In any dictionary research, it's possible to do twice as much work on a word, but only to advance our knowledge of it by 1 percent. That's not an efficient way to proceed. All research decisions—at some point—have to be bounded by practicality and resources. If you have to, give up (for now).

I t is commonly assumed that lexicographers have some advanced sense about which words are going to be the next big ones. We spend so much time staring at words, and analysing them, that people think we must develop some intuitive sense of what will be significant in the word market next year. Journalists like the idea that we can predict, and of course I don't. It only causes us trouble, as my chief editor demonstrated ably but unintentionally soon after I had arrived on the dictionary staff.

In 1978, the chief editor went on a lecture tour of the United States. The prospect engendered enormous excitement for him, but some trepidation elsewhere in the department in Oxford. He was slated to lecture in New York, Washington, and several of the other big cities in the States. As a junior lexicographer I was commandeered to supply him with detailed background information for his tour—not, as it turned out, on the state of the language in Britain and in America (which I was expecting), but on the unmissable sights in the various states he was visiting. And before the days of the Internet, there wasn't much I could do in the office in a hurry except to look on our shelves at the *Encyclopaedia Britannica*. (But then it's also possible that I wasn't motivated to do a whole lot more.)

A few days into the tour, the problems erupted. In a Q&A session after his lecture in Chicago, a journalist asked him where the English language was heading in the near future. This wasn't a question we had discussed back at the office, but our chief editor liked to startle. In retrospect, I have a feeling he may have wanted to provoke a debate on the issue. The first echoes of his response reached us back in Oxford the next morning. We awoke to learn that in two hundred years' time it was likely that Great Britain and North America would find their versions of the English language mutually unintelligible. We did a collective double-take when we heard that; it wasn't on our back-room FAQ prompt for his lecture tour.

But the media loved it. At last they had found a fearless, uncompromising lexicographer sticking his neck out and prophesying the future of language. It didn't matter that none of us would be around to find out if the prophesy was accurate. What mattered was that the broadcasters could have a debate.

Are there any signs now that the languages are beginning ever so slowly to slip towards mutual unintelligibility? Not really. There are bound to be words and meanings that are more common in British English, American English, Australian English, etc., than they are in other varieties of the language, but in general, English speakers around the world are quite alert to the salient features of other Englishes. Our work in Oxford was daily teaching us that English was undergoing a process of globalisation rather than fragmentation. When we prepared an entry for a term that originated in North American English (say *air guitar*, *hardball*, or *wacko*), the unavoidable, standard profile of these words showed documentary evidence beginning in America and gradually seeping over into British (or Australian, or other regional) sources as we became more familiar with the expressions. English speakers were assimilating words from other geographical varieties of English, especially through the media. We had witnessed this assimilation of American English in previous decades (*stumped*, "nonplussed, rendered at a loss"; or *slick*, or *to fly off the handle*). Over the years we had forgotten that there was ever anything odd about them, and we accepted them now, thinking that they had always formed a part of British English.

The furore in Chicago and elsewhere in America as the press started debating mutual intelligibility soon faded. But it reminded us that changes in language typically developed along well-worn trails. Although you might not be able to predict precisely which new words are just over the horizon, it is certainly possible to examine how new words arise, and to identify the general routes they take into English. If you do want to try your hand at prediction, you need to play the percentages—which means that you have to know two things: how words have been formed in the past, and which areas of the language are likely to generate new vocabulary.

Fewer than 1 percent of new words are actually new—well, far fewer than 1 percent, actually. There is no point in trying to create a new word from nowhere. They almost all have some sort of ancestry or association with words already current in the language. Language is for communication, and if you are brave enough to introduce a new word with no links to existing word-formation patterns, then communication more or less comes to an abrupt halt until the people you are trying to communicate with have learnt the new meaning.

A few years ago, the standard example of the word that fell to Earth from nowhere was *grok*: to understand intuitively or by empathy. In 1961, Robert Heinlein wrote: "Smith had been aware of the doctors but had grokked that their intentions were benign" (*Stranger in a Strange Land*, Chapter 3). No doubt there were lexicographers dancing in the aisles back then: spontaneous creation; the infant phenomenon; boldly going where no other verb had gone before. This is all that the laconic *OED* has to say about the genesis of *grok*: "Arbitrary formation by Heinlein." As simple as that. There wasn't really a lot else it could say, as Heinlein's word had no lexical relatives. But how do you manage to advance communication when you invent something with no known alliances to existing words, and with nothing for the user to grab hold of? It doesn't really work.

We often came across one-off instances of words which (unlike *grok*) had never managed to gain even the slightest foothold in the language. In fact, when we were sorting through the card files looking for potential dictionary entries, I would guess that we passed over more items than we set aside for inclusion. Occasionally people asked me which words we left out. I don't remember examples. In those days, they would have been instanced by fewer than five examples. It goes without saying that they were—as a group—instantly forgettable, because they had been instantly forgotten. If they had attracted an audience, and people had started using them, then we would have discovered more examples. Again, think of the practicalities. This is something else not to waste time on.

If new words aren't generally pure inventions, then where do they come from? You might think that they are mostly snatched from other languages. You would be wrong there, too, but not so wrong. Borrowings have been a significant factor in vocabulary change in English over the past millennium, but today they represent—statistically—a waning, less productive form of language change than in the past. Nowadays we borrow less than 10 percent of our new vocabulary. And what would be the reasons for this? The reasons are buried deep in economic and cultural adjustments that have spanned centuries. Major language change doesn't occur overnight. It's not dependent on some political decision taken on a particular day, but is an accumulation of small changes, sometimes over generations. Loanword or borrowing studies teach us that English was at base a Germanic language, and that at various times it has undergone significant change through invasion, trade, cultural developments, scientific innovation, and the like. Up until the nineteenth century, English was nothing like the high-prestige, global language it is today. As a result, if it wanted to follow the latest trends, it had to import words—especially from French, Latin, and Greek, which were higher-prestige languages in culture, science, and many other areas. I refuse to launch into long lists, but if—in the eighteenth century—we felt that we needed to bulk up our knowledge and vocabulary of military defence techniques, we didn't take words from Scandinavia or Welsh, but looked to French, the language of Napoleon: *abates* (defensive barricade), *deployment* (of troops), *pas de souris* (passageway from an outwork back to a defensive ditch). If we wanted to introduce a sense of artistic brilliance into English in the same century, we looked to Italian and Latin: *agitato*, *falsetto*, even *melodrama*. These—and many others—were areas in which English was not a market leader.

As we entered the twentieth century, things changed. Other geographical varieties of English, outside Britain, were now strong, and supported increasingly vibrant and self-confident cultures generating their own vocabulary; English generally was becoming the prestige global language, and the balance started to shift so that other languages were absorbing the vocabulary of this newly dominant English. Non-English-speakers aspired to the culture of Britain and America, and the economic strength of America pushed home this position. English has therefore, over the years, found less need to borrow words from elsewhere, and, as a result, looks to its own resources and creates new terms from its own word stock. It's not that we don't take on borrowed words at all these days—it's just that the percentage has, for this and doubtless other reasons, diminished.

The predominant factor in language change today is best described as minor adjustment—use what you know and tweak it slightly, so that you take people with you. Neither spontaneous creation nor word borrowing affect language so much as discreet innovations that make use of existing elements of the language. So, without a great deal of fuss, you can weld together old words already existing in English to form new compounds (*snowboard*, *halterneck*), and add affixes to words or word elements to create new terms (*microbrewery*, *interdisciplinary*, *rageful*, *selfie*).

Another major brand of word formation today is semantic drift, whereby one word develops a new meaning in addition to the ones it already has (including technological *arrivistes*, such as the computer *mouse*—which just happens to look like one of those cuddly furry beasts with a clutchable body and—unless wireless—a long, thin tail). I could produce a very long list of these, but not even I would be interested. Think of any word, and then think of the secondary and tertiary meanings it has developed (start here: *table*, *ladder*, *kid*, *rotor*).

To complete the list of major word-formation types, we should mention *conversion*, or switching part of speech (e.g., *impact* the noun becomes *to impact* the verb: we've had this change mode since the dawn of language, so please don't let it worry you). Then there is *blending* (e.g., *influenza* and *affluence* create *affluenza*), *shortening* (abbreviating), and the creation of *acronyms* and *initialisms*. The difference between these last two similar types of word formation is that acronyms (e.g., *NATO*, *AIDS*) can be and are often pronounced as words, whereas initialisms (e.g., *RSPCA* and *FYI*) can't be, at least without unnatural facial contortions.

The key fact about all of these word-formation methods is that they employ tried-and-tested routes for creating new vocabulary items from old, pre-existing terms. So if you are forecasting the vocabulary of the future, you would be well advised to stick within these guidelines. The relative frequency of use of the methods may change over the years, but they are likely to cover almost all new expressions for the foreseeable future.

We began by thinking about whether it was possible to predict the next big word—an activity I recommend avoiding. But thinking about it has drawn us into what factors do influence language change. Language change typically happens along well-established routes, and it takes place most vigorously in areas that are subject to the most change in real life: politics, medicine, computing, general slang, environmental concerns, SMS. I'm sure you can think of others. But in general, don't waste your time—my advice is to observe what happens without trying to change it.

I t is a strange and little-known fact, but as the New Words group was editing new entries for the dictionary in the mid-1980s, we found ourselves exposed to some of the curious policy decisions made by *OED* editors in the past. For instance, when we wanted to add some new material to the entry for *African*, we found that the existing entry was unnaturally brief. Way back in 1884, the original editors had intentionally omitted the word, and all that the dictionary now contained was a short entry hastily compiled in the 1970s for the *Supplement* to the dictionary. The reason the original editors omitted *African* was that they didn't really regard it as a word, but as a proper name turned into a pseudo-word by the addition of *-an*. If you included *African* in the dictionary, then surely you were opening yourself up to having to include an almost indefinite number of comparable terms based on place names and the names of people. But the original editors had a tremendous change of heart a few months later when they reached the word **American**—another place name plus *-an*. Even the objective and neutral *OED* editors could see that there was more to *American* than met the eye, and so they condescended to include a rather small entry for the term (about six inches of type).

The various versions through which the *OED*'s entry for the word *American* passed from that first appearance in 1884 up to the present day show a number of shifts of editorial and cultural perspective. Although the original *OED* was firmly based "on historical principles," the editors allowed themselves to deviate from these if they thought they knew better (or, more accurately, if they thought that as-yet-undiscovered evidence would back up what they felt). So they had a habit of presenting words based on proper names as if there were some universal law that the adjective would appear first in the language, followed later on by the noun. The evidence of real data—and especially from the fund of real data that has become available to us since the emergence of the Internet—seems, on the contrary, to suggest that these nouns typically predate the adjectives.

It turns out that this is an issue with the entry for the word *American*. The loyal old *OED* placed the adjective in first place within its entry, before the noun: "Belonging to the continent of America," dating the term in English from 1598. It then followed the adjective with the noun, of which the first meaning was, in the wording of the time, "An aborigine of the American continent; now called an 'American

Indian,'" but dated it twenty years earlier, from 1578. According to the editors' own historical principles, the noun should have been placed first. Look at those definitions, too, for further evidence of changes in editorial (or general cultural) perspectives. We use a different word-set these days to describe indigenous peoples (not *aborigine*, for example). It would no longer be accurate to call the original inhabitants of North America "American Indians," when a new vocabulary has been introduced for Native Americans. These are changes that have been working through society and language for decades in different regions of English, and they are part of a spectrum which will surely change again in future. It's intriguing to try to gauge how much these changes are based simply on the use of different words nowadays to describe things, and how much on the much larger issue of different mindsets. We think of things differently now, so we use different words: not new, borrowed words, but modifications of terms we already had in the language. I know it's a small thing, but it is a slight indication of how perspectives were different in those old days of certainty and empire.

As a universal rule for the *OED* of the past (when it was generally adhered to) and for today's editors (by whom it is rigorously adhered to), proper names, such as the geographical name *America*, or the personal name *Mandela*, are not included in the *OED* unless they are used to signify more than the one person or place to which they originally relate. The Duke of Wellington is noticed by the *OED* not as an individual—for his military prowess, or because he was a prime minister—but because of his boots, amongst other things. The Duke will be remembered for many things: he was, perhaps uniquely, a British hero with a celebratory door-knocker named after him—though that has so far evaded the all-seeing eye of the Pinkertons at the *OED*. This was an object which, in one of its many incarnations, possessed a stout iron knocker in the shape of a British Lion which came smashing down on a striker plate consisting of a defenceless Napoleonic Eagle, thus encouraging people to visit their neighbours at the same time as contributing to the war effort.

The "Iron Duke" (1830 onwards) left us a considerable verbal legacy: his knee-high military boots were called Wellingtons from 1816, and waterproof lookalikes were developed later in the nineteenth century; we also had Wellington trousers, Wellington hats, and Wellington coats from around 1810. We named a beef dish after him, and even an apple (which the *OED* slightingly likes to remind us was also called the Dumelow's seedling).

But for the past hundred years Wellington has perhaps been least remembered for providing the English language with the first example of the word *ganja* (Indian hemp, for smoking or whatever else you might like it for). And how did it come about that we have Wellington to thank for *ganja*? In his early career as a soldier he spent much of his time in India, needless to say the home of "Indian hemp." To keep the soldiers happy, the army ran bazaars at which anything Indian might be bought and sold. Wellington was an indefatigable dispatch-writer, telling his army fellows everything that was happening to him in India. In 1800 he wrote about the bazaars, to which local Indians brought ganja, "bhang," opium, "country-arrack," and toddy to sell. Wellington was concerned that the British redcoat should not become debauched or roué, so he enforced a blanket ban on alcoholic arrack or toddy being sold to the soldiers. He seems, however, to have let ganja and opium slip through the official net—perhaps because they were regarded as medicinal tonics for men wounded in battle. The *OED* is a dynamic masterwork: in due course, we will find earlier evidence for *ganja*, I'm sure. But just for now, the Iron Duke is credited with the introduction of the word into English—"mentioned in dispatches."

From time to time, as editor of the New Words group, I became aware of *big* words that would need addressing—words that dominated cultural or scientific debate. These were always difficult to edit, but on the other hand, they were good indicators of the strength of the dictionary's editorial policy. High-profile words often rush into public prominence, but their meaning and cultural significance can take a while to settle down—how we regard a word after fifty years can be very different from the way it is interpreted after six months (*AIDS, perestroika, online*). Our source evidence—texts from the real world—sometimes sends us mixed messages. Sometimes English speakers just alter the spelling or pronunciation of these words subtly as they embed themselves in the language.

By the mid-1980s you did not need to be a historical lexicographer to be aware that AIDS was a major social issue—and consequently one that the *OED* would need to address comprehensively and yet sensitively. *AIDS* was one of the trickiest new entries we ever had to confront, in terms of its social context. It kept on moving around. Even the way it was spelt caused problems. The earliest evidence we collected used the form *A.I.D.S.*, with a full set of full stops in the old style. But considerable uncertainty arose, as the term settled into the language. Some people preferred a lower-case form, *aids*, which came to be regarded as slightly confusing, as we already had a perfectly usable word *aids*, in the context of helping and assisting. Both coexisted in roughly the same semantic area (medicine). People tried *Aids*, too, but that didn't really stick. Eventually a consensus settled on *AIDS* in the late 1980s and early 1990s. In the early years of preparing and publishing the entry, we had to monitor our headword spelling almost daily to keep up with what our evidence told us was the most frequent spelling.

We had similar problems with the etymology. Early documentary evidence was confused over whether *AIDS* was short for "acquired immune deficiency syndrome" or "acquired immuno-deficiency syndrome." Read that again—there is a difference. Later evidence tended to prefer the former (*acquired immune deficiency syndrome*), but we couldn't establish definitely which form really was primary. Yet again, you have to accept that language development may not be absolutely straightforward.

The standard technique for establishing the details of the historical emergence and continuity of a term is to follow the documentary evidence. We would collect as much evidence as we could find and then submit it to a process of analysis. As time went by, we were able to pull in computer power to help with evidence-gathering, but in the end the decision still remained in the hands of a human (the editor). Put yourself back to this unstable stage in the history of the word *AIDS* in the mid-1980s: we didn't have the medical knowledge we had later, and we didn't have the defining terminology that developed as the condition was better understood, and we didn't have computer power to collect and sift through reams of documentary evidence. In addition, *HIV* wasn't coined until 1986, so aspects of the full picture only became available later.

Common knowledge dated *AIDS* to 1983. When we researched it we were surprised to find that the name did predate 1983, as it had arisen in medical discussions the previous year. That shouldn't really have surprised us. It is not unusual for research to uncover an unrecognised prehistory for any term. On 8 August 1982 the *New York Times* had published a pioneering article on the new condition, tentatively informing its audience about what would turn out to be one of the words of the decade, if not of the century.

That earliest reference from 1982 is another object lesson for users of the dictionary. We find it's not unusual for the gentle reader to assume that the *OED*'s first recorded quotation is the very first use of a term ever: to imagine that the expression *AIDS* was actually coined on 8 August 1982. If you ever find yourself thinking that, give yourself a sharp rap on the back of the head to return yourself to reality. In real life, that is just the earliest reference we have been able to find. Obviously, a reporter on a newspaper isn't likely to invent a term that is bubbling around amongst specialists at the time. But that is a fact it's easy to forget.

Once we had collected all of the documentary evidence that we were able to amass for *AIDS*, we faced the problem of its definition. As already noted, definitions can be problematic if your term has not established itself fully in the language. It was our science editors who were charged with the problem of defining *AIDS* for the first time. Their first efforts reached print (even then after many changes) in 1989. It now feels curiously dated:

> Acquired immune deficiency syndrome: an illness (often but not always fatal) in which opportunistic infections or malignant tumours develop as a result of a severe loss of cellular immunity, which is itself caused by earlier infection with a retrovirus, HIV, transmitted in sexual fluids and blood.

That was all very well at the time, but before very long I found that science editors would be knocking on my office door saying respectfully that the definition should be updated. Over the years we have made several changes to the definition to accommodate new medical knowledge and public perceptions about *AIDS*, and an altered sense of what the *OED*'s readership wanted to know about the condition. As public perception of the term changed, we needed to shift the tenor of our definition gradually from a simple statement of what was known about the condition to more complex information—only known later—about how the condition interacts with HIV. At the same time, the entry was expanding, almost daily, to incorporate other supporting data for related compounds (*AIDS crisis*, *AIDS awareness*, etc.) which showed that the term had a social weighting as well as a medical one. Compare that first effort at a definition with the 2014 version:

> A disease characterized by fever, weight loss, lymphadenopathy, and the occurrence of opportunistic infections and malignant tumours, associated with a reduction in the number of helper T lymphocytes in the blood, and now known to occur as a late stage of infection with human immunodeficiency virus (HIV); = *acquired immune deficiency*

syndrome at ACQUIRED *adj. Special uses.* Also (more generally): infection with HIV.

But then consider methods by which dictionary editors can quantify social significance. It's often the case, linguistically speaking, that you can't determine social or cultural significance simply by staring at the word itself. Words exist in context. We use context to help refine a definition. That's fairly obvious. There would be no point in the *OED* carrying millions of illustrative quotations showing how a word can be used in context if this wasn't somehow important to our understanding of the word.

Cultural context is bigger than that, and is something that applies to every word, however insignificant it might be. One of the best ways for the lexicographer to judge cultural context—in order to supply additional fact and nuance to a basic definition—is to investigate what compounds and derivatives a word can be found in over the years.

This probably needs a little more explanation. The basic sense of *AIDS* (with all of its accompanying quotations) represents only about a quarter of the full entry in the *OED*. So what is the rest, and what does it tell us about the word? As we carry on down the entry, we find a long tranche of compounds of which *AIDS* is the first element (*AIDS sufferer, AIDS test,* etc.). These can be subdivided (as lexicographers like to do—some more than others) into various types, all symptomatic of how society has come to think about and handle AIDS.

First of all, there are the neutral compounds which just help to explain what *AIDS* is, in the public perception: *AIDS virus* is the key one here. Then there are compounds that show that we have a basic medical approach to the condition: *AIDS treatment, AIDS drug, AIDS patient.* There is nothing surprising there. Next the detective lexicographer can see—from our word data—that the scientific community is busy researching the condition, which shows that it is a fairly significant problem: *AIDS research* and *AIDS researcher.* As a result of this medical research, people might be offered an *AIDS test*, which again raises the game slightly, and then we notice *AIDS awareness*, with its implication of public concern about the condition. Finally, a residual cluster of compounds takes us up to a new level: *AIDS crisis*, *AIDS hysteria*, and *AIDS epidemic*.

These days, with the OED Online, you can take this kind of analysis a stage further and look for definitions elsewhere in the dictionary that contain the word *AIDS*, in search of more information about popular perceptions and misconceptions. Among others, you turn up *buddy* and *gay plague*, which are reminders that the dictionary reflects a blunt, hard-nosed picture of what exists linguistically in the real world, not a pre-packaged and socially acceptable version.

The list of new words and new meanings that we worked on provided an arresting cultural index to the 1980s. But although I was now well and truly the New Words editor of the *OED*, I was gradually coming to feel that the real business of lexicography related to much earlier periods in the history of English. Much as it was fascinating to trace each of these modern and often frothy words back to their source (often many years before the general public thought they existed), and to add them like coat-hangers to the meanings already present in the main dictionary, hoping they might one day be published, there was always a feeling that most of them would disappear, to be replaced in a few years by a new crop of equally transient ephemera. I was beginning to feel that just working on new words and meanings was not a sufficient end in itself.

Maybe editing new words—like reading Christian Metz's *Film Language*—was just a phase I had to go through. It was a remarkable training in many areas of dictionary methodology, but you didn't end up with a complete picture. You were continuously painting images of shreds and fragments of language. We had selected the right words—it's not as if many of the words we worked on disappeared: they are predominantly still around in the language.

Some well-informed journalists, unlike the earlier ones who had seemed ready to accept any offering about the language, were becoming jaundiced about the lists of the latest dictionary additions that dictionary houses published. They suspected they were simply being targeted with glossy additions by the publisher's publicity department. It was a view I was tempted to share. It didn't worry me that aspects of language could be transient, but I did worry that concentrating principally on new words trivialised what we could and should be doing.

But there were always plenty of new lessons I could still learn from the work on neologisms. One of them was that it is preferable to document the language from everyday sources—the sort of sources that people encounter in their day-to-day lives—rather than from the classic authors. We didn't discover evidence for *bean-counter* (an accountant), *demo* (to demonstrate—new music, amongst other things), or *toastie* (the sandwich) at the time by reading the likes of Charles Dickens, J. D. Salinger, or Harold Pinter. Those terms are cited from sources such as *Ski Magazine*, *Hyperlink Magazine*, *Plow Snowboarding*, *Melody Maker*, and, of course, the *Lawton Constitution*—a newspaper in a south-western Oklahoma town, for *to demo*—and the *Glasgow Herald*—for imaginative new foodstuffs, such as the *toastie*. The *Supplement to the OED* had already pushed at this door and, as we grew in confidence, we now gave it a healthy shove. The *OED*, like many other things—such as the teaching of history—was undergoing a quiet democratisation. History no longer concentrated exclusively on the stories of kings and queens and grand political games, but now also on what everyday life felt like for the ordinary person. The *OED* was starting to do just the same by hunting out everyday sources to document language change.

While I was feeling as if it might be time for a change at work, my family was on the move, too. My father had retired from the Secrets Emporium in 1980, after moving ten years earlier to work for another of the outposts of the Government

Communications business in London. He remained more involved with numerical codes than with language ones throughout his working life. My mother taught office practice (shorthand, etc.) at Croydon Technical College, near where they lived in Surrey. My sister, Gill, and her husband were by then running a small family business with their children down in Lyme Regis, and my brother, David, was in any of three or four coastal venues, **bird-watching** and generally participating in conservation projects, such as plotting the migration patterns of seabirds, documenting the incidence of orchids in field sites, and enquiring into what butterflies had for dinner. Over the next few years we were all about to move on, but it didn't seem like that in those sunny late-1980s days.

I like to think there is something interesting that can be said about any word, however unprepossessing it may at first seem. *Bird-watching* originally appears in the language because there was a need for it, and more recently it has formed the basis for new types of *-watching* behaviour observed in humans. The *OED* credits Edmund Selous (1857–1934) with the earliest use of the term: he used it in the title of his book *Bird Watching* (1901). You can tell he didn't really think of the term as a familiar compound at the time because (*a*) he didn't hyphenate it, and (*b*) you can imagine that the stress of the compound was bird WATCHing, not BIRD-watching. The important thing is that Selous was trying to publicise a new way of interacting with birds—observing them scientifically, investigating their movements, feeding habits, nesting habits, etc., etc. And not shooting them. So he needed a new term, and the one that naturally suggested itself was *bird watching*. You can in fact, by going online, find earlier isolated occurrences of the expression before this, but generally speaking, you can do that with any compound. I was quite taken with the rather reclusive Selous when I found that he described the ideal relationship between the bird and the bird-watcher as that maintained between the lexicographer Dr Johnson and his biographer James Boswell: the target of interest was the bird and its behaviour, but everything was filtered through the observant eyes of his scribe. Selous's chapter titles may not excite the interest of non-ornithologists: the first one is "Watching golden plovers, etc.," the second is "Watching ringed plovers, redshanks, peewits, etc.," and the book generally appeals to obsessives by going on like this. But it marked a new era in our engagement with birds, and so a new word was appropriate.

Another mode of observing the word, from our ivory hide, is as a compound ending in -*watching*. Before *bird-watching*, the compounds have to do with watching the passing hours of the night: *midnight-watching* and *night-watching*. These two are quite ancient in English, dating from the sixteenth and seventeenth centuries, when there wasn't much else to do. But *bird-watching* in 1901 started a new channel of word-formation in which the objects of scientific study, or just of personal interest, can be introduced, like *bird*, as the initial element: *people-watching*, *whale-watching*, *weight-watching*, and *word-watching* are four of the "biggest" of these.

I had just started to feel—by the mid-1980s—that supplementing a big historical dictionary was, ultimately, an unsatisfying task, that it was only piecemeal work, and did not address the core of the language. There were larger objectives that the *OED* should be directing itself towards. We had previously been held back artificially for many years by our chief editor's reluctance to involve the *OED* in the computer revolution going on around us. But the winds of change could penetrate even Oxford, and when they came, they arrived in the form of a typhoon.

SIX

Shark-Infested Waters

The possibility of putting the *OED* on to computer had never really occurred to us back in the late 1970s and early 1980s. We had a sketchy impression that computers were being used elsewhere to assist lexicographers—by automatically concordancing texts, for example—but in those days the chief editor, Bob Burchfield, was simply preoccupied with leading the charge to reach the end of the *Supplement to the OED* and didn't want any of our editorial work to be subjected to unwelcome interruptions. We were already over three-quarters of the way through the project—what would have been the point of upsetting all of our routines?

But there were plans afoot to jolt Oxford out of the nineteenth century, where its denizens traditionally shambled out of bed in the morning, ambled off to the library to check a few facts (or maybe even ideas), had lunch in college, and then dozed until dinner. While we had been beavering away on assorted editorial matters in St Giles', things had been changing in the upper echelons of the University Press. Since 1980 we had been distantly aware of a brand-new head of reference at Oxford, Richard Charkin (soon to become our managing director), occasionally referred to whisperingly and behind closed doors as "the Shark." His word, according to those brave enough to have anything to do with him, was law, and once he had an idea he didn't drop it. That is precisely how dictionary types behave, but we weren't used to other people in the Press playing intellectual poker too.

Gradually the gaze of our new managing director alighted on the *OED*. Did the Press owe the *OED* a living, or did the *OED* need to start earning its keep? The smart money was on option two, but we had our heads down, and some of us didn't notice that the world was changing.

The Shark had come to the sleepy old University Press from a "real" commercial publisher, and he was intent on reshaping the destiny of the Press as a world-class educational publisher which would put any other university press around the world far into the shade. I didn't know anything about the larger politics, as usual, but one day back in late 1982 I had received a phone call from our chief editor to join him in his grand office with my former trainer, Lesley Brown.

It turned out that the future was opening up before our very eyes. I'm afraid the Chief's were tightly shut and mine were only slowly prising themselves open. Here was the task, as relayed by the Shark to my boss: take a look at that incredibly slow project you've been working on since 1957, with your quill pens, mechanical adding machines, slips of paper, and far too many editors, and see if it's feasible to put the whole diction-ary on to computer so that in future you can race through the work in no time at all (and produce a first-rate dictionary along the way), and then let the University Press concentrate on those other projects that respect-able academic publishers really want to do.

Of course I've got no idea if these were really the thoughts in any-one's head. You can go down to the University Press's archives and con-sult all of its records from the time, but I don't think you'll get a better picture. What you get there is recorded history as packaged by the offi-cial recorders. It's as dangerous a slant on the past as mine. But I like to think that even then I began to recognise that we might have a mech-anism for opening up the reach of the *OED*—people might be able to access the dictionary on their computers, rather than having to make a special journey to their local library (which many of them were clearly disinclined to do).

As the meeting progressed, it became clear that Lesley and I were being asked to test out the grand scheme that was slowly taking shape in the mind of the Shark. At first, the University Press had contemplated a mammoth paper-based cut-and-paste job on the dictionary, integrating the old Victorian edition of the *OED* with its modern supplements and then somehow updating and then republishing the whole thing as a book. The Shark was not interested in that. He could see that the only way to drag the dictionary into the present century was to update it with state-of-the-art computing. But, ironically, to test out the plan, Lesley and I had to pick up our state-of-the-art scissors and pretend that we were computers, literally cutting and pasting together entries from our two sources (the old *OED* and its modern *Supplement*). We reasoned that if we could do that in a fairly mechanical way with glue and staples, then maybe a computer could be taught to do the same thing automatically and at great speed, and then perhaps the end result would be worth publishing as a dictionary.

We produced page after page of stuck-together dictionary text that passed for the **blueprint** of the dictionary of the future. Then things went quiet for a while. I returned to my New Words work, and Lesley returned to her revision of the *Shorter*, both of us back contemplating the editorial issues and deadlines with which we had grown familiar.

Words develop out of the culture in which they are used, and *blueprint* grows naturally out of the scientific interest shown by the Victorians in light sensitivity (most easily appreciated in photography, of course, but also in any discipline that utilised switches operated by light-sensitive cells). The specialist sense of *blueprint* is now "a technical drawing"—in architecture, electronics, or anything that needs to display a structure through lines—but the word started off life around 1850 as something rather more specific: it was "a photographic print composed of white lines on a blue background, used chiefly in copying plans, machine drawings, etc." (*OED*). Here's the problem that people had back then: in the early nineteenth century there were no copying machines, no Rank Xerox, no Banda machines, no colour reproduction. If you wanted to copy an image, you had to do it yourself, or hire a humble clerk to do it for you. And then if you needed two hundred copies of the plan, you had to stay up all night to finish the job.

Photography was one of the great successes of the era. As early as 1839 John Herschel (the baronet mathematician, astronomer, chemist, and inventor) wrote exultantly, "I yesterday succeeded in producing a photograph on glass." This is significant both because it marks the invention of a new technological process and because it is the first known instance of the word *photograph*.

A *blueprint* was a piece of paper washed with the chemical ferro-gallate, which turns blue when exposed to light. If this paper is clamped under glass to a plan or a map drawn on light-transmitting paper, and then put out into the sun, it seems that a "blue print" is formed on the original document. There is one other little point of lexical interest here. The original pronunciation will not have been BLUEprint, as we have it, with the stress on the first syllable. Stress can drift to the front of a word over time. Originally we would have spoken the new compound as it was first spelt, descriptively—as two separate words with equal stress "BLUE PRINT," or perhaps "blue PRINT," with stress on the final term. How do we know this? Well, from analysing the older spellings of the term; from examining old dictionaries, which indicate stress patterns; from poetry (though you might struggle to find "blueprint" in early verse); from personal experience; from anywhere else that tells you directly or indirectly about accentuation. As usual, the *OED* takes its information and knowledge from wherever it can find it, and then makes sure to corroborate it.

By 1910 we realised that the word *blueprint* might have wider applications, and its domain expanded from the world of chemistry and design into general speech—anything could be a "blueprint" if it acted as a model or a template: a blueprint for the future, a blueprint for success. That original link between language and culture had weakened.

I had returned to my quiet dictionary editing, but over the next year Richard Charkin was orchestrating raging discussions in the higher echelons of the University Press about the future of the *OED*, and in particular about the possibility of computerising it. The *OED* was at the most alarming crossroads that it had seen for around one hundred years. Some senior members of the Oxford University Press and of the University of Oxford itself regarded the dictionary as a white elephant, and one that was stifling other exciting publishing projects. If the University Press could not agree on a computerisation plan, then this could mark the end for any future development on the dictionary, which would just be left to gather dust as an increasingly forgotten pillar of Victorian endeavour. But the momentum to transfer the full text of the original *OED* to computer, and in parallel the full text of the *Supplement to the OED*, was gaining ground. A tentative plan arose: that we might be able to transfer the text of the First Edition of the *OED* and the text of the *Supplement to the OED* into two separate large files, tagged to distinguish elements such as definitions, etymologies, etc., and then we might electronically merge the two files into a single, comprehensive, and enormous dictionary file, and the whole shooting match would be published on CD (the Internet not being available when these plans were drawn up).

There was no doubt that this computerisation project was a grandiose scheme, and a very risky one—almost certain to fail, given the University Press's lack of experience in all aspects of this completely new style of publishing. If there was any hope of it becoming accepted, then the Press needed an editor to represent the dictionary in its computerisation discussions. After a while I became aware that Ed Weiner had been asked to transfer from his editorial work in order to fill this role.

At this investigative stage there was no grand announcement. In one sense I was very disappointed that Ed had been offered this work and I had been left managing the New Words group. But at the same time I knew that it wasn't what I was best at. Although I was more than curious about the idea of computerising the text, I'd always been better suited to keeping systems running—and improving them—than to building new ones from scratch. In any case, our jobs were two halves of the same egg: Ed was edging into a project to make electronic access to the dictionary easier, and I was spearheading a parallel project to update and simplify the editorial content. Everything was linked up. It would doubtless have taken me ages to get to grips with all the intricacies of the computerisation project anyway, and I would be well advised—if I so wished—to edge my way into that side of the project slowly.

What followed was a period of extensive activity of a type unfamiliar to shy, retiring lexicographers. On the computerisation front, the University Press knew it needed active partners from the international world of software analysis and data processing to get the project off the ground. It just didn't have that level of expertise itself. The Press encouraged Richard to explore the options thoroughly, so that it might in due course decide on whether to give us the official go-ahead.

Ed was charged with writing a description of what we wanted to do, for circulation to any technologically minded organisation that might be brave enough to be inveigled into helping. Here he struck lucky, as the old *OED* editors had devised the dictionary as if they were just waiting for computers to be invented, and he uncovered a formidable information structure which in time yielded relatively easily to the fielded database structure of the computer. Databases like information to come in regular packages, and so do dictionaries. Dictionaries tell you whether you are looking at a definition, a pronunciation, or an etymology by their structure and by the way the page looks (by formatting—a change of typeface, size of print, special print characters, indentation, etc.). Because all of this information is presented regularly and repetitively, it proved to be relatively easy to pour the right pieces of information (the definition, etymology, etc.) into the right database buckets. Obviously it wasn't that easy, and we didn't have buckets. But you get the idea.

It soon became clear that my New Words group in St Giles' would have a major role to play in the computerisation. In one of the numerous meetings I attended as the project began, I was asked whether we might be able to contribute some new entries for the computerised version of the dictionary. This enquiry ran counter to the general ethos of the project, by which we planned simply to republish what had already been published in the past, but in a new format. But there was some sense in the request, and I realised that it was an opportunity to start getting the old dictionary more up to date. I cavalierly agreed to contribute 5,000 completely new words and senses to add to the thousands already in the *OED*. As it happened, many of these were the very same words and meanings which the New Words group had been working on anyway (*AIDS, computer disk, disinformation, black propaganda*, etc., etc., ad infinitum). Others were new ones which we discovered ourselves as we continued our searches through the word files. And so at that point the project expanded from "put the full *OED* and its *Supplement* on computer" to "put the full *OED* and its *Supplement* on computer and add another 5,000 words and meanings whether there's really time or not."

We had another meeting a while later at which the Shark introduced a new factor: it would apparently be beneficial if we no longer showed Sir James Murray's old handmade pronunciation system, but replaced it with the International Phonetic Alphabet. The Shark might be a management guru, but he also had his finger on the editorial pulse and knew a good idea when he had one.

To explain: the International Phonetic Alphabet (IPA)—which is the standard and neutral way of transcribing pronunciations—was devised just too late for the *OED* back in the 1880s. The first IPA system was published in 1888, four years after the first instalment of the dictionary had been published. In the absence of an acceptable phonetic transcription system, Sir James Murray had made up his own. In fact, it was roughly similar to the IPA, but in some cases too complicated (making vowels carry etymological as well as phonetic information), and in other cases too simplistic. As it was now a hundred years out of date and had been adopted by nobody except us, it seemed a good plan to replace it with the current industry standard. Obsolete words were not given pronunciations by the dictionary, but that still left us with about 140,000 pronunciation transcriptions to convert from the old system to the new one. In the end, we worked out a way to make these conversions automatically, by computer—most of the time. There was a problem, though. Words have stress—we stress the word *preliminary* on the second syllable. Murray's old system placed the mark indicating the syllable carrying primary stress just before the stressed vowel (i.e., *prel'iminary*). The new system placed it before the stressed syllable (*pre'liminary*). So Ed had to spend a while working out how to tell the computer where syllables began. This isn't always easy when you are talking to a machine.

And so the project expanded yet again to "put the full *OED* and its *Supplement* on computer and add another 5,000 words and meanings whether there's really time or not, and then make sure that all of the tens of thousands of pronunciations are converted to IPA from the *OED*'s own home-grown system."

There are often good reasons for avoiding meetings if you could manage it.

Despite all of this additional work, the prospect of being able, at some point in the near future, to revise the dictionary online was extraordinarily attractive to editors such as myself. But what intrigued me and my colleagues just as much were the possibilities that would be opened up by enabling people (ourselves included) to search the entire content of the dictionary instantly for information relating to the language. Since the dawn of dictionaries, access had only been through the word you looked up. If you wanted to know what *strategy* meant, you found your dictionary and turned to the letter *S*, struggled to find *st-*, etc., and then read the brief definition which (you hoped) enlightened you as to the meaning of the word. But supposing you suddenly developed wider interests. Supposing you were interested in finding all of the words in English that ended in **-ology**? You had to start on page 1 of the dictionary and read every entry until you reached *Z*. And there was quite a good chance that you would miss one or two as your eyes glazed over or the telephone interrupted your concentration. Once you'd spent an unconscionable amount of time discovering how many words in the *OED* ended in *-ology* (the dictionary currently knows of 1,011), you might then want to compare this with the number of words ending in *-ography* (508 this time). So then you would have to start all over again. Obviously this was far too difficult and time-consuming for the ordinary person to do, so it wasn't done.

Hundreds of other questions which might have been asked about the language were not asked, or were only answered falteringly by considering just a sample of the data. What if you could dream up more or less any question you wanted about the language, ask it, and receive an answer seconds later? What if you could impose a historical dimension, too, on your questions? It was a dream worth working towards, and one that to most would have seemed impossible at the time.

When we think of words that end in -ology we are actually looking at a mixed bag of words with a mixed history. Historically, -ology words derive ultimately from Greek, where *logos* meant "word" or "discourse," interpreted eventually as "field of study." The very earliest word included in the *OED* with this termination is the word *theology*, recorded from the mid-fourteenth century. But we borrowed this word in its entirety: -ology was not at that early time a suffix which could be added to other words in English—we borrowed whole words which already ended in -ology (or its equivalent in their own language). In the fourteenth century, any word with a hint of scholasticism in it tended to enter English from French, as French and Latin were the languages of informed debate in Britain at the time. So it is not surprising to find that we hired the word *theology* from French *théologie*. It seems the word was quite new to French then, and that the French had received it from the Latin *theologia*, which is in turn a borrowing from the Greek.

Other early *-ology* borrowings were taken wholesale, directly or ultimately, from the classical languages, and not forged in English from their component parts: the words entering English (from Latin and French) before 1500 were *amphibology* (ambiguous discourse; a quibble), *astrology*, *etymology* (word derivation), *mythology*, and *tropology* (figurative interpretation of the Scriptures), which gives you some hint of the subjects of discussion around the High Tables of Oxford and Cambridge in those years. Later formations on this model tended to be words from the sciences (which rather liked creating words from classical elements) and philosophy, which was clearly too rarefied at the time to use plain Anglo-Saxon terms.

But what we are looking for is the turning point: when *-ology* first became an *English* word-formation element, not one just carried in as part of borrowed words of foreign extraction. *Demonology* (1597 in English) is a possible example. Although it might have been formed in late Latin, we don't yet have any evidence for this earlier than the first English use, and it can therefore be posited tentatively as created in English from *demon* and *-ology* (or perhaps *demono-* and *-logy*). It is not until the late seventeenth and early eighteenth centuries that we begin to find true English creations, and these are often playful ones, such as *trickology* (1723) and *punnology* (1744).

Through the eighteenth century we started to create new *-ologies* for branches of study. These were mostly formed on classical elements, but in compounds unknown to Latin and Greek. France was busy creating its own *-ologies*, and we also borrowed some of these, not liking to see them go to waste: *entomology*, *morphology*, etc. Nowadays we still create many *-ologies* on classical elements, but we also allow ourselves freedom to form them from English words (*Egyptology, musicology, oceanology, reflexology*). Next time you come across one of these, see which of the possible routes it has taken into English.

We put the word around in Britain and internationally in our search for partners for the new dictionary project—or at least those in serious positions of power in the Press put the word around. As usual, the silence resounded throughout Oxford and more widely in Britain, but it did eventually generate some interest in North America—which was at the time considerably more wired than the British Isles. And I carried on quietly writing entries for new words.

To capitalise on the North American interest, and to investigate how it might pull together to help the computerisation project, in November 1983, Ed, the Shark, and one of the University Press's computer managers flew out to the United States and Canada for further discussions with potential partners. We had acquired three new friends: IBM, which offered equipment and personnel; International Computaprint Corporation (ICC), in Fort Washington, Pennsylvania, which undertook to have the whole text of the multi-volume dictionary keyed on to **computer**; and the University of Waterloo in Ontario, Canada, which became interested in the obscure question of "what sort of electronic database could most efficiently hold the mass of structured data of which the *OED* (theoretically, at this time) consisted." Unbeknown to us, while we in Oxford had been busy publishing books on paper, the University of Waterloo's Computer Science Department had been building a worldwide reputation for handling and processing electronic data. At the same time that the language was going global, and so—of necessity—was our search for project partners. The attraction to our partners was principally the size of the *OED*, eventually measured at around 67 million characters when stretched end to end, which was hard to do even then. For the time, this was big data. And if we couldn't transfer this international interest in the dictionary into something that opened up the text to the masses, then we weren't worth the paper we were written on.

Computer wasn't really much of a word in the past. It didn't make any serious inroads into the history of the English language until the second half of the twentieth century, though by then it had already been around for four hundred years. In terms of its development, it's one of those words that moves from meaning a person who does something (i.e., who computes) to meaning a device that carries out an equivalent operation (i.e., that computes)—especially with the help of new technology. Printer and scanner followed the same route, as did typewriter, which in the late nineteenth century could mean both the machine on which a person typed and the person who did the typing.

For some reason I have a soft spot for words that entered English in the Early Modern period. That's from, say, 1500 until the early 1700s—though my personal interest often wanes as we move into the eighteenth century. Computer (and its base, the verb compute) rings all the right bells for me. Except for an odd and very Latin-based meaning from the late Middle Ages, the verb really kicks into action in 1531; in 1613, without any fanfare, the noun computer slips into the language. But the meaning back then, before we had any electronic wizardry, was quite different. A "computer" was a person who computed, or made calculations. We didn't know that machines could do that back then. The very first recorded occurrence of the word computer doesn't fill you with any sense that this would be one of the biggest words of the late twentieth and early twenty-first centuries. Here it is (in its old sense of "a person who computes"):

> I haue read the truest computer of Times, and the best Arithmetician that euer breathed, and he reduceth thy dayes into a short number.

That's from the snappily titled Yong Mans Gleanings Gathered Out of Diuers Most Zealous and Deuout Fathers, written by the enigmatic

"R. B. Gent. [i.e., Gentleman]" in 1613. This meaning carried on unin-
terrupted until the middle of the nineteenth century, when people
started applying the name *computer* to devices that performed calculations, such as slide-rules (earlier alternative terms included the obvious *calculating machine* and the mechanical *mill*). It wasn't until the
1940s that developments in electronics meant that we could start
applying the word to the sorts of things that we nowadays think of as
computers.

Once we had international partners on board, things started to look
more promising, and to move forwards faster. I, too, was becoming
much more involved in the computerisation project, while still maintaining my new-words work. Although Ed and I could oversee anything to do with the content and structure of the dictionary, we
recognised (as did others) that we didn't have the expertise to manage
the entire project ourselves. Fortunately other people in the University
Press were good at that. So at the start of 1984 the Shark appointed an
OED project director, Tim Benbow (affectionately known as the Admiral), to keep us on track, on the perceptive reasoning that if you
show a lexicographer a track, he (or she) will wander off it without a
director to keep them on the straight and narrow. Under Tim's management, the University Press had by the end of 1984 given official approval to our risky and radical new project.

This achievement deserves a small round of applause. I was enor-
mously pleased when the news came down the line that the Delegates
of the Press had approved the project. At last we had a budget, and
soon we would (we presumed) have a detailed plan—or at least more
of a plan than we had etched out to achieve the project's approval. No
one knew if this decision heralded the end of the print tradition of the
OED: opinions differed, but the right answer seemed to be "wait and
see, and don't call an end to print publication straightway." If publishers can sell you the same thing in two or three different versions, it will
make them happy. At the same time I took an A-level in computer

science at night school in Oxford, on the reasoning that I didn't want to be flummoxed by technical colleagues under pressure to curb our ideas. I discovered that when a software analyst said something wasn't doable, my job was to call their bluff and to find the loose brick in the wall of obscurity they erected to prevent us from proceeding. It was the easiest course I ever took. I knew there would be dark nights ahead, but here at last was our chance to set the dictionary on the road to recovery and a viable future.

All of a sudden, the Shark was best friends with Ed and me. I knew this for certain when he started asking me to play for his village cricket team in Oxfordshire. It was rubber-stamped in gold when he asked me to turn out a few times in the annual Oxford Publishers v. London Publishers cricket match held on the John Paul Getty estate at Wormsley in Oxfordshire. It was good to be asked, but technically speaking I was at the edge of my competence—much as I loved the game. Each team was bolstered by one or two international players of the sort you normally only see on television. The games were generally a ritual humiliation for the Oxford crew, as you can imagine that there are rather more publishers in London than there are in Oxford, so they had a far larger pool to draw from. The Shark kept wicket and nonetheless tried to encourage us to put on a good show.

There was one event that happened at that time that symbolised two things for me rather violently: firstly, the way we were shuffling off the old traditions of printing and dissemination in readiness for the new; and secondly, a worryingly dismissive attitude held in parts of Oxford towards the icons of the past. The Shark and Ed and I had joined one of the educational visits made from time to time by Oxford editors into the print-works at the back of the University Press. Although some of OUP's printing was done by third parties around the world, many texts were still printed in Oxford. In those days the enormous printing machines stood two storeys tall, like the massive machines you see in old clips of newspaper offices, rattling out sheet after sheet of text for binding and then publication. It was a very impressive sight, and one that was swept away by new technology and working practices at the very end of the 1980s.

We were walking with our group along a narrow corridor on a gallery halfway up the print room when we came across an old man throwing squares of metal into a roaring furnace. On further investigation, it appeared that this was not some job-creation scheme, but part of the Oxford printer's recycling initiative. In the past, huge storerooms had been stocked with these old copper printing plates. Over time the plates grew worn and were no longer of any use. Eventually they were recycled by being melted down and reused.

To our alarm, we discovered that the heavy copper plates which the lonely old man was committing to the **inferno** were in fact printing plates once used to print the *OED*. Needless to say, Ed and I were horrified by what seemed to be the wilful destruction of the dictionary's history. The Shark was also shocked: though doubtless he shared our concerns, he clearly in addition lamented the loss of the windfall revenue that this Götterdämmerung of the *OED*'s heritage would precipitate. We halted the burning and salvaged what we could. To recoup some revenue, the Shark sold some of the plates through the University Press's bookshop in Oxford. Lucky lexicographers, I well remember, carted others home on their bicycles.

Every word has a shape, or profile, and the historical lexicographer has to be attuned to this. When we looked at *AIDS*, we saw that it had arrived very recently in the language, had one basic and very strong meaning, and that it had developed a wide-ranging collection of compounds, such as *AIDS virus*, etc. If we visualise it as a tree, it has a short trunk and a large canopy of leaves. Words which entered English in the Middle Ages or earlier have had a long time to develop, and their profiles often resemble old oak trees, with extensive ramifications (literally, branch-like structures).

Inferno is an important, powerful word today, but curiously, it does not have an extensive profile. According to the *OED* it has a single meaning, and no compounds worthy of note. It is more like a nursery sapling placed in the ground awaiting the chance to develop than a bona fide tree. And the reason for this odd profile is that *inferno* entered English late (1834), and as a result of conscious literary borrowing from Italian. We knew the word *inferno* before the 1830s, but only as the title of the first part of Dante's *Divine Comedy*—the section where Virgil takes Dante down through the nine circles of Hell (the Inferno), to find Satan bound in its very heart. But until the early nineteenth century we do not seem to have thought to use the word for Hell itself (or anything resembling it, such as a fiery furnace); we reserved its use for the title of Dante's text (which alone wouldn't merit inclusion in a dictionary—which is not intended to be an encyclopaedia of knowledge). *Inferno* derives directly from Italian *inferno*, itself developed—after the Fall of the Roman Empire, from late Latin *infernus* (= Hell).

Why didn't we use *inferno* earlier in English? Well, being a culture with a long Judaeo-Christian tradition, we already had a long stream of words for "Hell" (the *OED* lists ninety-seven, starting chronologically with the good Old English *Hell*, then *perdition, welling woe, Tophet, Avern, Hades, Sheol*, etc.). There wasn't necessarily room for a new one until Gothic literary types from the early nineteenth century saw fit to introduce another.

On the other hand, *inferno* slid into English relatively easily, as we were already perfectly familiar with its relations. *Inferno* is a cousin of the adjective *infernal*, which we absorbed in the Middle Ages from French *infernal*, where it had developed by the twelfth century from Latin *infernalis* ("of the realms below"—i.e., Hell). Italian *inferno* came by a separate route from Latin to that taken by *infernal*. *Infernal* is a word with a strong profile in English, to the extent that we sometimes forget its link to Hell when we use it in exasperation to mean "blasted" or "confounded."

With the new *OED* computerisation project approved, and with the Shark on our side, the message reached Ed (as chief editor) and me (as New Words editor) back in our offices that if we could manage to pull off the coup of computerising the dictionary on schedule and on budget—which became the mantra of the day—then we could more or less choose what we wanted to do in the future: the resurgence of the dictionary would be assured, as would our place with it. Promises like that have a short half-life, but we believed them enough to want to get on with the job.

The *OED* had reached a turning point. Over the past year our new managing director had galvanised support for the ageing and rather infirm dictionary both within the Press and (more importantly) more widely in the University. We had worked on plans to transfer the dictionary on to computer, and had found that its contents would fit reasonably easily into a database structure. We—and here I need to give much more credit to Ed and the Admiral than to myself—had conjured up project plans which the venerable scholars of the University were prepared to back. Before the Delegates of the University Press, orchestrated by Richard Charkin, had voted funds for what became known as the New OED project, we had been given to understand that there was a serious possibility that the grand old *OED* would simply be allowed to sink into obsolescence and decrepitude. The Press had no stomach for other long-drawn-out supplements. But now, at last, there was a chance that the dictionary might just pull through.

SEVEN

OED Redux

The new *OED* computerisation project received the official bless-ing of the University Press, and that approval came with an un-derstanding—agreed by all parties—that the Second Edition of the *OED* (as it came to be called) should be published in 1989. So we had about five years—working with IBM, International Computa-print, and the University of Waterloo—to put the text of the dictionary and its supplement on to computer, to merge these two texts together into one seamless whole, and to do whatever else was needed to publish the dictionary in print and on time. It would not be a new dictionary editorially. The key point for the future was that the merged text was to be published *from the computer database*, not from copper plates, or by phototypesetting from paper-based camera-ready copy. This had never been done before for such a large reference work, so we were venturing into the unknown. Once the Second Edition had been published in print, we could then think about disseminating the text as a searchable CD. That would come after the print publication, but as part of a sep-arate project.

We set about announcing the project to the scholarly community, at first through journals, newspapers, and budget-free word of mouth. (You will see that the syntax of *word of mouth* is extraordinarily un-English; not surprisingly, it is a straight translation of the medieval Latin *verbum oris*, first recorded in English in the 1450s.) I think someone had already booked the dining room at Claridge's for the launch party in 1989, just so we appreciated that the date was serious and inflexible. Sometimes it seems that publishing projects creep on beyond their planned completion time. The Shark and the Admiral constantly reminded Ed Weiner and myself that that wasn't an option for us.

In order to help us concentrate even better, we were moved into new offices—new offices being generally thought to be motivational. And so the New OED project was now proudly housed in what was then known in the University Press as "The Old Post Room." This was not a title of antique distinction, like "The Old Rectory" or "The Old Bakery," accorded the room to remind us of its picturesque aspect and quaint and charming history. It was called "The Old Post Room" because it was a big, square, utilitarian room which used to be the Post Room, in which old-fashioned incoming post was sorted and delivered to the Press's departments, until the Post Room staff found more suitable premises in the basement of the Press. At this stage there were never more than a handful of us, and I was officially moonlighting between the *OED*'s new offices and our old offices back in St Giles', where the New Words group was still located. Our new premises had little character and we had no budget to create one.

For me, the *OED* was at last heading in the right direction. It wasn't that I thought the Second Edition was the be-all and end-all of lexicography. In truth, for me it was a mechanistic project—though tough and imaginative for all that. I wanted to see the text of the dictionary safely housed on computer so that we could start updating the *OED* comprehensively, rather than making piecemeal additions through supplementary volumes. It was all, of course, still very uncertain. Ed and I didn't really know whether the University Press would countenance a big update project in the 1990s. Even if it did, we didn't really know how to carry out such an extensive historical overhaul of a dictionary that had arguably been neglected for decades. We hadn't sat down and thought out in detail how we might adjust the editorial policy for a modern national dictionary.

But first of all, we had to get the dictionary on to computer by 1989. If we couldn't do that, there was little point in trying to write a happy ending beyond. I thought of the project until 1989 as Phase One; Phase Two was our secret dream of what we wanted to do with the dictionary in the longer term. We thought that perhaps we could engineer an *OED* **redux**—an *OED* reborn. If you wait long enough, most things make a comeback.

> I had worked on the curious word *redux* in the late 1970s, for the *Supplement to the OED*. The original edition of the *OED* contained just a single meaning for the term, magisterially and rather obliquely defined as "Of crepitation or other physical signs: indicating the return of an organ to a healthy state," and squeezed in between the words *reduviid* ("belonging to a family of predaceous bugs") and *redvore* ("a variant of *radevore*; the precise sense is not clear"). The editors found that *redux* was a Latin word that had been borrowed directly into English by learned medical men during the Renaissance. By the twentieth century the *OED* editors knew that this old medical term was falling out of use, but that a new use—reborn from the original Latin and easier for the ordinary person to understand—was now known, from the titles of novels such as Anthony Trollope's *Phineas Redux* (1873) and John Updike's *Rabbit Redux* (1971): "brought back; restored, reborn"—as when a character in an earlier novel by the same author reappears and is "reborn" in a novel later in the series. It was naturally a usage associated mostly with literary types. I liked to think that we were going to be taking the dictionary through a process of rebirth.

Quietly, under cover of the Old Post Room, we planned a revolution in lexicography. This was the office where the Second Edition of the *OED* (*OED2*) would be prepared, spun from the text of the old dictionary, and nursed through to publication by Ed, myself, and Yvonne Warburton. We were joined by several other hand-picked colleagues, including Julia Swannell (silently present earlier in this narrative as the person who was actually appointed to the post on the *Pocket Oxford Dictionary* for which I long ago applied) and Veronica Hurst (later to become the *OED*'s bibliographer). If we could pull it off, then dictionaries could take a quantum leap to the benefit of both readers and editors. Up until now, dictionary readers had been restricted to "single look-up" (finding out information about the specific word they wanted to look up) and serendipitous browsing; now they would be entering into what we thought of as a new language universe, based around the *OED*. For editors, we would be creating a massive, dynamic, and updatable language resource: we wouldn't be restricted any more to alphabetical, paper-based updating, but could edit in whatever mode we wanted. That was the hope, anyway.

You need to bear in mind that this emphatically wasn't a project to put the dictionary *online* in the way we understand that term today. Going online wasn't something that anyone knew about back then; the Internet didn't exist if you were not part of the US military. The Shark's big project involved putting the dictionary on computer and seeing how the land lay computationally when that had been achieved. The real possibility of online publication came later. We talked then about *computerising* the dictionary. It sounds old-fashioned now: later on we understood that we were *digitising* the dictionary. It's much the **same** thing.

Little words like *same* cause enormous problems for lexicographers. This is because, however it is used, *same* always means the same thing. It is a word with Germanic antecedents which has had a long time to develop in English, as first records of *same* date from the Middle English period (though Continental parallels indicate that it is likely to have been known but unrecorded in Old English). The *OED* defines it with a broad, catch-all sweep as "not numerically different from an object indicated or implied; identical." You can see it's having difficulties from the very start, because it begins its definition with a negative ("not numerically different"). That is generally regarded as bad practice.

But lexicographers like to be helpful. They know that the contexts that *same* can be used in differ widely. Here are two sentences: "The same observations are true of all other contracts similarly circumstanced"; and "All the planets travel round the Sun in the same direction." In the first sentence, "the same observations" carries with it a reference backwards in time (probably earlier in the paragraph) to other, comparable "observations." In the second sentence, the planets are orbiting in the "same direction," not in reference to anything in the past, but in reference to each other. Some people like this sort of distinction, and they become lexicographers.

Here is a slightly different poser, but an easier one. Can you see how you might go about describing the difference between these two usages: "the sailors in the fleet all received the same pay as the soldiers"; and "the Greeks and Macedonians . . . looked on the Egyptian Ammon as the same god with their own Zeus"? *Same* has a very similar meaning in both sentences, but in one it is used in a syntactic construction with *as*, and in the other with *with*. There is enough of a chink of light between the two for the kindly lexicographer to wish to explain the history of each separately.

The end product is that if you examine the documentary records for *same*, you can separate the data into tens of different contexts and syntactic constructions, and define them all by describing the context and not the meaning. This happens with lots of little words, such as prepositions and conjunctions, and also with many adjectives and adverbs. Here is how one of those examples of *same* we just looked at is defined: "Followed by *as*. Now the commonest construction." If you look at entries such as *same*, you'll find this sort of technique used regularly. It reminds you that lexicography and language aren't only about meaning, but also about context.

Ed had relocated his office to the Old Post Room a few months before me. With the assistance of various computer types from left (OUP), right (IBM), and centre (Waterloo), he had devised a routine for transferring the *OED*'s text safely and elegantly on to computer in preparation for *OED2*. Under his oversight, the twelve volumes of the very old dictionary (1884–1928) and four volumes of the *Supplement* were being keyboarded in America to be ready for the publication of *OED2* in 1989.

The very basic decision to have the full text of the dictionary keyed manually (rather than automatically scanned) on to computer was one that the project team had made early on. But before we made it, we listened to advice from industry insiders. Several told us that we would be daft if we didn't scan the text on to computer (using optical character recognition), rather than waste time and risk introducing error by having it painstakingly keyed by hand. We always gave these obliging consultants a few pages of the *OED*, and said we would be delighted to check over the results when they had run it through their state-of-the-art text-scanning equipment. Curiously, we never saw any of them again. Perhaps some went mad, and maybe others were sighted selling ice creams on the sea-front in Brighton. But they certainly didn't come back to us with scanned text that we could make use of.

In the end, we had the whole text keyed on to computer by hand. But even then it **transpired** that there was no company in Britain big enough and courageous enough to take on the job of keying the entire text of the *OED*. Fortunately this was an activity that one of our potential partners offered to do: International Computaprint Corporation, in the home of the brave and the land of the big (Pennsylvania). They had our text keyed down in Florida by around 150 of their keyboarders, working over eighteen months. We required a high accuracy rate: no more than 7 errors in every 10,000 keystrokes. That in itself was suitably challenging. And at the same time the typists had to introduce tags before each element of the dictionary entry (the definition, the etymology, etc.), so that a computer could recognise it for what it was.

And how could we police that? Twenty thousand pages of type, each with three columns of tiny print. And it was difficult text. It wasn't Jane Austen. There were swathes of quotations dating all the way back from the Old English period up through Chaucer, Shakespeare, and all stations to the present day: it was not the sort of text with which the normal keyboarder in Florida would be familiar. And once the text was keyed, we then had to proofread the whole thing—which was a major project in its own right. Managing the keying and proofreading operation in Oxford became the responsibility of my colleague Yvonne, who set up a band of fifty freelance proofreaders to do the job. They could be seen shuffling into the office every now and then to collect their work and to hand back what they had just completed. And all this needed to run precisely to the clock, given the tight deadline we were facing.

In the mid- to late eighteenth century, the verb *to transpire* caused no end of arguments between otherwise healthy individuals. There are people who think that words should mean what they used to mean, and that any deviation from this is heresy (the "etymological fallacy": that *nice* is still somehow related to its origin in Latin *nescius*, "ignorant"; or that *logic* is only argument over "words," from the Greek *logos*, a word). *Transpire* (or at least its aged equivalent) has a literal meaning in classical Latin, but over the centuries English speakers have, to use the technical word, mangled this. The word *transpire* is known in English from the latter end of the sixteenth century, and it derived from Latin *transpirare*: *trans-* as in "across" (*Trans-Siberian*, etc.) and *spirare* as in "to breathe" (*inspiration*, *spirit*, etc.). So you would expect it to mean something to do with transmission by breathing.

Here's how the *OED* views that old meaning: "To emit or cause to pass in the state of vapour through the walls or surface of a body; esp. to give off or discharge (waste matter, etc.) from the body through the skin." As we move through the seventeenth century the range of contexts in which the term could be employed grows, but the core meaning remains constant: perspiration comes into it rather frequently—liquid passing from inside to outside or from outside to in. It turned out to be quite a useful word in the emerging sciences of the Early Modern period, and was heading for stardom.

The first hiccup on the road to immortality occurred in 1748. It concerns Lord Chesterfield, who—as a style leader—later annoyed the volatile Dr Johnson by withdrawing support from his proposed dictionary when the noble lord realised that it was veering off plan (i.e., Johnson had accepted that language changes and wasn't necessarily inching nearer and nearer to perfection, and that dictionaries should be open to this). In 1748 Lord Chesterfield (rather ironically and despite his general qualms on language change) decided to use the verb *transpire* in a figurative way that was new to English (though not to French *transpirer*), when writing to one of his correspondents. This is what he wrote: "This letter goes to you, in that confidence, which I . . . place in you. And you will therefore not let one word of it transpire."

Now there is absolutely nothing wrong with that (should you be the sort of person who finds things "wrong" with language), and the French had developed this use slightly earlier in the eighteenth century. What Lord Chesterfield was saying was that he did not want one word of the contents of his letter to permeate from its current private, secret state through to public view. The development from the physical transpiration to the metaphorical one is easy and unexceptionable. But when he came to address the word in his dictionary, Dr Johnson rather pompously found even this minor semantic shift too much ("a sense lately innovated from France without necessity").

What happened next, though, set language purists into a deep decline. According to the *OED*, it was an American lady—Abigail Adams, wife of the second president of the United States—who is credited with writing in 1775 to her husband at the Continental Congress in Philadelphia: "There is nothing new transpired since I wrote you last." I'm sure others used it in this way before she did, but at the moment she has all the credit.

Language purists hated this new meaning "to occur, to happen." What, no permeation—or at least only permeation and transmigration of the very loosest variety, in the sense of something moving from one state (nothing happening) to another state (something happening). Organic change like this should not happen in a polite eighteenth-century salon. The fact that it might well be an Americanism—and Americans were not really top of anyone's dance card in Britain around 1775/1776—probably made the usage even less popular in Britain than it might have been. The First Edition of the *OED* despairs: it is a "misuse." The dictionary offers some assistance: "Evidently arising from misunderstanding such a sentence as 'What had transpired during his absence he did not know,'" which is itself a rather enigmatic and confusing way of explaining something. In observing the usage, the *OED* was following in the footsteps of earlier lexicographers, such as the American Joseph Worcester, who wrote in 1850: "This novel use of the word is pretty common in the United States; nor does it appear to be very uncommon in England, though it has been repeatedly censured by judicious critics, both here and there, as improper." Worcester didn't seem to mind too much, though. It transpires.

In the autumn of 1985, I was invited—along with Hilary and three-and-a-half-year-old Kate—to Waterloo, Canada, on the notion that—as an *OED* expert—I might advise the Waterloo computer

gurus on their job of thinking theoretically about possible structures for the planned *OED* database. Actually, my role was simpler than that. While the gurus were discussing how best to organise the dictionary's mass of data inside a computer, I was expected to supply in-depth information on the structure and content of the print version of the dictionary, in case by any chance it had implications for their work.

At the same time I was to be addressed as visiting assistant professor in the Waterloo English Department, and was expected to hold post-grad classes on the history and practice of lexicography. Hilary was also invited to teach a first-year class on her speciality: the modern English novel. Kate was expected to go to day care: she remembers helping me clear mounds of snow from the drive of our house, but she doesn't remember the educational benefits of day care.

I love the conventional eighteenth-century spelling *gooroo*. *Guru* is another of these Early Modern English words (so it gets an extra tick from me). Like *juggernaut*, it is one of many Indian words that early travellers and traders encountered in the Indian Subcontinent. The austerity of the gurus' lifestyle, and the deep respect in which they were held, struck the Europeans as surprising—the wise men that they knew didn't look quite like the Indian guru. So naturally they wanted to tell their audience back home about this new phenomenon. The *OED* defines *guru* primarily as "a Hindu spiritual teacher or head of a religious sect," from 1613 (the same year as the first "computer"). Samuel Purchas, an indefatigable recorder of travellers' tales at the time, refers to "a famous Prophet of the Ethnikes, named Goru." The dictionary sensibly thinks that this is a common noun, not the gentleman's personal name.

Normally Indian gurus seem to be slight, thin gentlemen. This is not always the case with computer gurus, where too much sitting down at the keyboard and being sedentary broadens the beam. In twentieth-century English we started to extend the meaning of *guru* from its original Hindi sense. H. G. Wells writes: "I ask you, Stella, as your teacher, as your Guru, so to speak, not to say a word more about it," in his *Babes in the Darkling Wood* (1940). After that, the word was available for use generally as "any influential teacher or mentor." Computer administrators at the time rather liked to be called "gurus"—not to their face, necessarily, but they liked to know it was going on out of their earshot.

These were exciting days for the digitisation of the *OED*. The dictionary had previously often been the subject of informed comment and criticism from literary scholars, but in Waterloo the way that the dictionary held and presented its information was rigorously probed by computational logicians. They asked me simple but awkward questions about the dictionary that I hadn't necessarily heard before. Like: "What is the generic structure of a definition?" or "Would it be useful to link from an entry to full, digitised versions of the texts it references?" "Would you always want to present entries in alphabetical order, or should there be other options?" "Would you ever want a computerised assessment of which entries are most out of date?" "Do you want us to tell you computationally which twentieth-century compounds seem common enough in real text to be added to the dictionary?" I knew that my answers would help shape the *OED* of the future. It was a good match, and a very productive one.

Waterloo had already devised some lightning-fast search software for the dictionary. (This was years before software of this kind was available off the shelf.) Although the software searched almost instantaneously over the massive amounts of text residing in the dictionary, the dictionary's text was complicated enough that a human brain (in this case mine) was needed to unscramble problematic issues.

The problems we tussled with were esoteric, but they had to be resolved if we wanted to be able to search the digitised database more efficiently and discover new information about the language that was just lying hidden at the moment, waiting just below the surface. Take dates, for example. Traditionally, if the *OED* couldn't allocate a precise

date to one of the texts it was citing in support of a word (often an un-
dated manuscript text deriving from before the invention of printing),
then it would date it imprecisely—say, circa 1400. That caused no
problem to human readers consulting an entry. They used their common sense. But that was no use to a computer, because they weren't
born with common sense. The computer didn't instinctively know
what circa implied, and it wanted a real number or number range to
work with. So we had to come up with one. After experimentation, we
devised an idiosyncratic system which told the computer that at one
period in early history (when you generally only had a very sketchy
idea when the manuscript was actually composed), then circa should
be assumed to imply a date range of fifty years, but that when you were
dealing with post-medieval texts (and you might generally be more
confident of your ability to date the text), then circa might suggest a
twenty-five-year spread, or later in time just five years. It wasn't perfect,
but with that information nestled in its software, the computer could
work happily with the dictionary's apparent inexactitude.

I was introduced in Waterloo to a culture in which texts were the
object of a new form of analysis: where looking for patterns in language was paramount. We began to think about how computers
could be taught to extract information from texts so as to improve dictionary content and to benefit language analysis generally. Obviously
we weren't alone in this, but it was something of a revelation for me,
coming from a long-standing editorial project in Oxford that was really
a throwback to the 1950s, when the *Supplement to the OED* had originally been established.

All of a sudden we were familiarising ourselves with a host of new
ways by which we could investigate the dictionary. Shakespeare is always a good example. We looked at all the words and meanings said to
have been coined by Shakespeare (around 8,000 in all): What could
that tell us about authorial creativity (was it greatest in nouns, adjectives, verbs?)—Was Shakespeare's lexical creativity most active in his

early work or later, in the comedies or the tragedies (we found 210 neologisms in *A Midsummer Night's Dream*, but 480 in *Hamlet*)? We revealed that Shakespeare was credited with augmenting the word-stock
of English with meanings for 2,900 nouns (such as *partner* = dancing
partner), 2,350 adjectives (*Nestor-like*), 2,250 verbs (*to waddle*, applied
to a person), 146 phrases (*too much of a good thing*), 40 interjections
(*bow-wow!*), 39 prepositions, etc. We discovered how many English
words had been coined between 1600 and 1610 (8,400, at least according to the *OED*'s record). We looked at the aggregate number of nouns,
verbs, and other parts of speech before this date and after: Was there a
difference, and, if so, what did that tell us about the language? Did we
lose many words in the fifteenth century through obsolescence? If so,
what sort of words were these? Why did we lose them? What was happening to our society to cause this to happen? And how do those words
compare with the ones we gained over the same period? Sometimes the
data wasn't really strong enough at the time to answer our questions,
but it was exhilarating just to think of the questions, let alone discover
the answers.

It was in discussions of this sort that I spent the busy days of autumn
with the computer scientists at Waterloo. There were two gentlemen
who led the pack: Frank Tompa and Gaston Gonnet. Frank knew considerably more mathematics and computer science than was good for
him, and Gaston knew the rest. Frank was so good at it that he's had a
street in Waterloo named after him, and Gaston had already invented
his own computing language, which he named, with the true generosity
of a Uruguayan to his adopted country, Maple. The professors were as
excited about the project as the lexicographers were. We thought of it in
the same breath as the Human Genome Project, getting off the ground
at around the same time: pattern-matching through huge swathes of
data was crucial to both adventures.

One of the most unexpected things about going to Waterloo was
that suddenly I was in an environment where lexicography was regarded as an important new area of progressive language research led

by a computerised *OED*. The computer science professors in the University of Waterloo's new Centre for the *OED* were helping to wrestle the *OED* towards a brave new future.

My English Department master's students were also curious about and excited by this new field of research, and not fixated on the fusty British stereotype of lexicographers. In England, the media often couldn't see beyond the sepia images of *OED* lexicographers as old men with trailing white beards, amnesia, and chalk dust. My postgrad class investigated the history of antique English lexicographers, from Robert Cawdrey in the early seventeenth century, through Dr Johnson, to Noah Webster (not a beard among them), but they also had access on campus to the early reaches of the *OED* on computer. They soon came to realise that examining this database could give their literary and language studies a new perspective.

I n those days, there were only a few dictionary courses available in universities and colleges. Before the digital revolution, historical dictionaries were something of a cosy end in themselves, admired by literary scholars but often overlooked by others whose interest in language would be gripped by the new technology. We needed to look at the tradition of dictionaries before we broadened out into options for the future.

Dictionary history can be taken all the way back to Akkadian/Sumerian wordlists in the third millennium BC. But to do so is not particularly enlightening for the student of the English dictionary, so we started our course at a more recent date.

There are several basics that you need to know. Bilingual glosses, and then bilingual dictionaries, predate monolingual dictionaries such as the *OED*, because people encountered a need to understand foreign languages before they worried unduly about the definition of words in their own language. The first language that the early English needed to gloss was Latin, the language of the early church and of instruction. In order to assist their pupils' understanding of the Bible, Anglo-Saxon teachers would write the English equivalents of Latin words (or some-times just simpler Latin words) between the lines of their manuscript texts. These glossaries are very rare, but we know of several works of this nature. The surviving Leiden Glossary, for example, was copied in modern-day Switzerland around AD 800 from a lost Anglo-Saxon manuscript.

But there is little doubt that, despite indicating a need for reference texts to help understand language, the interlinear glosses of medieval manuscripts were never going to be international successes. We had to await the invention of printing, in the mid- to late fifteenth century, before a medium was available through which dictionary (and other) texts could be made more readily accessible.

Even then, the British were not ready for their first English dictio-nary. The medievals had been more interested in classifying knowledge in thesauruses (literally "treasure houses" of knowledge) than in dictio-naries. But the need for translation remained strong. In the sixteenth century, bilingual **dictionaries** (involving Latin, English, French, Ital-ian, or Spanish) fed a market in Europe (including Britain) eager to make sense of the changing world: important titles at this time include the Latin-English *Dictionary* of Sir Thomas Eliot (1538), which was published in many editions throughout the sixteenth century, as well as Claudius Hollyband's *Dictionarie French and English* (1593) and John Florio's Italian-English *Worlde of Wordes* (1598).

We first meet the word *dictionary* in the thirteenth century, in its Latin form *dictionarium*. But at this stage it wasn't used in the way we know it today. It was introduced by the Parisian teacher John of Gar-land (born in England, it should be noted) as the name for his elemen-tary guidebook to Latin composition. The *OED* and others have investigated this matter in some depth, and report that the author's introduction states (in translation) that the book "is called *Dictionar-ius*, not from [Latin] *dictio* in the sense of 'single word' but from *dictio* in the sense 'connected speech.'" So John of Garland intended it to mean a book explaining the mysteries of "connected" Latin composition, not a "word-list" with glosses or definitions.

It used to be thought that the first occurrence of the word *dictionary* in English was in William Bonde's *Pylgrimage of Perfection* (1526). But a recent surprise discovery uncovered evidence of the word's existence from around 1480 (the *Medulla Grammatice*, or the "Marrow of Grammar," a collection of Latin-English glossaries held in the British Library). So we now have the word from the very late Middle Ages. It feels significant when research causes a word to pop back into an earlier band of the language, as has happened here.

Dictionary is the first word recorded in English to mean "a dictionary." That may sound like an obvious statement, but often other words occur sporadically before a keyword is settled on. In the case of *dictionary*, the next word that was tried, in 1568, was *calepin*, from the name of an Augustinian friar who wrote a famous Latin dictionary first published in 1502. It was a well-known word in the early sixteenth century, but fell into disuse after that. Other synonyms include *world of words* (1598–), *lexicon* (1603–), and *thesaurus* (1823–).

As expected, the word *dictionary* (like *lexicon* and *thesaurus*) comes from the Romance rather than the Germanic tradition. Scholarly medieval and Renaissance words tend to arise on that side of the language divide. Once established in English, *dictionary* did develop new meanings over time. By the 1570s it was comfortable enough in the language to sprout two new meanings—or really just adjustments of the old meaning. In 1576 the *OED* notes that it could be used of any alphabetically arranged reference book or encyclopaedia, not just one with headwords and definitions; and in 1579 records show that it made a larger jump, to mean the personal vocabulary of any individual person—your "dictionary" was the sum total of words you knew. We still use a variation of this sense when we say "Purple is not in my dictionary" (and other things like that, obviously). By 1609 the poet and dramatist George Chapman starting referring to someone as a "walking dictionary," and that is a use also preserved today. By 1829,

if you were a know-it-all user and consumer of jawbreakers, then you
might be said to have "swallowed a dictionary."

I explained to my students that the book traditionally regarded as
the first English dictionary was not published until 1604: the *Table
Alphabeticall*, by schoolmaster Robert Cawdrey. In truth, this wasn't
what we think of as a dictionary. It was almost a translation dictionary,
for it only contained what the author regarded as "hard" words—usually words of Latin or Greek derivation—with which the untutored
Briton might need help. It was, as its author candidly stated, written
principally for women and children.

The hard-words tradition dominated the early scraps between the
lexicographers who were competing to publish small dictionaries in the
early seventeenth century. In order to satisfy a growing market, each
dictionary had to be slightly larger than the last, or have some new feature—scanty etymologies, regional words, slightly more common
words, classical allusions, geographical names, proverbs and phrases,
and gradually—by the latter end of the seventeenth century, and in
works such as Elisha Coles's *English Dictionary* of 1676—we started to
find dictionaries that we might classify as dictionaries today.

There was no theory of lexicography in those days. Definitions were
normally lists of synonyms or brief descriptions of the term defined;
the etymologies were only as good as the etymological dictionaries of
the day (and some were rather good); there was as yet no help with
pronunciation. Dictionaries in the seventeenth century were very
workaday works, often produced by almost anonymous schoolmasters,
for use in the classroom.

The eighteenth century saw English dictionaries become more obviously commercial. The great English lexicographer of the early eighteenth century was Nathan Bailey, who dominated the market with his
cramped, stocky, and yet perversely attractive dictionaries of the period. Bailey would from time to time in his entries cite famous authors
who had used the words he treated—as if to give his words a renewed

legitimacy. His *Universal Etymological Dictionary*, first published in 1721, was extraordinarily popular, and not particularly etymological. He is well known for some of his evasive definitions, such as the *spider*: "an Insect well known"—which harks back to the seventeenth-century amateur tradition. This is to do him a disservice, though, as for most of the time he was operating on a much higher—though often equally conversational—level than this. Take, for instance, his definition of *hook-pins*: "[in *Architecture*] taper Iron Pins, only with a Hook Head, to pin the Frame of a Roof or Floor together." Generally speaking, it helped if you already knew the meaning of what you were looking up, though, before you searched for it in Bailey.

Nathan Bailey was worried about Dr Johnson. He knew, of course, that the great man had been compiling a dictionary to beat all dictionaries, and he had tried to shore up his own market by publishing a spoiler—a large folio format dictionary that might equal Johnson's projected two-volume production of 1755. It didn't, and when Johnson's dictionary was published, it was rapidly accepted as the standard. Johnson's page format was elegant, his definitions were elegant—as befitted a journalist and literary man—and were amply supported by quotations from the "best" authors. He was not responsible for introducing our modern spellings for many words, as is sometimes thought, but his choice from among variant spellings of his day was wise, and reinforced their status as the standard spellings of the time (and often of today). Dr Johnson gave the English dictionary—and to some extent, the English language—a legitimacy which it had not possessed in the smaller world of schoolmasterly lexicography. The fact that he introduced a small number of rather quirky definitions (such as the well-known *oats*: "a grain, which in England is generally given to horses, but in Scotland supports the people") only seems to have endeared him to his audience.

The new United States of America developed its own dictionary tradition, led by Noah Webster, an ardent spelling reformer and a citizen and supporter of the Union. His most famous dictionary, *An American*

Dictionary of the English Language (two volumes: 1828), had a political as well as a lexicographical purpose: Webster wished it to be understood that the United States was as independent of the British Isles in terms of language as it was politically. His dictionary doesn't feel like a piece of elegant typography, but his definitions are clear, and he was able to introduce words and meanings characteristic of the new America. It didn't sell particularly well when it was first published, but after his death it was acquired by the brothers George and Charles Merriam, who with new editors gradually took it successfully in hand.

Webster had not availed himself of the new comparative linguistics which had developed in Europe from the very late eighteenth century. Comparative linguists in Germany and elsewhere had started to work out how some languages that might appear on the face of it to be very remote from each other (such as French and Sanskrit) could be distantly related. Often the links dated from times before the languages were written down, which made this rather an esoteric subject of study. Rules were worked out which demonstrated how the English word *fish* was genetically related to the Latin word *piscis* (= fish), for example, and once the initial discoveries had been made, it was possible to envisage a network of related languages in language family trees and their conjoined cultures spreading back for many centuries into the past.

British scholars followed these developments with great interest in the early nineteenth century. Many of them were members of the Philological Society in London. These ideas about the network of comparative languages informed the discussions in the society about what later became known as the *Oxford English Dictionary*.

The line of development from 1857, when the Philological Society debated the state of English dictionaries, through to the completion of the *OED*, in 1928, is straightforward. The *OED* draws on this comparative knowledge to investigate the prehistory of English words in other—often related—languages, and then uses the equivalent of a genealogical tree structure, with meanings branching off from the base over time, to illustrate linguistic developments within English.

The digital, searchable dictionary project takes this historical tradition to a new level. The result is as significant for lexicography as were the changes brought about by the invention of printing and the development of monolingual from bilingual dictionaries. Whereas in the past the dictionary had been a static text, at which the reader would sometimes gasp in excitement when discovering some interesting new word by browsing serendipitously through its pages, the digital dictionary offered the possibility of a cognitive upgrade to new avenues of information and research at the level of the whole language, not just the individual word, as well as—eventually—links outwards from the dictionary text to whatever world (of text, knowledge, etc.) the reader wished to explore.

One of my ongoing issues is with people who "love words." As a language scientist, I generally avoid commenting words which simply amuse and entertain, which don't contribute anything useful to the language, and which certainly don't represent the important words of language study. I take the hardline view that words are not there to be "enjoyed" or purred over. They are not dolls: who cares about *antidisestablishmentarianism* from the point of view of real language, or *floccinaucinihilipilification* ("the action or habit of estimating as worthless"—at one time the longest word in the *OED*), or *mallemaroking* (look it up)? Why waste time on them? Concentrate on the real words of the language. But it seems no one else shares this view with me.

Maybe I think of these show-off words as elitist, or at least undeservedly attention-seeking. They are easy to like (or so it seems). But they are outliers—not central to the real language.

Working with the computer scientists at Waterloo, I was able to start investigating—on computer—what seemed to me much larger language questions. What I wanted to investigate was how words evolved in their passage through time. I wanted to explore patterns: How did what happened in society generally affect language? Why did some words succeed while others didn't? Which Anglo-Saxon words went underground for centuries after the Norman Conquest, only to reappear—still alive and kicking—five hundred or more years later? Why did Americans need some of the traditional English words as they developed a new, independent country in the eighteenth century, but not others? These aren't questions for crossword buffs. And you could only hope to answer them if you had collected and correctly analysed enough of the everyday data of English.

Let's look briefly at just one of the questions I wanted to investigate: What sorts of words did those early voyagers bring back to English in the sixteenth and seventeenth centuries? The sixteenth century was a period during which the English language reasserted itself as the language of Britain and became a cultural artefact in which great literature, great thoughts, and great invention could be expressed. That sounds like an odd thing to say, but in previous centuries English had been struggling against the French of the Conquest and against the Latin of the church and officialdom, and had never really been able to breathe for itself. Sixteenth- and especially seventeenth-century Britain experienced a sense of expansionism, which in turn led to empire and a more stable relationship between the home country and the numerous locations from which new words might enter English. One of the most important arenas of British expansionism was the Indian Subcontinent. After initial explorations, the British East India Company was awarded a charter in 1600 to trade on behalf of Britain in India. Over the years its role changed, and it came to exercise administrative control across large areas of India from its bases in Calcutta, Madras, and Bombay (to use the old names of these cities). The company was granted tax-raising powers by the British government, and even maintained its own army to support its predatory ambitions. Things came to a sorry halt for the East India Company with the Indian Mutiny (now normally called the "Indian Rebellion") in 1857, after which the power of the company waned, and the British government and the new Indian Civil Service took over the role of managing those parts of India under the sway of the British Raj.

What does the *OED* tell us about how the English language tracked these momentous changes? The dictionary shows absolutely no borrowings into English from Hindi (for example) from the dawn of time until the second half of the sixteenth century, before which there was clearly little or no interaction between the nations. From 1550 until 1599 there are five recorded borrowings of words into English from Hindi. And the method of transmission is revealing—all but one are found in English translations of foreign works, so the English-speaking people were introduced to a new area of interest at second hand. It was a symptom of Britain's early position in the politics of expansionism that when they arrived in the East, or in the New World in the West, they often found Spaniards, or French, or Portuguese there before them, and this has a significant effect on the mediation of words from the original language of the country into English.

The first borrowing recorded from Hindi is *kotwal*, an Indian magistrate or police officer, dated from 1582 in English. The word appears in a translation of a Portuguese work by Fernão Lopes de Castanheda (c. 1500–1559), a Portuguese historian who had spent much of his childhood in Portuguese India—the Portuguese were well ahead of other Europeans in India at the time—in the region of Goa. Castanheda's work was mostly published posthumously and was not translated into English until thirty years or so after his death.

Four of the remaining sixteenth-century words from India come from another translation, which is from the work of the Dutch merchant and historian Jan Huyghen van Linschoten (1563–1611). Linschoten's account of a voyage to Portuguese East India was published in Dutch in 1596, and because of growing interest in the region it was translated immediately (1598) into English. Linschoten also published trade routes to India, and he was instrumental in opening up the region to the Netherlands and Britain. The words we take from him are trading terms (*paan* and *supari*, relating to the betel nut) and *Kunbi*, the name for a member of an Indian agricultural caste. The fifth and final term loaned from Hindi into English in the late sixteenth century is *hing*, better known by its older name *asafoetida*, a resin-like latex gum used as a spice in Indian cookery and medicine, and recorded in the journal of English merchant Ralph Fitch. *Hing* was a traders' name for the product, used while it was being manhandled as a cargo on its way to Europe; the apothecaries and cooks in the West preferred the more familiar *asafoetida*. These few words do not represent a massive onslaught of vocabulary, but they were a straw in the wind.

The pervasive intrusion of the British into India until Partition in 1947 and beyond, into *Hinglish*, meant that many other words—after this slow start—could permeate into English. The *OED* records just over 800 of them from Hindi. That surprised me—I only knew the more long-standing expressions, not those which meant so much to the early history of the British in India, but have faded from our memories. The wealth of borrowing from other Indian languages surprised me, too: 80 words from Bengali, 25 from Gujarati, 61 from Marathi, 49 from Panjabi—as well as the 550 from the formal, "official" language of Sanskrit. In the past it had not been possible to obtain the instant and panoramic view of these languages and their relationships with English that we could now access with the computerised data. We knew the significant words (*jungle, Sikh, crore, rupee, Jain, raj,* etc.), but there had been no easy way to find the minor players (*war*, the banyan tree; *musseet*, a mosque; *jugger*, a type of falcon—all at the bottom of the dictionary's frequency list of Hindi borrowings); and yet these minor players need to be examined before we can speak confidently and precisely about this and other comparable areas of language and social interaction and development.

While I was busy advising computer-science professors and teaching budding lexicographers, Hilary was hard at work with her first-year class on the English novel. She had essays to mark, and lessons to prepare, and new students to get to know. She remembers the term for four things (I am reliably informed): the first three were seeing her first-ever student wearing shorts; being challenged on a grade she awarded; and being laughed at for suggesting that a meeting take place at "tea-time." But she remembers that term principally for a banal sub-headline in the university magazine, the *Waterloo Gazette*.

The editor of the *Gazette* had decided he would notify the university of our arrival through its columns, and to do so he wrote a sterling front-page piece on the new collaboration between Waterloo and Oxford, which included a few paragraphs about me and my role in the project. The problem arose when he generously decided to add a short section on what Hilary was teaching in the English Department, which he incautiously and patronisingly subheaded "Wife is Prof." As you will appreciate, Hilary was a no-nonsense feminist; back home, my former chief editor, Bob Burchfield, had whispered to me one day that she was the only dictionary "partner" of whom he was seriously in awe, so heaven knows how the editor of the *Waterloo Gazette* was about to feel. There was a certain amount of seething at home, and sharp letters were written to the editor of the *Gazette* decrying the sexist undertones of the passage. He, in true journalist style, hid behind the fact that it was the truth—she was my wife, and she was a professor. When the **hue and cry** had died down, we wore T-shirts printed with "Wife is Prof" emblazoned across the front.

> *Hue* is a fossil nowadays. That means that it doesn't have a life of its own any more, and is only found in set phrases which we just repeat with little concept of their original meaning. It's not unusual for a word to become fossilised: sadly, it's one of the ways we retain the shape of the past while forgetting its content (you might compare *beck* in *beck and call*). *Hue* did once have a meaning, as you would expect. You need to travel back to the time when the Normans and their descendants ran England after the Conquest. Law was transacted in Anglo-Norman French, and those French had an expression *hu e cri*, which meant (according to the *OED*): "Outcry calling for the

pursuit of a felon, raised by the party aggrieved, by a constable, etc." Well, there's no doubt that was what it meant, but when the English used it, they altered the Anglo-Norman French into the more English-looking *hue and cry*. They'd know *cry*, and would understand it as a frantic shout after a criminal who was in the process of legging it, and at the time they'd even know what *hue* meant (much the same, in fact). By the mid-seventeenth century, this meaning of *hue* had effectively faded from the language, but the English still went on using it—fossilised—in the expression *hue and cry*. Their descendants were so puzzled by this phrase in the seventeenth century that they even thought it might be one word, or perhaps *hewing cry*. It's an instructive example of what happens as a word turns into a fossil.

I returned to Oxford in early spring 1986 filled with confidence about the computerisation project. I had learned during my months in Waterloo that what had seemed like a brash effort to force the old *OED* out of the comfort of the nineteenth century and into the twenty-first might actually work.

My return also marked a major change in my position on the project: I was appointed co-editor of the *OED*, alongside Ed Weiner. As before, this meant that I retained my responsibility for running the New Words team, but added a shared responsibility for the computerisation project. As someone who is naturally cautious, the magnitude of my new responsibilities should have alarmed me to the core. But my trepidation was outweighed by the thrill of having a major role in breathing new life into the Victorian dictionary.

Back in the Old Post Room at the University Press in Oxford, the project had moved on during my absence. Everything—the twelve volumes of the original *OED* and the four volumes of the *Supplement*—had now all been keyboarded. The next task was for our computer and its accompanying software to merge these two streams together for us into a seamless alphabetical whole (we fondly called this "integration").

But the software for making seamless wholes was in fact making seamless holes. This wasn't a surprise—we had known all along that we would at times need to intervene heroically to save the situation, when the system was unable to achieve the appropriate level of microsurgery. If the *Supplement* wanted its new sense 4c to fit after the existing senses 4a and 4b, then the computer could usually cope with that. And suppose the old dictionary contained senses numbered 1, 2, and 3, and the *Supplement* wanted its new sense to be shoehorned in as a new sense 2, bumping the old 2 and 3 down to 3 and 4. The computer could normally handle that, too. But there were flourishes it didn't seem to understand. Sometimes the instructions which the *Supplement* had provided for its human readers, notifying them where a new piece of the dictionary jigsaw was intended to go, were not logically consistent enough for a computer, or sometimes they were just wrong and the computer hit a **brick wall**. So we immediately introduced a new editorial stage—in other words, from time to time we would carefully unpick what the computer had done and redo it ourselves (we should have called this "disintegration"). And so, as each section of the text was processed through 1986 and beyond, we were on hand with an artist's brush and a conductor's baton to reintroduce the seamlessness.

Remarkably, there are two completely different terms *brick wall* in English. You wouldn't think there was a need. They are a good example of word growth, word decline, and word death—with some healthy behind-the-scenes competition thrown in for good measure.

Brick wall in its original meaning—"a wall constructed of bricks"—dates from the end of the Middle English period, around 1440. Although compounds are much better attested in later centuries, that certainly doesn't mean that they didn't exist in Old and Middle English—it's just that there are fewer of them. And they often relate to everyday things, like *cupboard* (think about it), *love-drink* (don't think about it), and the aforementioned *brick wall*. *Brick wall* is such an obvious expression that the original *OED* editors hardly thought it was worth shelf space. They gave us the earliest known reference (around 1440: Osbern Bokenham's translation of the monk Ranulf Higden's *Polychronicon*, a universal history down to his own time), added one quotation from the Bible and another from Shakespeare (and a third from Ephraim Chambers's eighteenth-century *Cyclopaedia*, for the sake of solidarity), and then signed off the entry. They didn't even bother to illustrate it later than that. It was as if the dictionary wanted to say, "If you need to be told more about this, then you're reading the wrong sort of book." To help stragglers, the editors even defined it in the simplest of terms: "a wall built of brick."

Brick wall is compounded of *brick* and *wall*. Although *wall* is Old English, *brick* is later. The *OED* isn't 100 percent sure about the etymology of *brick*, but it thinks very strongly that French is involved. So as *brick* isn't known to the Old English, we wouldn't expect to find *brick wall* in Old English. This is not the case with *stone wall* (yes, there is no end to the twists and turns that a lexicographer can take). Both *stone* and *wall* were well known to the Old English, and doubtless to many Germanic tribesmen and tribeswomen before Anglo-Saxon times. So it comes as no surprise that *stone wall* is also recorded in Old English.

There is another term in English, *brickwall*, written as one word, which is not composed of the word *brick* and the word *wall*. As it comes from a different origin, the *OED* logically makes it a completely different dictionary entry. This second *brickwall* tells us other things about language. It doesn't date from the Middle Ages, but from the early years of the Early Modern period (1500–), when English speakers began to use a variety of English which is more recognisable as the language of today. This *brickwall* means "the rebound of a ball from the wall of a [real-]tennis court." It dates from around 1570 in English and is actually a corruption of the Early Modern French word *bricole*, which originally meant "an ancient military engine or catapult for throwing stones or bolts," but had moved on to mean a rebound off the wall in real tennis. Because the rebound involved bouncing off a wall, the English (in their comical wisdom) had decided that it was more fun to reuse their existing and similar-sounding open compound *brick wall* than to get used to saying the outlandish French word *bricole*. And so we did.

This was the heyday of real tennis (called just "tennis" in those days, as there was no need to distinguish it from lawn tennis, which cropped up—originally known rather hopelessly as *sphairistike* = "ball skill"—late in the nineteenth century). Gradually, real tennis waned in popularity, and we found as a nation that we had less need for the word *bricole* and for the new word *brickwall*, and so it was unsuccessful in the struggle for survival against the more established and considerably more useful *brick wall*; it fell out of common use in the middle of the seventeenth century—whereas the successful *brick wall* branched out into new metaphorical expressions, such as *banging your head against a brick wall* (known since 1697), and coming up against a *brick wall* (an impenetrable barrier), in the last half of the nineteenth century. With its workmanlike but elegant simplicity, *brick wall* shows no signs of wilting today, in either its literal or extended uses.

The whole business of keyboarding the dictionary from *A* to *Z* had taken eighteen months. Proofreading the text had taken us another six months (sentenced to run concurrently). Then Ed and I shared the big read-through of the final, integrated text at the end, checking the content and approving it for publication. That means that we read ten volumes each, which isn't something either of us wants to do again.

The year 1986 was also the year my old chief editor, Bob Burchfield, retired. He'd notched up just under thirty years on the dictionary, and had brought the *OED* from what was effectively a point of stagnation in the 1950s to the brink of the future, without wanting—or being in a position—to push it over into the digital era. In the end he seemed to us to leave quietly. He had already moved off to another building to work on his edition of Fowler's *Modern English Usage*, and his final departure was quite a muted affair. He came along to one of those dictionary tea sessions shortly before he left his office in St Giles', where he launched into an extended metaphor about Piccadilly Circus and Victoria Station in London. It seemed that it was intended to symbolise the difference between the hectic excitement of digitisation (Piccadilly Circus) compared with the quiet regularity of old-style lexicography (the railway station at Victoria). I think the metaphor needed more work. With his departure, one of the residual links with the everyday life of the Victorian editors finally snapped.

I n the Old Post Room, we knew we were getting towards the end of the computerisation project in two ways. Firstly, the much-heralded publication date of 1989 was getting relentlessly closer and closer. And secondly, a cardboard progress chart that we had devised had almost reached the corner of the office by the window. This, you will appreciate, was our cosy alternative to professional online management software, which even in those days gave you advance warning of when to put one foot in front of the other. Our progress chart evolved naturally from a piece of cardboard to a fully-fledged piece of cardboard with empty squares on it. Technically, Yvonne Warburton or her colleague Veronica Hurst would be in charge of filling in each empty square once a batch of work had been approved. So without even needing to turn on our computers we could tell exactly how far along we were with the project—and whether we were on schedule—just by staring at the wall. I have heard that some of our managerial colleagues within the University Press were less than impressed by this improvisation, but oddly enough, it had more motivational potential than the reams of continuous stationery that the real project-planning software disgorged in some of the better-appointed offices we occasionally entered.

By now, we were battling hell-for-leather to meet our regular and draconian deadlines for processing the text, and checking the proofs that were rolling off the old-style printing presses to form the pages of the Second Edition. The full dictionary text existed on computer at this point, but it was only accessible internally, to *OED* editors. The printing of the Second Edition was carried out in Britain—by Film-type Services in Scarborough in Yorkshire—but the binding and final production of the twenty volumes were entrusted to Rand McNally in the States, a company that was quite familiar with the enormous print quantities and the marbling of end-papers and the speckled patterning of the edges apparently necessary for the American audience, which was still rumoured to be our largest potential market.

We knew from our calculations that the new edition would be twenty volumes long. What we didn't know was which words would fall, by chance, at the beginning of each volume, and so would appear for all to see on the spines. Within minute limits we were able to in-fluence this. The old edition of the *Shorter OED* had for many years sported a first volume which announced proudly that it ran from *A* to *markworthy*. *Markworthy* seemed a more important word because of this. (My former colleague John Sykes had apparently been tickled that many dictionaries said *atom* in the spine. It turned out that this was "A to M." It doesn't take much to make some lexicographers chuckle.)

We set out in a small way to see if we could engineer language-related words on the spines of our volumes. *A* was an obvious start. As the pages rolled on towards the end of the first volume, we realised that we could bring down the guillotine just before *B.B.C.* (as in *B.B.C. English*, etc.). And so *B.B.C.* became the lead word on the spine for Volume Two. For Volume Three, we had to be more cryptic and chose **Cham**, from a nickname applied to Samuel Johnson.

There are nowadays only a few people who will have any idea why the word *Cham* might be relevant to the *OED*. But sometimes words are plucked out of obscurity and associated with some new person or thing, and that is what happened with *Cham*. The *OED* defines it as follows: "An obsolete form of KHAN *n.*[1] formerly commonly applied to the rulers of the Tartars and Mongols; and to the emperor of China," from which you might surmise that it has little to do with the study of language.

The link with language comes through Tobias Smollett, author of numerous picaresque eighteenth-century novels, such as *The Adventures of Peregrine Pickle* and *The Adventures of Ferdinand Count Fathom*. In 1759 Smollett wrote to the radical politician and journalist John Wilkes that Samuel Johnson's black servant, Francis Barber, had decided to leave Johnson's service for a life on the open wave. Johnson was desolate, and worried that Francis would not stand up to the rigours of life at sea. According to Boswell, Johnson pronounced that "no man will be a sailor who has contrivance enough to get himself into a jail; for being in a ship is being in a jail, with the chance of being drowned." When he wrote to Wilkes, Smollett referred to Samuel Johnson, the great dictionary editor (amongst many other things), as "that great Cham of literature," a phrase which Boswell dutifully republished.

I'm sorry to say that that *Cham* was where our ingenuity ended as regards appropriate catchwords for each volume. Volume Four of the Second Edition of the *OED* started with the word *creel*, which even we couldn't invest with serious relevance to the study of vocabulary. When we had finally approved the contents and spine of the twentieth volume (*Wave* to *Zyxt*), we were ready to publish.

Just for a moment, we felt on top of the world. Over the previous five years we had commandeered the text of the dictionary from its old-style book form on to computer; we'd proofread it, added 5,000 new entries, and altered the pronunciation system (despite almost terminal worries that we would not be able to); and we'd got it all to the point at which it could be published. Curiously, it was going to be published again as a book, and not (straightaway) as an electronic resource. We still had some work to do.

EIGHT

The Tunnel and the Vision

F inally, the day arrived—Thursday, 30 March 1989, the launch date for the Second Edition of the *OED*. (Publication days were always Thursdays, since time immemorial. I think this was so that people had a couple of days to assemble their pocket money to be ready to go to the bookshops on Saturday.) A few weeks prior to this, our publicity colleagues had stormed into action. Ed Weiner and I found ourselves travelling up to London to have our picture taken by Lord Snowdon, formerly the husband of Princess Margaret and at that time a very successful commercial and society photographer. The photograph was to accompany *The Times*'s article on the publication of the dictionary. We were new to the world of modelling, and naively imagined ourselves progressing swiftly from Lord Snowdon's celebrity studio to the front cover of *Vogue*, before having our image flashed across one of the illuminated hoardings in Piccadilly Circus. But to our surprise, Lord Snowdon was more interested in how we had managed to squeeze all the data in the First Edition of the *OED* on to a little compact disc (which we had been instructed to take along as a prop, to contrast with the row of twenty enormous Second Edition volumes) than in his unique opportunity to make the editors style icons. In his vision of the photograph, all that would be seen above the dictionary volumes would be Ed's disembodied hand holding aloft and in triumph the tiny CD-ROM ("compact disc—read-only memory": technically, a data CD rather than an audio one).

A quiet word about CD-ROMs: nowadays we tend to forget them, and we have certainly wiped from our memories almost everything about data storage on magnetic tape, which nowadays we associate with audio technology. But in the days before we had minute storage disks, we stored data on large magnetic-tape spools and hooked these up to mainframe computers. CD-ROMs and mag tape were the two new mediums by which the digital *OED* introduced itself to the public in the late 1980s and early 1990s, before the emergence of the Internet. We had produced a rather basic version of the First Edition of the *OED* on CD-ROM in 1989 (containing everything edited up to 1928)—almost just to prove that it could be done. You could buy it, but it was more of a beta test for the real thing. This was the one that Lord Snowdon wanted us to hold exultantly above a sea of books.

Despite Lord Snowdon's preference that the compact disc should be centre-stage in his photograph, our publicity minders refused to be coshed by a genius more creative than themselves, and insisted that the image (which the publisher was, after all, paying for) should feature the real-world characters, Ed and myself. So the vision changed. The CD was relegated to its rightful place in a jewel-case off-set, and Ed and I regained the photographic high ground. But once the twenty volumes had been arrayed neatly in stacks on the table in Lord Snowdon's studio, and we had been asked to drape ourselves elegantly behind them, you could only see the tops of our heads. In my case, that is not a feature. This gave Lord Snowdon another chance to suggest that Ed might hold the CD up in his outstretched hand, reaching towards the light above the books. Once again that plan was vetoed, though it did remain in shot. Eventually it was necessary to find two chairs for us to stand on, so that we could appear as if we were in complete control of the mass of volumes arranged car-boot-style beneath us, with the two of us proudly surveying them like nineteenth-century European princelings.

This was one of the best publicity shots we managed. Numerous other journalists and their photographers thought it would be comical for us to hold half of the volumes each and for their photographer to snap us just as a stack started to topple and we were about to drop them. After one or two experiences of that order, we toughened up and refused to act as construction workers, as bookends, or as mannequins holding open books of condolence.

The **launch** itself, many years in the planning, was at Claridge's. It was rather a damp squib for the editors. All the exciting work had already been done and we were unused to sticking our heads out of our offices to talk about it in public. But the University Press was delighted with how things went. Literary critic Christopher Ricks, author Malcolm Bradbury, and former Librarian of Congress Daniel Boorstin were amongst the guest speakers, and they praised the University, and the University Press, and the editors generously for their endeavour and their commitment to scholarship. They had not at that point had an opportunity to read all twenty of our volumes, so what they said must have been based on first impressions. The first impression, in fact, of the Second Edition sold out within months—mainly to university libraries around the world.

There is something impenetrable today about the word *launch*. It is not one of those words you can look at and say, "I know where that comes from." Fortunately, the sage old editors of the *OED* knew better back in 1902, when they first published their entry. It's a word that doesn't come from the ancient Anglo-Saxon word-hoard, but from post-Conquest French. It's of interest to dictionary types, though, because it derives from a historically important variety of regional French. The knowledgeable editors tell us that *launch* entered English in the Middle Ages as another of the mass of French words to arrive after the Norman Conquest. The verb derives from Old Northern French *lancher*, "to lance."

It's important for us that we record that *launch* derives from the Northern French form with a -*ch*-, and not the Central French form *lancier*. These varieties of French were distinguished by aspects of pronunciation as well as of vocabulary. Old Northern French was the language of Normandy and incorporated features of the Norse (Scandinavian) language of the Norman settlers in Normandy in the Middle Ages. Since William of Normandy came, you might guess, from northern France, his troops brought over many northern forms. We have the regional *poke*—a bag or sack, as in buying *a pig in a poke* (i.e., unseen)—in parallel with the standard *pouch* (Northern French *poque*, Central French *poche*), and *warranty*, not *guarantee* (ultimately from Northern *warrant*, not Central *guarant* and *garant*).

To *launch* meant "to hurl (a missile)" or "to pierce (as with a lance: NB lance/launch)." When it was applied in the Middle Ages to people, it meant "to rush, plunge, dart forward." *Launch* developed metaphorical uses, and from the seventeenth century we launched ships, or careers. By the time the publishing world had got its act together around 1870, we developed the concept of launching books (and later, other products). In the West of England in the nineteenth century we launched leeks, meaning "to plant them like celery in trenches," though I cannot see any evidence that that sense has clung on.

A short note on pronunciation: even into the twentieth century in Britain it was standard to rhyme *launch* with *branch*. It doesn't seem possible now, but there you are.

In the weeks following the launch, Ed and I had to enter a smiling publicity mode, something with which we were not entirely comfortable. We flew over to North America to introduce the populace there to the importance of the digital dictionary. Our North American publicity was always managed by the indefatigable Royalynn O'Connor, who, against all odds, thought that we were newsworthy and were at least promising communicators. Before she had time to be disabused of that notion, she set us up an exhausting media schedule. Ed had the unfortunate experience of being woken by a phone call in his hotel room one morning to find that in his bleary-eyed state he was broadcasting live to regional America. We were both annoyed by a journalist who insisted on publishing a warts-and-all verbatim transcription of precisely what we said in response to his questions in a face-to-face interview: all of the ums and ahs and false starts, as well as the regular stream of connected discourse.

More demanding for us still was our publicity tour of Japan. In those days, Japan was the second-largest market for the printed *OED*, after the United States and before Britain. That might stop you in your tracks. It's obvious why North America was our top market: the American university and college system has always been fascinated by the English language—the language of the old country, and the language they had pioneered themselves in post-colonial times. And they recognised British scholarship at its best, as we liked to think. But Japan?

The secret was that the Japanese also love detailed information, and apparently especially when it relates to the English language: Japanese professors are held in high respect in their educational system, and Japanese professors of English seem to be at the top of the tree. The Japanese admired the close work that had created the *OED*—and they were a little sorry and down-in-the-mouth that they didn't have their own historical dictionary of Japanese, to demonstrate the strengths of their own culture to the world. They also had ample money within their corporation budgets, and so their love and respect for the English language was matched by an ability to acquire it. Britons, on the other hand, have never been quite sure whether the *OED* is a work of monumental scholarship or simply opens up to the world the British at their most obsessive.

The tour in Japan got off to a bad start, when we were introduced to the Japanese gentleman who ran OUP's branch in Tokyo. We soon discovered that we were far too young for him, and (in his view) for the Japanese public, who thought that the best things came in old and dignified packages. Nevertheless, it was too late to send for replacements, and he was stuck with us for two weeks. He proceeded to entertain us royally with saki, seaweed, and barnacles—or at least that was the impression we had of some of our evening fare, as he played his own game of trying to establish at just what point an Englishman would refuse to taste "traditional food" of the sort that would not be eaten by any self-respecting Japanese.

Despite official misgivings, the Japanese remained—as we had expected—extraordinarily polite, and those who came to hear us speak were willing to listen in silence for long periods of time while we explained the methodology and content of the new dictionary. But there was a problem. Our speeches were simultaneously translated. That doesn't mean that Ed and I were speaking at the same time, but that in my section of the lecture I would say a sentence, and it would be immediately translated into Japanese for the benefit of the audience. We gave the same talk (I have to confess) in several places. In Tokyo the translator regarded us with regal respect, and so used a form of Japanese—with all sorts of ingratiating circumlocutions—that made each Japanese sentence take three times as long as the equivalent English one. With all of this gross politeness, the talk overran by about half an hour. In advance of a repeat performance in Kyoto, we drastically pruned the text so that the same disaster could not recur. But this time the translator turned out to regard us as colleagues and equals, and used a less verbose and possibly more racy form of Japanese when translating our text. As a result, the talk was wrapped up early, and our host found it necessary to hold sway over the longest question-and-answer session in recorded history.

I f you look closely enough, you will find that the *OED* has plenty to say about Japanese loanwords in English, and this was one of the subjects of my talk. We saw earlier that the dictionary plots the course of around 500 Hindi words in English, especially from the period of British expansionism and consolidation in the Subcontinent. The history of Japanese loanwords has its own peculiarities, due to the particular course of Western exposure to that country. Historically, Japan's isolationalist policy of *sakoku*, in effect between the early seventeenth and the mid-nineteenth centuries, meant that the country was to all intents and purposes closed to Western traders and other visitors. By the same token, Japanese were forbidden to leave Japan in this "Edo" period. Word borrowing occurs through contact, and at that time, especially through geographical proximity or physical contact. If Japan was effectively closed for business to the West, then we wouldn't expect any words to seep from Japanese into English.

And so we have one Japanese loanword in English in 1557 (*Kuge*, the nobility attached to the royal court at Kyoto) and, as with early Hindi borrowings, this occurs in a translation from an intermediate language—in this case Italian. Then there is a micro-boom of other Japanese terms (21 in all) from 1600 until 1650: *inro*, an ornamental set of boxes; *miso*, soybean paste; *shogun*, a hereditary commander in the Japanese Army; and *tatami*, the rush-covered straw mat used endemically on Japanese floors of the day, and indeed a standard unit of measurement. The *OED* records 508 words from Japanese in English from 1557 to the present day. But precious few of them entered English between 1650 and 1800, when there was no official travel to Japan.

A trickle of new words starts to enter English again from Japan in the early nineteenth century, but the real rush starts around the middle of the nineteenth century, and especially after 1870. Between 1870 and 1910, we find over 200 words arriving from Japan. And how has this happened? Yet again, the language follows culture. Japan had lifted its *sakoku* policy in 1868, and the West had been gradually developing an interest in the arts of the Orient: the *OED* has the style nouns *chinoiserie* from 1883, *Japanesery* from 1885, and *japonaiserie* from 1896, for example. Now these new Japanese words were acquired in English not only directly from travellers who experienced the culture and preoccupations of the Japanese at first hand, but also—at home—through the influence of Japanese art, literature, and costume (prominent for Western art-lovers through books and exhibitions): *haiku, judo, ju-jitsu, Kabuki, netsuke,* and *Noh* on the art front, and *futon, hahama* (loose-fitting trousers), *haori* (a short, loose coat), *happi* (a loose outer coat), and the flowing *kimono.* The influx of Japanese words into English continued throughout the twentieth century, with new foodstuffs (*edamame,* or soybeans), martial art terms (*ippon,* from judo), and a slight shift towards technological innovation: *emoji, karaoke.*

Why have some of these words stood the test of time in English? Not because we intuitively understand their etymology, which, in almost all cases, is a mystery to Western speakers (few people know that *emoji*—literally, a pictogram—comes from the Japanese word *e,* "a picture," and *moji,* "a letter, a character"), but because Westerners have become very interested—if not obsessed—with the material manifestations of Japanese culture, and we need the words to describe these. And the easiest words to use are those that the Japanese already use.

Once the hype surrounding the Second Edition died down, we began to realise that the *OED* was no longer the University Press's top priority. When you are absorbed, as we were, in an all-engrossing project which has international ramifications and treats the language from its earliest days up to the present, it's easy to imagine that everyone else thinks it is as important as you do. Well, we were wrong there. Gradually I appreciated, probably a bit later than everyone around me, that what I had been itching to start on—the next phase of updating the old Victorian *OED* comprehensively, in all its nooks and crannies, turning it into a modern, dynamic reference resource—was going to be put on hold until the University Press had cleared up several other projects that had been awaiting funds which we had been gobbling. After five years of being in the international spotlight, we found ourselves parked in the back streets for several years, with editorial staff drawn away to other projects.

It's not that the language was quietening down, so the New Words editors just carried on recording the language we saw flashing past us. That's something I always told editors: if there are problems around the project—financial, personal, whatever—just concentrate on the text. Nothing else really matters in the long term. Concentrate on getting the text right, and the other things will, at some point, fall into place. I used to find that thought reassuring around this time. But nevertheless I found OUP's reasoned delay almost a betrayal, and I was not happy. We made representations to all and sundry for new staff, for new software, just for support—but in large measure it was not forthcoming. All we could do was carry on editing more new words, knowing they might not ever find their way into an updated *OED*.

And the new words kept on coming. We were moving out of the Thatcher years and the language was beginning to experience (I almost said "suffer," but we don't like value judgements) its social after-effects. Pubs were changing—from the old spit-and-sawdust locals to *gastropubs* (1996). The gastropub could perhaps be peopled by *new lads* (1991 onwards), redolent of the brash self-centredness of the post-Thatcherite early 1990s. By 1995 we had *ladettes*, showing that once a word like *lad* creeps into the limelight, it develops in ways we might not have expected. We were *on message* (1992) thanks to President Clinton's *policy wonks* (1984; origin unconfirmed), and this Americanism soon became part of the vocabulary of *Blairism* (1994–). We heard *babelicious* for the first—and sadly not the last—time in 1991; we could *text-message* by 1994, though we apparently had to wait till 1998 before we could just *text*. Who can deny that these were days to be proud of? (Not!—popularised particularly by the film *Wayne's World* in 1992.)

Although dictionaries were preoccupying most of my time in the wake of the 1989 launch of the Second Edition of the *OED*, Hilary and I now found that we were expecting another baby.

Kate was seven and doing well at school, as the teachers told us at our regular meetings. We were all set for Baby No. 2 around New Year 1990, to cap a triumphant year. There were no problems when Eleanor (Ellie) was born on the morning of 10 January 1990. And since Hilary and I had already had one child, we felt fully equipped to handle anything that the new baby would throw at us: early mornings, late nights, midnights, screams, colic, rashes, nappies, more nappies—all the usual stuff.

For the first six months, everything seemed to be going along just fine, until my mother came to visit in the summer of 1990. We didn't see very much of our parents at this point. Hilary's were away in Norfolk, where they'd retired several years earlier; and my parents (also retired) were deep in Surrey, where my father was futilely dreaming about establishing a vineyard on the south coast. But one day, when Ellie was about six months old, my parents came over for one of their lightning visits on the way to somewhere else, and Mum took her out for a stroll in her buggy. When she returned, she said she thought there was something different about Ellie; something she hadn't been expecting. For a six-month-old baby, her eyes weren't responding as sharply as you might expect to the various stimuli around her—trees mostly, clouds, birds, things that hove into and out of view from the perspective of a baby in a buggy. That was the first inkling we had that something might be wrong. It was only later, though, that the full extent of Ellie's **disability** became clear.

Ability is another of those words that entered English in the Middle Ages from French. But the French didn't give us *disability*. We had to work that one out for ourselves. Our first record of the term dates from 1545, in the general sense "lack of ability (to do something)." But the specific application of the word to a person's mental or physical incapacity also comes from around the same period: it was first noted in 1561, and contrasts strongly with many of the other words used at that time (such as *imbecility, dumbness,* etc.) for personal-disability terms which are now no longer regarded as acceptable. We might be surprised that a "neutral" word was so prevalent in the sixteenth century.

The vocabulary of disability changes with the generations, as one term rises to acceptable prominence, displacing those employed earlier. When Ellie was diagnosed, *disability* had become the preferred term amongst professionals, superseding *handicap*. There were times when we wanted to use *handicap*, almost to shock people out of the complacency that a neutral term like *disability* can engender ("We have the right term now; that shows how caring we are").

Why did *disability* become the more acceptable term? The word *handicap* dates from the seventeenth century, over a century after *disability*. It comes from a time when the English enjoyed experimenting with new vocabulary. But at first the term had nothing to do with disability. In the beginning, *handicap* was a game. As the *OED* says, it was "a game in which one person claims an article belonging to another and offers something in exchange, an umpire being chosen to decide the difference of value between the two articles, to be made up in money by the owner of the less valuable one." The handicap, then, is the difference between the value of two items, or the value you have to add to one to make it equivalent to the other.

The main definition doesn't explain why the game was called a "handicap," but if we read on we find that the contestants put equal wagers into a hat or cap. The umpire and the two players put their hands into the cap (and even I can see *handicap* taking shape here). The umpire declares the value of the less valuable item. The two contestants take their hands out of the shelter of the cap. And they take out their hands either full or empty, to signify agreement or not with the valuation. If both agree, then the umpire takes the money. If not, the pot is taken by the contestant who agrees with the valuation.

I didn't follow that, but I've seen a TV quiz show based along similar lines and it seemed to work pretty well, though I think I must have been waiting for the show following it.

By the eighteenth century, the word *handicap* attached itself to horse-racing, on the same logic. An official decided the extra weight to be carried by a horse to equalise its chances of winning. Originally the agreement was conducted between two principals with a cap, as in the game, but later bureaucracy took over. The meaning seeped into various sports in the eighteenth and nineteenth centuries.

It wasn't until around 1888 that the *handicap* was first applied to physical or mental disability. The earliest records for this come from the United States. At first it was regarded as a perfectly normal expression—an acknowledgement of the difference in ability between two people. But, by the later twentieth century, *handicap* had come to be considered generally unacceptable: an unfamiliar-looking word implying too marked and dismissive a distinction between the able and the disabled. Maybe the expression also seemed to imply going "cap in hand" to beg for public assistance.

Soon enough, people stumbled over phrases like "differently abled," as they tried to develop a new vocabulary for disability. The history of *handicap* doesn't lend itself to the sensitive description of disability, so it's probably for the best that we don't hear it all that often nowadays. It appears to offer a crushing value judgement on someone "different" from the average. But it would be wrong to forget what it tells us about how we responded to disability in the past. *Disability* has a negative prefix, so maybe it, too, will have a relatively short shelf-life. However the vocabulary changes, we need to remember words as tinder-boxes of their time.

The nature of Ellie's disability emerged over time. At first the doctors noted that her weight gain was not keeping up with what was considered normal. After a few visits, we found ourselves directed towards a neurology consultant. Ellie's new consultant was supportive and puzzled. (Hilary used to note that whenever we met him, he and I were always wearing identical clothes. We used to register that sort of thing, no doubt as a kind of counterweight to the tragedy that had overtaken our lives.) The consultant had batteries of tests run, and we became familiar with a stream of vocabulary that I'd never encountered before. He decided that Ellie wasn't autistic, but that she had some genetic abnormality—at the mitochondrial level—perhaps Angelman or Rett syndrome. She was tested for these, but the tests came back negative.

Against the backdrop of this bewildering medical uncertainty, I wondered about putting these expressions into the *OED*, since the dictionary generally didn't seek to cover the enormous range of syndromes and diseases that can afflict us. But I felt that had I included them, I would have been skewing the traditional word-selection process and letting details of my own life interfere with the neutrality of the dictionary. Nevertheless, both later found their way into the dictionary. *Angelman syndrome* cropped up as we worked through the files for *A*, and it made its way through the editorial procedure into full *OED* publication. It's a short entry, giving brief background information about Harry Angelman (1915–1996), the British paediatrician who first described the condition in 1965. Angelman syndrome is a rare genetic disorder causing severe mental disability and characterised by ataxia, creating a person who is affectionate and cheerful but blissfully unaware of many things, most especially the need for speech. The first quotation from the *OED* reminds me even now of the dreadful habit people had of giving conditions extremely unkind informal names: the *American Journal of Diseases of Children* (1972) speaks of "Angelman's ('Happy puppet') syndrome."

The searchlight beams of the *OED* also fell on *Rett*, when we next waded through the waters of the letter *R*. Nowadays the dictionary tells us that Rett syndrome is first recorded as an expression in 1983 (in the *Annals of Neurology*)—and is named after Dr Andreas Rett, an Austrian physician who first described the condition in 1966. Predominantly affecting girls and starting at between six and eighteen months, it is sometimes called a "locked-in" syndrome, in that whilst the patient's understanding is not occluded, she is unable to convey messages from her brain to her body. It is disturbing to find the neutral procedures of the *OED* sweeping into its maw the uncertainties of your own life.

Ellie's disability didn't hit us suddenly, at that breakthrough moment when my Mum noticed that something was wrong. Things are never as simple as that. Over the next few months—even years—we experienced more and more indications that something was amiss, and we would attend increasingly frequent appointments with her consultant. Her mental development had stopped, as far as we could see, at around six months of age. She wasn't learning. No words; no sense of recognition or understanding except the very barest. She wouldn't play; she didn't pick things up, except to throw them gently away ("casting," as the specialists liked to say), so she can never be given a cup to drink from without support. She smiled and laughed, but didn't speak (she never has). We couldn't easily tell if she was unwell, or had a headache, or had accidentally cut herself. Her natural recourse, if even slightly injured, was silence. But she was very precise in her movements, as if she recognised dangers but could do little to prevent them.

So there wasn't one moment that we can turn back to and say, "That was the moment we knew." And there wasn't a particular day when the future seemed to fall apart. What we did experience, Hilary and myself, and our daughter Kate, was a growing sadness and helplessness about Ellie's condition. Many parents must experience this. There is absolutely nothing you can do. Kate remembers reading a book about a baby who only talked when no one else was around, and she apparently convinced herself (without telling us) that this was what Ellie was doing. As it was a gradual process, we had time to come to terms with it, as much as you can. But there's a void which won't be filled.

We have never discovered a cause for Ellie's condition. She is a beautiful child. Other people—including myself—are better people because of how she is, but that's no help to her.

As time went by, we discovered that it wasn't that she was hard to look after, but that you had to watch her every waking hour of the day, and then make sure she wasn't a danger to herself at night. That's the same with any young child: it's only later that the strain starts to show.

She's in her mid-twenties now, but still has the developmental age of a preverbal toddler. Opposable thumbs, fine motor control—those were the first milestones she failed to make, or any after that. She's happy in her own wordless world. I always thought I would be able to break in. I'm still trying to, because you can't give up.

As far as the dictionary was concerned, once the Second Edition of the *OED* was out and published we took down our cardboard progress chart from the wall and contemplated the future. We'd expected that once that progress chart was removed, we'd replace it with another one—which would allow us to plot how we were comprehensively updating what was in essentials still a Victorian dictionary. That had been the understanding throughout our work on the Second Edition: it was just the precursor to the real job of updating the big dictionary, to which everyone seemed committed and which we assumed we would move on to the moment the Second Edition was published. But now we realised that that was not the case. There could be no tangible commitment by the University Press to the immediate revision of the dictionary, because there was no approved plan. We had been naive, but someone could have told us how these things worked. Other projects needed to be completed, and the *OED* needed to wait its turn. Realistically, that was sensible strategic planning, but I didn't like it at all. So, with the progress chart and all that went with it removed, I moved back to the main dictionary offices in St Giles' to work on new words more or less full-time, while others remained in the Old Post Room preparing data for their next big thing—*OED2* on CD-ROM.

This was a very active period for the New Words group. Rather than selecting our own words for *OED2*, we became a central post office located in an editorial no man's land in St Giles', receiving requests for work on new words by the editors of other, smaller Oxford dictionaries—which seemed (in contrast to the stately *OED*) to rush through the alphabet at a remarkable rate, and continuously to want more new words. There was a race towards informality: *achy-breaky, anoraky, badassery, fusion* (of music), *happy-clappy* (in religion), *janky* (of poor quality), and *kikay* (a flirtatious woman). Health, fitness, and extreme sports were becoming top of everyone's agenda: *hoverboard, rollerblade, snowblading, Tae-bo, three-peats* (the third of three successive victories), and *oversupination* (running on the outside of your feet). Well, at least to me these seemed extreme sports.

I was trying to think which word I most remembered from this period. The sorry state of affairs is that it is the term **burpee**. This was, somewhat remarkably, a word with which I was quite familiar, from my athletic, hockey-playing days, but of which—under close examination—almost everyone else that I spoke to refused to admit they had ever heard. In case you are rolling the word around on the tip of your tongue, the stress normally falls on the final syllable: bur-PEE. If anything, that only makes it worse.

Those of you who do or have done circuit training or any physical jerks prior to a sports match will be quite familiar with press-ups, star jumps, running on the spot, and all of the other muscle-stretching activities that are supposed to make you more able to race into and around your opponents during a game. You'll also (I presume) have heard of the burpee, but will not know where on earth the term comes from. *Burpee*—despite its unusual form—is an example of a word derived from a personal name, and in this case we know the person.

First of all we need to understand what it is. So stand up straight, looking towards the front. Bend down and place both hands on the ground in front of your feet. Once your hands are planted on the ground, jump your legs backwards so that you're almost in the press-up position. As if that isn't enough, then jump forwards again so that your feet are back where they were before you bounced backwards (athletic training is reductive like that), and then return to the normal standing position. At some point in the procedure you need to ensure that you don't bump your knees against your nose. Repeat this in a continuous easy motion ad infinitum. To the advanced-level linguist, that's a squat thrust performed from and returning to a standing position.

How did this exercise receive such an irregular name? Here, we find ourselves in the realm of Major General Henry Shrapnel (1761–1842), the British army officer who invented an explosive shell which scattered its contents (bullets) all over the shop when it went off. So we get the word *shrapnel* from him. I'd like to be able to say that *shrapnel* is Old High German for a knight armed with a fearsome multi-pointed lance, or that it derives from the metallic sound of the projectile when it detonates, but neither would be true. *Shrapnel*—unlikely as it may seem—comes from a person's name.

You can see where I'm leading. *Burpee* also comes from a person's name, not from Major General Shrapnel, but from Dr Royal H. Burpee (1897–1987), an American psychologist. He devised a test, which came to be called the *Burpee test*, to measure a person's agility and muscular coordination. Although the *OED* dates *burpee test* to 1939, we had to wait until 1957 to encounter the worn-down simplex *burpee*. And we had to wait until the 1990s before the *OED* took any notice of it, because—I suspect—previous editors gave little weight to the notion of sport.

The success of the Second Edition of the dictionary did give us one opportunity to expand. Our base had always been in Oxford, and yet more English was spoken outside than inside Britain. But if we really wanted to capture the changing face of English more widely, then we needed a stronger presence in America.

It would of course be wrong to claim that I noticed all of this single-handedly. We had decided several years earlier, in the mid-1980s, that it would be a good idea for the *OED* to have a North American crash pad. There were innumerable reasons for this, and here are three. Firstly, it seemed to us and to other language commentators that most language change was taking place in American English (and, indeed, that American English was exporting its vocabulary, even sometimes its syntax and morphology, in ever-increasing amounts, to Britain and other varieties of English). Secondly, North America was still light-years ahead of Britain technologically. And thirdly, America had been traditionally the *OED*'s largest market and greatest supporter.

It's not hard to see why the United States was the focus of so much change. The more people there are using a language, the more the language changes. That's a basic rule. Furthermore, if several language communities interact within a single linguistic space, then even more change happens. The number and mix of people in the States means that words are constantly interacting, and bending American English into new shapes (semantically and syntactically). Added to this, people generally like change: it's symptomatic of growth and success, and so they proudly embrace new modes of expression.

Beyond the boundaries of the United States, American English had started to push change across the English-speaking world generally (and even beyond that). America was an economic success story that others wanted to share and emulate. Its culture had a high prestige; its language—a major symbol of its culture—was attractive as the purveyor of a lifestyle. American economic success, American music, American literature and films, and American cars were admired internationally and gave American English a sense of glamour abroad. If there is a weakness in American English (unlike British English), it's that it has a tendency only slowly to accept external influences—words from other varieties of English—which is something that has always made British English strong.

We elected to take a softly-softly approach as far as the *OED*'s takeover of America was concerned, and so rather than filling sheds in the Midwest with unpractised lexicographers, we decided to appoint someone to run a reading programme of North American sources for us, so that we could begin to fill our files with vocabulary of a type we simply could not amass from our incident rooms in Oxford. I initially assumed that we would be espoused by one of the big American universities, and given office space, help, funds, staff, probably our own baseball caps—but offers never came. There was sometimes a feeling that for an American university to offer historical Oxford academic shelter on an American campus would only be at the expense of the homegrown American dictionary houses. For me it wasn't a competition, but something we needed to do on our own.

To find the right person to head our American operations, we advertised throughout the American university circuit. We caught the attention of several likely candidates, who were not particularly dissimilar to the interview applicants we knew from Oxford (though sometimes perhaps slightly more advanced in years and experience). We wanted someone to manage the reading programme and, more importantly, to run it as a computer-based operation. We didn't want more index cards choking our card-quotation cabinets.

In the end the task of appointing a director for the reading programme was easy. Jeffery Triggs was a poet and an enthusiast. He seemed to me to have the manners and style of a perfect southern gentleman along with the digital acumen of an advanced software analyst. As it happens, he was neither of the two (southern or software analyst; the manners and style can stand), and I soon learnt that whilst you were talking to him he was usually busy trying to work out how to write a program to solve whatever you were talking about. So if you asked him the time, it was sometimes quicker to look at your watch.

Yet again, Oxford and the *OED* were way ahead of the game in the data-collection business. It was 1989, and with Jeffery's appointment as our North American Reading Programme director, we effectively shut down the card-file system that had served us so faithfully for 130 years. The files were (and still are) technically left open, but the vast majority of new data from then on arrived electronically. In almost all ways this method was an advantage, so we were all looking forward to working in the new computerised environment. But there was one thing that was never the same: you can't sort online "index cards" for a word into their separate senses in the same way that you can physical cards. People tried to develop the relevant software for us. But you never have the flexibility to make adjustments to the content of the various "piles" you create. It's hard to explain. In the old days, you could fan out the index cards in your hand, and tinker with sequences—as if you were playing poker—or you could build up piles on the office floor. You always remained in control of the data. They were present all the time. On computer, they sank or swam depending on what was observable on your screen.

From the start, Jeffery insisted that all of his "readers" key their findings directly to computer. The files were processed and then regularly sent to Oxford for incorporation in a growing database of raw language data for the editors to use when working on their words. There were numerous advantages of the new data-collection method over the old card-based one. By now, editors had desk computers for aspects of their work—though not yet for editing entries. They had purpose-built software (originally from the University of Waterloo) that let them search these reading-programme files. Having the files on computer meant that at last every word in the file was searchable: you'll remember that the card-files were only searchable in their heavy card cabinets by catchword.

There were other advantages too. We started to write software to look automatically, by algorithm, for words (especially compound words, such as *computer-assisted*, or *doomwatcher*) which the program judged possible entrants to the dictionary—based on frequency in text. We could total, average, list, order, reorder; we could introduce thematic source tagging to help in our search for evidence; find all instances of the word *narrative* in literary theory (rather than in other contexts), or quotations for *post* in football (rather than horse-racing), and this saved editors' time quite dramatically. We were starting to move into a new world of language study. Jeffery's reading programme served the *OED* admirably for many years to come.

Despite this expansionist optimism, Ed and I recognised in the very late 1980s and early 1990s that we would not be handed the future on a plate. Instead, we would need to argue convincingly for the sort of *OED* we had begun to envisage, and for where we wanted to take the dictionary, now that it had at last become a digital resource. The publication of the Second Edition in 1989 had long been just a staging post for us. We'd computerised the data, but it still consisted mainly of a book (though now spanning twenty closely printed volumes) which had been planned in the late nineteenth century, completed in the early twentieth, and added to incrementally and in piecemeal fashion since then.

In fact, the outline of our vision for the *OED* was encapsulated in a little time bomb we left in the introductory text of its Second Edition. At least we thought it was a time bomb, committing the University Press to the further enhancement of the dictionary, but looking back, I realise they could easily have disregarded it. Right up there on page 55 of the printed introduction, we inserted a tiny sub-subsection entitled "The Future of the *OED*." This was where we stated that not even *we* thought that the Second Edition was the end of the road, but that it was really only a new beginning. The dictionary had been dreamt up in the 1850s, and compiled from the 1870s onwards, but had never been comprehensively revised. This had, sensibly, been considered far too big a job by the masters of the University Press, who had continued to issue supplements without attempting a root-and-branch revision. So in "The Future of the *OED*," we systematically listed many of the things that we thought needed to be done to the text of the massive dictionary to drag it out of the nineteenth century and then into the twentieth and subsequently even into the twenty-first.

Everything needed to be looked at again in the light of modern knowledge: definitions needed to be rethought; quotation sections needed to be updated to the present day; bibliographical details needed to be checked and standardised; entry structures needed to be reconsidered; references to outmoded systems of currency, geographical names, and so on needed to be fixed; some people whose birth years were given in old nineteenth-century *OED* etymologies had now died, and we needed to give them closure in their entries; label names needed to be reconsidered; more new—and especially old—words needed to be added. So it needed not just a tune-up, but a complete service. I don't think we thought that many people would reach page 55 of the introduction, as introductions are consistently overlooked by anyone who opens a dictionary. In fact, dictionaries must be one of the few types of books that are more or less opened at random—or where the user thinks, for example, that particular words might be found—rather than at page 1. But you miss things that way.

By now we had a clear sense of where we wanted the dictionary to move, but we had no budget to fund this, and certainly not enough editorial staff to help bring it about. At the same time we were relieved to find that people in the real world were starting to take a greater interest in what we were doing. Scholars were fascinated by the possibilities of the *OED* on CD-ROM and the idea of an enormous online dictionary, constantly updatable, incorporating all of the documentary evidence on language that had been missed while the main *OED* remained in its mothballed cocoon throughout most of the twentieth century. The Second Edition of the *OED* on CD-ROM had become a reality in 1992 (superseding the beta-test version of only the First Edition, produced in 1989), after months in which editors were fully stretched, pushing and shoving the data into new tags to make searching more efficient. Researchers started to knock on our door, at first just in **dribs and drabs**, but then in numbers, which helped to feed our sense that the dictionary had a bright future.

> *Dribs and drabs* is an odd expression. Nowadays we don't really use the two principal terms in other contexts. Do we say, "I'll just put a drib of butter on the toast," or "Clean up that drab of mud from the floor"? I don't think so. These are effectively fossilised words, only used in this expression (like *hue* in *hue and cry* and *beck* in *beck and call* earlier). Still, there's no harm in finding out what they used to mean.
>
> As far as we know, *drib* and *drab* were not drafted into English from abroad, but arose amongst the tussocks and streams of Britain. We can start with *drib*. The *OED* first passed its investigative eye over the word in 1897, when it found that its first occurrence in English was actually in Scots, in around 1730, where it meant a drop, or a small quantity. Casting far and wide for a possible etymology, the editors noticed that the verb *to drib* predated it—right back to 1523, but not characteristically from Scottish sources. The verb is said to derive ultimately from *drip* or *drop*, and here the *OED* comes up with another of its masterfully cryptic statements: "The modified consonant express[es] a modification of the notion." So a *drib* is not quite the same as a *drop*, it is more of a drip or drop forming part of a dribble. (Unfortunately the dictionary does not contain illustrations.) To cover itself, it sums up by saying that *drib* itself may come straight from *dribble*. These words aren't invented on paper, so you have to piece together the early history from later records, and you can't expect exactness every time.
>
> Now we've tied up *drib*, we need to unpick *drab*. Obviously it means much the same as *drib*. The *OED* tells us that it found our *drab* from dialect records in 1828, in the sense of "a small sum of money." That meaning seems to persist. It's not a one-off contextual example.

What we don't know is how these two words *drib* and *drab* colli-ded. The First Edition of the dictionary didn't even include *dribs and drabs*. We added it very much later, in 1993—when we swept up lots of our interim unpublished material into two occasional *OED Addi-tions* volumes. And then we found the expression in 1809 (so we'll have to review that first dialect example for *drab* in 1828). What is starting to look likely is that *dribs and drabs* is one of those nonsense pairs where both elements sound similar but one or both make no real sense independently: *hurdy-gurdy, hubble-bubble, higgledy-piggledy, riff-raff, bits and bobs*, etc.

One of the first of this wave of new academic researchers to knock on our door, an educator from Canada, John Willinsky, had obtained some seed money to start a pilot study on the *OED*—not by looking at page after page of tightly printed definitions, but by analysing the ma-chine-readable data on which the dictionary was based. He was able to make use of the database held at the University of Waterloo in Canada since our work there in the 1980s, and with our assistance had come up with some interesting early stats and tables about the language and the dictionary, published in his book *Empire of Words: The Reign of the OED* (1994). He used this data to indicate which parts of the dictio-nary needed further specialist care and attention.

For example, he examined the most-cited authors in Burchfield's *Supplement*. Top of the league tables of authors cited here (as opposed to elsewhere in the dictionary) were George Bernard Shaw, Rudyard Kipling, James Joyce, and P. G. Wodehouse. Given the world of text available to the editors, this is generally (apart from Joyce) rather a con-servative, conventional list. The first American author pops up at No. 6, in the form of Mark Twain. How about the top twenty women au-thors in the full (unrevised) Second Edition? Right at the top comes George Eliot, with 3,310 quotations (her top-cited work was *Daniel Deronda*, not the equally long but more popular *Middlemarch*); then Harriet Martineau, Elizabeth Barrett Browning, popular Victorian novelist Mary Braddon, *OED* contributor Charlotte Yonge, Fanny Burney, Jane Austen, and Mary Mitford. There was scope here, I think, for the new editors to search out other kinds of female discourse. In case you think these stats are all helpful, bear in mind another table, of titles given to authors in *OED* quotations: the league table omits "Mr." (because—in the manner of the day in the nineteenth century—that was assumed), and runs from the most popular—"Sir," down through "Mrs.," "Bishop," "Miss," "Lord," and "Lady." But even this table is of interest, in that it highlights the assumptions and deference of nineteenth-century bibliographers and lexicographers (and of the reading public generally). This old-fashioned classificatory system has now been consigned to the dictionary's editorial dustbin.

This sort of information hadn't been easily discoverable until now, though we had heard of a legendary Anglo-French scholar who spent much of his adult life working slowly through the print dictionary isolating all of the words in English which derived from Anglo-French. Nowadays that work can be done almost in an instant.

The *OED* on CD opened up the dictionary to questions that people had not been able to ask before—simply because there had been no hope of receiving an answer: not just "What does this word mean?" but larger ones, like "How did the set of words first used in English in the early fifteenth century differ from those first encountered in the late eighteenth century, and what does this show about how language and society differed in these two periods?"

When you consider this question, you see extensive differences between the concerns of language and society in the two time-periods. Back in the earlier period, late Middle English, we are still heavily dominated by post-Conquest French. The concerns of language users at that time (at least in the documentation that has survived) were with the details of everyday life in the Middle Ages: the day-to-day issues of feudal life, the concerns of the lord of the manor, activity in the law courts, religion, farming, food (especially amongst the upper layers of society), and, increasingly, shifting thought patterns towards modern analytical discourse. It's arguable whether that last one was something everyone was aware of, and it's perhaps an odd addition to the list—but the vocabulary of French (and its source, Latin) brought with it an intellectual culture that had largely not troubled the Germanic Anglo-Saxons up to this date, with words that we still use: *abstraction, debater, negotiation, sentiment.* Manuscript texts—you have to remember—typically recorded the language of the successful classes of society.

Here is a snapshot of some of those words first introduced into English in the early fifteenth century, mostly from post-Conquest French: some are religious (*abbatial*), some legal (*abetting, abjure, above-written*), some characteristic of the lives of feudal villeins (*abasement, abject*). If we move further into the alphabet, we just find more religion and conflict, pain, publishing, and pseudo-science: *pacification, pact, paganism, palliative, palmistry, pamphlet.* There are over 11,000 words I could choose from in this category. Don't forget *papelote* = "porridge," which is probably another welcome donation from Anglo-French. You might think that we didn't necessarily need another word for porridge, as we already had a perfectly good one (i.e., *porridge*), but in 1450 we didn't know about *porridge*, which only came on the scene in the sixteenth century, and even then only in the meaning "soup" or "broth." Our oatmeal concoction was so named, according to the records, around 1640.

That gives you a mini-picture or cameo of life on the ground in the late Middle Ages. If you now switch to the second set of words, from the late eighteenth century, you find an entirely different reality. English is under the influence of classical models; it has an international role, evidenced by vocabulary from across the world; its interests are far more "modern" than they were in the late medieval era. If we look at words starting with *A* entering the language in the early eighteenth century, we find long, Latinate terms—ways of describing things in a fairly complicated fashion: *aberrating, abevacuation, abruptedly* (rather than the simpler and earlier *abruptly*), *absenteeship, accountability.* The French influence is still there, but it's overlaid with the Latin of the Renaissance and by a patina of learning. Music shows Italianate influence, as in *a cappella* (literally "in the style of the chapel," i.e., unaccompanied).

And if we head off again into the letter *P*, it's not *pacification*, but the abrupt and perhaps redundant *pacificity*; not *above-written*, but the elegant and technical *pagination*. The arts of the Continent influence British fashions: *paintbrush* and *palette knife*. Instead of inventing the *pamphlet*, as we did in the Middle Ages, we now find *pamphleteer* as a new verb and *pamphleteering* as a new adjective. But those eighteenth-century types still enjoyed their simple entertainments, as attested by the staunchly non-classical *able whackets*, nicely described by the *OED* as "blows given on the palm of the hand with a twisted handkerchief."

Researchers were fascinated by the patterns and statistics they could find. Sometimes these patterns told you structural information about the English language; at others they just told you things about how the dictionary was compiled. As John Milton was one of the top-cited authors throughout the dictionary's twenty volumes, did this translate into a towering role for him as a shaper of the language? There are dangers in ascribing lexical creativity to writers on the basis of their position in *OED* league tables, because their appearance there may not in fact be related exclusively to their influence on the language. This is something that I only worked through to slowly, and it surprised me, because I had been guilty of accepting stereotypes.

Take Milton, for example. At the moment he ranks as the fourth most-cited author in the *OED*, with 12,400 quotations (Shakespeare is way out front with 33,000; some way behind in the chasing pack are Chaucer, Dickens, and Tennyson). How did writers achieve such a high position on the dictionary's leader board? Largely through their popularity as writers to the Victorian readers of the dictionary, since the vast majority of those references were in place in the First Edition of the dictionary. And how did they achieve this popularity? In different ways, but not just for their use of words: it was also because they had written outstanding plays, epic poetry, heart-rending novels, etc. Arguably, the writers at the top of the *OED*'s league tables are there simply because they were the most-read authors, and therefore quotations from their works were avidly carded, and therefore readily available to *OED* editors when they came to compile entries, and so by default they float to the top of the dictionary's statistics mill.

Are authors who are cited *first* for specific words and meanings in the *OED* inherently more creative? This seems a promising line. Milton is shown, on this reasoning, to be the earliest reference for just over 2,000 terms (remember Shakespeare had around 8,000). But again there is a strong caveat. The original *OED* tended to "read" authors who had entered the literary canon at the expense of other authors who may have been more experimental but less finished and less popular. There is statistical evidence that canonical authors were over-invested with lexical creativity. James Joyce is cited as the first user of around 575 terms in the Second Edition of the *OED*, but the revision of the dictionary currently in progress has found earlier references for over 40 percent of these. The original data was flawed, or at least it was not intended to be used to make value judgements of this sort. It is not, of course, that the information to be derived from the dictionary is wrong; it is just that it needs to be interpreted sensitively, in context, and on its own terms—and not brashly used to create new, incorrect stereotypes. Milton is a towering figure of English literature, but not necessarily for his language. The case isn't yet proven.

As well as asking questions about authors, we could—as a matter of course—ask questions about words. Which words had the most sub-senses, and did they develop rapidly, or over a long period of time? It's often the shortest words that have the most complex history (*can, do, set, make, pull, put, red, to, out*). There are thirty-eight words which have forty or more main meanings in English: 66 percent of these entered English in the Anglo-Saxon period, and all of them are monosyllables in their basic form; of the remaining 34 percent, only the noun *quarter* is not monosyllabic. These Germanic words from the earliest period of English have had many years to shift meaning, enter collo-quial phrases, and generally act as the glue for the language.

How many words entered English from Russian, and why? As of today, the *OED* says 404, peaking in the years following the Russian Revolution and going into the Cold War. (Again, this is a good question, and one which can tell us much about cultural contacts and mutual respect—or even distrust—between two language groups over history.)

Are there more adjectives than nouns in English? The dictionary thinks there are twice as many nouns as adjectives. This means that there are more things named (nouns)—whether abstract or concrete—than there are words to describe them. Some adjectives are based on earlier nouns anyway, and so often depend for their existence upon pre-existent nouns. But figures suggest that overall there are about two nouns for every adjective, and yet in the seventeenth century it seems that the figure is reduced to 1.5 new nouns to every new adjective. Why? In the nineteenth century, the ratio is higher again: 1.8 nouns to each adjective. These questions are as yet unanswered. Statistics are always right, but we may sometimes be asking the wrong questions of them. Was the data faulty for the seventeenth century, or was this a period when derivative adjectives were particularly likely to be formed, or was there another reason for the fall-off in the introduction of new nouns?

As we entered the early 1990s, we embarked upon what I regarded at the time—and also in retrospect—as a dark phase of the project, which lasted perhaps for the first half of the decade. The Second Edition of the dictionary had been published to acclaim, but we had been working with our sights set so closely on this goal that we had completely overlooked the need to plan for—rather than just to expect—a future involving the comprehensive update to which computerisation was only the prelude. And my dark mood paralleled something of a dark period at home, as Hilary and I gradually realised that our younger daughter, Ellie, had severe developmental problems of the sort that no amount of funds, effort, care, support, or love would overcome. Not everything can have a happy ending, but at this point we were deep in a tunnel with no sign of light ahead.

NINE

Gxddbov Xxkxzt Pg Ifmk

By 1993, the dictionary had outgrown its palatial surroundings in St Giles'. We moved back on to the main University Press site into two long and uninviting corridors in a characterless modern building which only existed as a passageway between two of the more historic parts of the Press. These gloomy corridors had been abandoned by another group that had gone on to more satisfactory premises. As usual, the office mirrored the sort of work we were doing, which was now linking, preparatory, in transit.

By now, our old friend and supporter the Shark had left the University Press to become a director of a major London publisher, so we needed to activate our remaining Oxford friends to convince the assembled dons of the University and the executives of the University Press that updating the dictionary was the right and only thing to do. They would then, we assumed, loosen the institutional purse strings for us. Our primary editorial objective was to develop our new policy and then to test-edit a range of dictionary entries, updating them according to the tenets of our new vision. The University Press would then, we assumed, enter some sort of internal conclave, and with luck decide to give the enormous update project the go-ahead.

With prompting from two or three of the dictionary's friends—senior professors in the University—the Delegates of the University Press, that body of professors ultimately responsible for approving the Press's academic publishing policy, kindly enquired of us how we were getting along, and in due course our business director, the Admiral, was formally asked to develop a project plan. The University Press was bending our way, mindful of the expectations it had raised that we would be able to work on the big dictionary once the *Shorter* had been wrapped up. After the Delegates met one long day in 1993, we knew that a project plan could be sketched out. It was politely intimated to us that a satisfactory project would involve a completely revised and updated *OED* by the year 2000, and that a budget to show that this was feasible would be even more satisfactory.

In order to develop a project plan, the Admiral needed facts (not yet available in any quantity or with much reliability). We couldn't generate facts without a detailed editorial policy, and so the business of hammering one out—which would guide us in transforming a nineteenth-century dinosaur into a twentieth-century thoroughbred—became our No. 1 priority.

Finally, there was a chink of light. After three years in limbo, there was once again a palpable sense of excitement and optimism amongst the small group who constituted the project—Ed Weiner, Yvonne Warburton, and I, and several others, had at last been invited by the University Press to consider the options for forging ahead with a comprehensive update of the big dictionary. Starting from now, we could plan the changes we wanted to introduce to the dictionary. With those changes, we could open up the content, increase access, and free it from the dusty air of the nineteenth century.

We busily divided the number of words defined in the existing dictionary (414,800) by the number of years until 2000 (7), and came to the conclusion that (*a*) it couldn't be done, and (*b*) we'd better see if we could do it. Maybe we thought that if we more or less achieved this target, then that might be okay. It turns out that isn't how businesses work.

It being a universal truth acknowledged by anyone managing a dictionary project that lexicographers should not be permitted to control the flow of facts themselves, it was agreed that a number of the University Press's Delegates, or their representatives, would meet regularly with senior members of the dictionary staff (the Admiral, Ed, and myself) as the *OED* Advisory Committee. This group would establish a comprehensive editorial policy acceptable to all parties. It made sense: you can't start revising a dictionary at *A* and just wander hopefully through until you reach *Z*. You have to plan the whole structure before you start. We were updating an antiquated mammoth of a dictionary, but we needed to have a vision of what our new version was meant to look like. We certainly had our own vision—but did it square with that of the University Press's Delegates? The Advisory Committee also had another, unwritten function. Back in those days, there were people who were extremely resistant to *any* change being made to the text of the dictionary: they regarded it almost as biblical writ. So the committee would, by its approval of our plan, confer upon us academic licence to revise the Victorian tablets of stone.

And so it happened that on regular occasions over the next two years the Admiral, Ed, and I participated in a series of meetings with some of the sharpest, no-nonsense professors that the University could throw at us: their specialisms included the history of English, English literature generally, comparative philology with particular reference to Linear B (the syllabic and ideographic script used to write early Mycenean Greek), and (almost the easy option) sociolinguistics. Several were reputed—even in the rarefied world of Oxford scholarship—to have extra toppings of academic rigour. We certainly did not enjoy the prospect of the first of these meetings: they were such a powerful group of academics—some of whom we only knew previously by name and reputation—that if they took a position in opposition to our vision of ourselves, then we would be in deep trouble.

First we had to decide whether the dictionary as it stood offered a satisfactory general model for the future. Were the current components of the entry the right ones—definitions, etymologies, illustrative quotations, all set within a historical structure? Or did some other structure suggest itself? Should we throw away the mould and start from scratch?

There were alternative options, one of which was that we should completely reassess all available sources and start afresh. Fortunately, it was generally agreed that the current dictionary, if properly updated, would still provide an excellent model for its users, and that it would be madness to discard what we already had and begin with a clean sheet. Scholars still wanted the precise, detailed information that the *OED* had always contained, but they wanted that information to be up to date, not (as in many cases) over one hundred years old. Even to the academics of Oxford one hundred years sounded a long time. And could we start to imagine what budget would be necessary for restarting from the beginning all over again? That, to all of us, was a no-brainer. It would be enormous, and well beyond the resources of the University Press.

Another big question we needed to discuss: Should the *OED* continue to order its subsenses historically, or would it be best—as some people argued—if the most common meanings were to appear first, with the rest presented in order of frequency further down the tail of the donkey? Well, frequency order helps you find the common meanings, but isn't much help (in a big entry) if you want to find anything else. How can you come up with a ranking order of word meanings that is relevant for all varieties of English, where frequency order is different, and constantly changing over time? Anyway, if you want the most common meaning first, go to a dictionary where this is all that matters. It's not the *OED*. With the *OED*, historical order leads on from the etymology, and should demonstrate how meanings change over time. Consider **magazine** (or *nice*, or *table*, or *watch*). Commonest first? Sometimes I just get slightly cross.

Here's a good example of how meanings change over time, along a logical but unpredictable route: the word *magazine*. What is the commonest meaning today? A periodical publication with feature articles and glossy pictures. But go back to the seventeenth century: What was the commonest meaning then? The same? I think not. The modern "publication" meaning didn't even exist until 1731. In the seventeenth century *magazine* meant "a storehouse for goods," especially provisions or explosives (preferably not at the same time).

The purpose of the *OED* is to show that *magazine* came into English in the sixteenth century (in the "storehouse" sense), and that we got the word from Middle French (*magasin*), which derived it from Italian (*magazzino*), and that it comes ultimately from an Arabic word (*makzan*) for—guess what—a place where things are stored, i.e., "a storehouse." Arabic influences (architecture, literature, etc.) along the southern Mediterranean are an indication of contact between Arabic people and Europeans (especially in medieval Spain). And where you have contact between peoples, you have language interaction and borrowings (also from Arabic: *algebra*, *giraffe*, *mohair*, etc.). The later senses of *magazine* in English are tendrils from the original "storehouse" meaning, leading up to the present day.

If you want to follow the evolution of *magazine* from Arabic to now, you don't start with the glossy periodical publication. Maybe not a no-brainer, but a brainer involving only a modicum of reflection.

The committee also considered another issue, involving one of those wild suggestions which sound ludicrous but from which you learn (in the Oxford way) simply by discussing and rejecting it. The idea was proposed by one of our senior academics on the committee that we would get the whole job finished earlier and with a considerable slashing of the budget if we disregarded everything in English before, say, 1500, and refocused the *OED* for the future as a dictionary dealing only with Modern English. There was no doubt that we would finish sooner that way. It was a bit like saying you could beat the Olympic hundred-metre sprint champion if they gave you a ninety-metre start. When the idea was proposed, we looked at each other as if someone had asked if we could squeeze Esperanto, Vulcan, or the language of fishes into the *OED*. But this was a deadly serious suggestion. And certainly, nothing would have made our financial colleagues happier than our truncating the project in this way.

The idea was not completely madcap, however: elsewhere in the Western world (Toronto and Ann Arbor, Michigan) there were already large dictionary projects whose objective was to capture—in much more detail than the *OED* could expect to manage—the entire vocabulary of English in the Old and Middle English periods, respectively. Shouldn't we just cede anything before 1500 to these dictionary projects, and simply concentrate on the later period? The idea was that we could save ourselves from dipping even a toe into the murky waters of Anglo-Saxon and Middle English vocabulary, and the equally murky culture of those early days. We could start with fresh pencils at 1500.

But that's not how English works. You can't start right in the middle and forget the distant origins. If we fudged everything before 1500, we would not be able, authoritatively, to comment on deeper etymology or even earlier meanings that influenced the senses of post-1500 words. We'd break in on important meanings halfway through their existence, unable to speak from proper knowledge about their early life. What we would be doing, in fact, would be representing English as if it were mainly a Renaissance creation—Latinate, or with words from modern Dutch, or French, or German, and full of English-only compounds, but without the organic complexity of its early Germanic and Romance past, where the real questions about English are set and have to be answered.

After a few minutes' discussion we had one of our rare votes, and all—including the wily proposer—agreed *nem con* against the stripped-back and curtailed *OED*. At a stroke, we had committed ourselves to a further ten or fifteen years' work.

A ll of our discussions with the Advisory Committee were premised on the assumption that our principal objective was to illustrate—through the dictionary—the complex emergence and flowering of English as a major world language. This objective had been present in the days of the *Supplement to the OED*, but had not been right at the forefront of our minds back then. Moving back in history to the earliest days of English ensured that we all had a new focus on our work.

It was easy to be blinded by the superficial attractiveness of later French borrowings in English and not to pay proper attention to the Germanic bedrock of English. Our committee was largely peopled by Anglo-Saxonists and Germanists, so there was little chance we would be allowed to forget this, even if we had been inclined to. English is called a Germanic language because it was brought to the British Isles by Germanic invaders and settlers (northern European tribes) speaking Germanic dialects—from an area much larger than Germany today. After the departure of the Romans from Britain in the early fifth century AD, Britain was once again peopled for the most part by Celts, and in the far north by grumpy Picts.

There are very few Celtic words in English nowadays. The *OED* offers just five from the earliest period of the language, Old English from before 1150 (*brat*, "a coarse or makeshift over-garment"; *mind*, "an Irish neck ornament"; *bannock*, "a northern round or oval home-made bread"; *pen*, "a hill, a height"; and *conveth*, "a Scottish land tax"). The better-known ones, such as *clan*, *pet* (a tame animal), and *slogan*, for instance, date from well after the first Germanic incursions. We used to think that this was because the German invaders obliterated all trace of the older Celtic language as they stormed through Britain. But in the absence of written records, it can be hard to interpret how the original Germanic invaders and the invaded Celts jostled along. Modern scholars tend to think that after the initial incursions, the Germans probably spent decades intermarrying with the Celts and learning from them how to tame the land. At the same time they effectively and probably almost unwittingly eradicated the Celtic language from large parts of its original domain, and Germanic English became the "prestige" language. Ironically, after the Viking invasions from the eighth century this new language underwent a comparable change itself—at least in the north and east of England (the area of the Danelaw)—as Scandinavians eventually settled and brought their own variety of Germanic to bear on the new Anglo-Saxons. And then again, after the Norman Conquest of 1066, the new Germanic English suffered a trough in fortunes and visibility similar to that which the Germanic invaders had inflicted upon the Celts. The Germanic Anglo-Saxon language almost disappeared from official records, subsisting principally in the mouths of the "ordinary" people outside the court and the aristocratic, legal, and religious elite—by whom, of course, the documentation was preserved.

By 1500—as we enter the earliest period of what is now known as Modern English—the records show English reasserting itself as the symbol of an expanding, more self-confident nation. Even today, words of Germanic origin dominate large areas of our basic vocabulary: the number system; most of the short prepositions and conjunctions we use; the basic verbs *be, can, do, have, may, must*; the "strong" verbs which change their stem vowel in the past tense (*swim/swam, ride/rode*)—in fact, out of a list of the one hundred most frequently used words in English today, not far from 100 percent are of Germanic origin, and only one or two (such as *nation*, or according to some lists, *people*) are of post-Conquest French origin.

The incursion of French after the Conquest brought English into immediate contact with the classical heritage of medieval Europe; French is often regarded as a more beautiful, sonorous influence than the guttural Germanic. The *OED* tells us that we have two and a half words of Romance origin in English today for every word of Germanic, but that doesn't reveal the whole picture—those Germanic words are still often the big-hitting, high-frequency ones.

The expansion of English has meant that it has gradually become a major language in many parts of the world which had, at some point in their history, come into extensive contact with English speakers, normally at the expense of the indigenous peoples (North America, Australia, New Zealand, South Africa, and numerous other places). But those original Germanic/Romance percentages have still generally held good into the modern, international era of English. In the new world in which such a large number of non-first-language speakers of English may be found, it is possible that speakers of Romance languages (French, Spanish, Italian) will naturally choose to use a higher proportion of English words of Romance origin when they speak English (speaking words with which they feel more comfortable). In the longer term, perhaps that will unsettle the old percentages.

Some of the policy decisions made by the *OED*'s Advisory Committee confirmed areas where the *OED* had been doing the right thing all along: its historical principles, the necessity for evidence rather than subjective impressions, the grand scope and detailed implementation. It was in one of these meetings that we agreed that the *OED* should not omit any of its entries during its update, that it should not jettison entries which some people might consider no longer significant, perhaps because they were only attested once or twice, or in a very specialist discipline, or—worse still—only in poetry. We decided that once you started peeling layers away from the dictionary, you would never know where you were going to stop. So we stopped right at the beginning, and decided that nothing should be jettisoned if it was already on board our lexicographical Noah's Ark—though we should continue to **vet** words very carefully before allowing them on board in the first place.

There aren't many things we like doing as a language group more than shortening words, to hurry us along in our fast-paced lives. We don't have the time for all those syllables and, in the case of SMS messaging, even for most of those letters. The *OED* knows of about one hundred new words coined by "shortening" in the first decade of the twentieth century, including *Aussie, auto, benny, demo, home ec, pneu,* and *post-op.* That's about the same number as during the previous decade. It seems that the number of new words created by shortening had progressed at roughly the same rate from Shakespeare's time (*arith.* for "arithmetic"; *cit* for "citizen") up to around 1800 (*advert, mag* for "magnitude" and "magpie"; *van* for "caravan"); then the rate started to increase in the early nineteenth century (perhaps as the pace of life hotted up), before hitting and maintaining a peak from around 1900 (*ad* for "advantage" or "addict"; *path* for "pathology"). The late nineteenth century was when this linguistic radicalism took a strong hold, and the mass of evidence for these shortenings gave them a place in the dictionary. Nowadays there are many forces producing abbreviations and initialisms: text-messaging , email, and websites (*FAQ, LOL,* etc.), technology (*DVD, SIM, SMS*), medicine, politics—and more or less any area which wants to present jargon as short and approachable.

The original editors of the *OED* wouldn't have known this meaning of this verb *to vet*—at least not before 1904. That's when the first reference to the word occurs, in the works of Rudyard Kipling ("These are our crowd. . . . They've been vetted, an' we're putting 'em through their paces"). It's a good example of a word that rapidly developed numerous usages.

The verb derives, as the historical documentation shows us, from the noun *vet.* And the noun *vet* is a shortening of *veterinarian* or *veterinary* (which are long words, and so of seventeenth- and eighteenth-century origin, respectively). The verb *to vet* originally had what you would imagine (correctly) was its literal meaning—to examine or treat a sick animal. 1891. It was a throwaway contraction, but the humorous British decided as early as 1898 that you might want to "vet" a person to see if there was anything wrong with them. And from there it was only a short hop to *vetting* things—examining them carefully for problems.

These *vet* words are not related to *veteran*. The former derive from Latin *veterina*, "cattle," and the latter from Latin *vetus*, "old."

There was one area where we did want to innovate extensively and to open wide the ground base upon which the dictionary was raised, and that was in the choice of texts from which we would find information about the language. We knew of old that the dictionary had favoured classic authors (at top of its list came William Shakespeare, Alexander Pope, Jonathan Swift, Walter Scott, and John Milton—not to the exclusion of all others, but enough to make some people think that the dictionary was based principally on "good" sources). This practice had skewed the analysis of the language, since not everything was written by literary giants. We planned to rewrite the policy and rebalance the typical sources from which we would seek evidence in future. We weren't out of line with the spirit of the age. Since the nineteenth century there had been something of a proliferation in the publishing of more informal sources such as diaries, journals, and private letters. We were also well aware that there were many unpublished texts residing in archives which could yield a slightly different picture of the English language if they were studied properly from a linguistic perspective.

Sir James Murray had tried to move along this track, and had found himself heavily criticised in Oxford for citing newspapers (which he continued to do unabashedly all the same). We told the Advisory Committee how we proposed to broaden the catchment area of our sources, and fortunately there was no dissent. It was the *OED* that was behind the times, not the scholars—this time. We didn't tell them how far we would move in future, because the issue—for example—of citing web pages didn't exist. In due course we did open up the floodgates even further, accepting evidence of the language from the Internet—from personal web pages, for example (retaining a copy in our files in case it disappeared from our screens over time). The first reference today for *LOL* = "laugh out loud" comes from a source (as you might expect) that was only distributed electronically (a glossary in the *FIDONews*—an early computer bulletin board—of 8 May 1989: "*LOL*—Laughing Out Loud"). We didn't want to miss factual information like that just because we insisted on citing only printed sources. I'm glad we didn't have to argue that one to the Advisory Committee back then—in the mid-1990s it might have been a step too far.

This was a small decision made one rainy afternoon in our meeting room overlooking the OUP's green quadrangle, but it validated our plans; although it would be a long time before the legacy effect of the canonical authors might be significantly eroded, we now had approval from Oxford to make this momentous change. Oddly enough, we felt that we were not so much veering from the unwritten policy of Sir James Murray as we were turning back to Murray's ways from the more recent literary-lion policy of our former chief editor, Bob Burchfield.

By the early 1990s, I had been working at the *OED* for over fifteen years, rather pleased that I had no particular links with the University of Oxford except through my employment at the University Press. The University Press was a department of the University, but it was the "publishing department," rather than one of the academic teaching and research departments. It operated regular office terms for its staff—we didn't receive long university holidays or research sabbaticals, even though we sometimes thought that a research break would benefit us and also benefit the dictionary in the long run. I was happy enough to be an onlooker squinting askance at the strange activities I saw outside my various office windows, as students wandered off to examinations in their dark uniform (***subfusc***). University politics and arguments were for others. About half of the dictionary's editorial staff had taken degrees at Oxford or Cambridge, so that left a reasonable proportion of disinterested observers such as myself.

I think I did resent the pressure that an effectively closed academic community could exert both on the city of Oxford (by owning so much property it had tended to hold back urban development over the centuries) and on learning (by appearing to restrict rather than disseminate knowledge outside its ranks). But worse was the obscurantism of the University administration. This seemed to be where the oldest and most inscrutable customs were preserved: they felt exclusive simply through their terminology—"Hebdomadal Council," which met (after the Greek, you understand) every seven days; they advertised strange posts, such as the "six-hour stipendiary lecturer in English" (with *stipendiary* from the Latin, naturally); the sets of professors charged with overseeing the publishing activities of the University Press were called "the Delegates," and the Press's CEO was known as "the Secretary" (to the Delegates). This wasn't a big issue for me, but I had been happy to remain on the other side of the fence, and I was also happy to steer the dictionary whenever I could away from this apparent exclusivity. I'm afraid I even vetoed the use of Scriptorium (Murray's term) for our editorial offices.

There are numerous words which derive from the universities and colleges (and the private schools) around the English-speaking world. Sometimes they remain within their circumscribed and rarefied ambit, and sometimes they break out into the real world: *bed-sitter* (British universities: single-room accommodation combining bedroom and sitting-room), *beer pong* (North America: a drinking game in which table-tennis balls end up in beer cups), *funk* (Oxford: state of cowering fear), *moby* (American colleges: large), *skiver* (Notre Dame University: student who leaves campus without permission), *noughth week* (Oxford: the week before the first week of term), and *viva* (British and other university traditions: an oral examination following on from written papers)—to name a handful. Slang is often a way to exclude others and to reinforce your herd mentality (sorry—shared subculture).

In the sixteenth and seventeenth centuries you might have used the adjective *fusk* or *fuscous* to mean "dark (in colour), sombre," especially if you were of a poetical persuasion or were engaged in natural history research. In their search for something mysteriously Latin and known only to the initiated, the University authorities in Oxford and Cambridge of the early nineteenth century let it be understood that the formal attire worn by undergraduates for examinations and other official occasions would be referred to by the adjective *subfusc* ("somewhat dark in colour"—not jet black). By around 1850, the adjective had developed into a noun as well, so you would don your subfusc for your Moderations (first examination). It's still the standard word in that context today, though poets and natural historians have largely moved on.

Although I had worked alongside the University for many years without attempting to integrate with it, the time came when some rapprochement seemed in order. Needless to say, it made absolutely no difference to the University, but I thought it would be beneficial to the dictionary. One option would have been for me to offer classes in lexicography within the University. But it was generally agreed on the project that lexicographers should edit, and not break up their day with academic teaching commitments, as these would deflect them from the most important part of their lives. This seemed to be a rule when I joined the dictionary in 1976 and had worked well. If you wanted to, you could teach outside office hours, but that never appealed to me. There were enough other odd souls drifting around Oxford to pick up any additional teaching that the college or University authorities offered, without upsetting the dictionary's apple cart. But as I had never regarded myself as a natural teacher, I chose not to take this route.

As time went by, however, I did develop closer connections with several components of the University: the English faculty (naturally enough), the Department for External Studies, and the new Kellogg

College. The Department for External Studies was the department of the University that dealt with real people—mostly part-time mature students who only occasionally had to dress up as penguins in their gowns. From time to time my colleagues or I would hold day schools for the department on the history, or the practice, or perhaps the future, of dictionary-making. *External Studies* was an old and characteristically not "inclusive" term. The University is changing—now, it refers to External Studies in the acceptable idiom of the day as "Continuing Education" and "lifelong learning." In Oxford, teaching departments (such as Continuing Education, which run the faculty staff and most teaching administration) are quite distinct from colleges (to which students are attached as their base).

After the first one of these day schools in which the *OED* had become involved, Ed and I heard the phone buzzing in our office. Ed answered it and, unusually, adopted something of an obsequious tone. It sounded like University business, as indeed it was. The upshot of it was that the president and Governing Body of the recently founded Kellogg College (the student base most closely associated with Continuing Education) had met together in conclave the previous afternoon and had (in our ignorance) elected Ed and myself as Fellows. Fellows are the senior members of a college, whether they hold teaching posts in the university or are associated with the college in an honorary capacity; a college in Oxford is based around the concept of its "fellowship" of academics. Ed and I came from different traditions. He was delighted with this honour and I was, in keeping with my traditional misgivings, both suspicious and dismissive. Why did I need to involve myself with University politics when I was quite happy as I was?

It turned out (again) that there wasn't much room for discussion, and it seemed I was wrong to be churlish. Soon we were being measured up for our caps and gowns and whatever else was required. We clocked on as "Supernumerary Fellows" and started to involve ourselves in the life of the college as far as we were able. *Supernumerary* really does means "surplus to requirements," so we knew our place.

The president of Kellogg, Geoffrey Thomas, told us that he wanted us as Fellows because the college catered mainly to part-time, postgraduate, mature students—typically students who were returning to learning after a period at work. His thinking in appointing us was, as he explained, that both the college and the dictionary provided access to knowledge for the ordinary person: they were trying to unwrap what might be regarded as the arcane and privileged world of scholarship and to empower the interested student. He was a cunning president who had created a college for part-time students in the face of stiff opposition within the broader University. He was being cunning again now. But what he said made sense, and we were glad to be there.

For myself, the Fellowship meant an important shift of emphasis, as it gave me a perch close enough to the University but not too close, and it brought the dictionary into direct contact with real people who were interested in acquiring knowledge. Many of the students had missed out on the chance to pursue higher-level studies during their first time round the educational system. The connection brought new specialist consultants for the dictionary within easy reach and, without intending to, also gave the dictionary a boost from within the University at a time when external support and acclaim could do the dictionary no harm at all.

At the same time, Ed and I were trying to edge our Advisory Committee towards approving the initial, pilot, and experimental work we were doing. We wanted to steer the committee to the stage where they stopped talking about things, and required us to produce a stretch of revised and updated text—taking the original nineteenth-century entries and subjecting them to whatever policies we had hit upon for the comprehensive revision. If the committee liked what it saw, then it would give us the thumbs-up and would recommend to the full body of Delegates of the University Press that it back us with some serious money.

It would be nice to be able to say that we really steered the committee to this stage, but of course it got there by itself. After two years of meetings, we had to produce something definitive. There was a certain amount of nervousness in the editorial corridors as we dutifully—but also with great excitement—applied the policies we had developed to a range of dictionary data. We reviewed the documentation and predated and updated each entry in our subset; we rewrote etymologies, trying to drag as much standardisation into the procedure as we could (as we had a feeling that this would make the finished product more tractable to computation); we added new meanings and new expressions; we rejudged whether words were formal or informal English (and we found quite a bit of movement towards informality in the language as we worked along). Definitions needed rewriting to drag them out of their nineteenth-century idiom. And at last we were done.

We submitted our efforts to the next meeting of the committee. They went away to consult amongst themselves. A few weeks later we reformed and heard the good news that the pilot study was acceptable. They would recommend to the Delegates and to the University Press that the project for the full-scale updating and revision of the dictionary should be funded. If we could have held a street party in celebration, we would have done. After many years, we were ready to start.

Even at their most trivial, the discussions we had with the Advisory Committee were vitally important, and the decisions we made there would have tremendous consequences for the future of the *OED*. This was the job we had all been waiting for. At last we saw ourselves embarking on a history of the whole language—not just supplementing the dictionary this time, but taking it by the scruff of the neck and forcing it into the twentieth (or, soon enough, the twenty-first) century. But we were well aware, even then, that we couldn't solve everything in committee. We wouldn't be able to make all the decisions at the start. Some you make as you go along. *Solvitur ambulando*, the Romans said: solving problems by practical experience. (The *OED* provides chapter and verse on the expression: "originally an allusion," it says, "to the reported proof by Diogenes the Cynic of the possibility of motion.") So we laid the foundations, but expected to make modifications as we actually worked with the language data.

One of the best ways to see how the emerging editorial policies and procedures we were hammering out worked in practice is to look at the results for a specific word. We can see how they held up several years later when we came to update the entry for *fuck*.

This was one of the words that the original *OED* deliberately omitted back in the late nineteenth century, when the instalment for the letter *F* of the First Edition was published. If the editors had worked on *fuck*, then it would have been published in 1898, which was when the entry immediately preceding it alphabetically was published (*fucivorous*: "eating, or subsisting on, seaweed"—a mid-nineteenth century Latinate word introduced temporarily into medicine). The closing years of Queen Victoria's reign in Britain were not known for their liberal and enlightened attitude towards sex, and the inclusion of *fuck* would probably have involved the editors and the publishers in a short walk to a long stretch in prison. So they were probably right to skip jauntily from *fucivorous* to *fuco'd* ("beautified with fucus, painted," mid-seventeenth-century mock Latin, *fucus* being—as well as a type of rock lichen—a rouge or dye for painting the face and generally titivating yourself in a way deemed suitable and attractive in the seventeenth century). With neighbouring entries like that, who would have missed one or two taboo words?

And so it wasn't until the *Supplement to the OED* in 1972, in Volume One (*A* to *G*), that an entry for *fuck* first found a legitimate place in the dictionary. In fact, the original *OED* had slipped in the word *windfucker*—"the kestrel," a bird of prey frequently seen hovering in the air for prey, often against a steady wind, but also a general term of abuse for a person—at the very, very end of the First Edition. This is likely to contain our word *fuck*: *windfucker* was first published towards the end of the Roaring Twenties—maybe they thought they could get away with it then, citing truth, and evidence, and responsibility to the scholarly community. Most likely, they thought no one would notice.

You might think it surprising that the cautious editors had waited until 1972 to include the word, but, other than for a brief moment in 1933 (the first supplement to the dictionary), they didn't have any other chance. In Britain, they and their publisher would have been arrested for gross indecency at any time before 1960, when the publishers of *Lady Chatterley's Lover* (Penguin Books) successfully resisted a legal action brought by the powers of darkness to prevent publication of their edition of D. H. Lawrence's novel as an "obscene publication." Once this prosecution had failed, the parameters of what constituted an unpublishable obscenity—in Britain at least—became less austere.

Six years later, Penguin followed up its *Lady Chatterley* success in the sort of minute way that matters to lexicographers—but that also acts as a touchstone for the direction society in general is heading—by including the verb *fuck* boldly in its *Penguin English Dictionary* of 1965. The editor of this dictionary was the celebrated Anglo-Saxonist Norman Garmonsway, a fit figure to lend his academic weight to the inclusion of such a taboo term. (The co-editor of the second edition of the Penguin dictionary was a J. Simpson. I've often wondered whether this was me, but it seems it was not.)

With the principle of publication established, Oxford was right there on the second bus. But that *OED* entry for *fuck* back in the days of the *OED Supplement*, Volume One (1972), was short and tentative: just three numbered senses. The dictionary dated the first use in English to the early sixteenth century and defined its meaning daintily in terms of the scientific "copulation" (generally applied to animals and humans alike) rather than the more familiar "sexual intercourse" (itself something of a euphemism). Once it had nailed the lid down on that sense, it passed on to various "profane imprecations" and exclamations (again tiptoeing rather gingerly round the issue, but providing several colourful examples: "tell whoever it is to go fuck themselves," "fuck the bloody thing"), before venturing off to numerous unrefined phrases in which the word is used with adverbs such as *about*, *off*, and *up*. The *Supplement* could have done better, if it had had a mind to, but *fuck* fell in the first volume of the dictionary to have been published for almost forty years, and the editors were still operating in a very cautious marketplace.

When we came to review the entry for the *OED3*, we did at least have a small shell of an entry to use as a basis for our own reassessment. But at last we had the opportunity to do the entry proper justice, by investigating in detail and with modern resources its pathways into English, and the mass of—often scatological—twists and turns it took once it had arrived here. We were producing a technicolour version of the entry, when our predecessors had omitted it entirely or only managed a black-and-white, two-dimensional simulacrum. And at the same time our new policies would open up the entry and make it less cryptic.

As with most *OED* entries, the real story begins with the quotations we had been able to obtain—as these underpin the dictionary entry itself. Remarkably, what appears to be the earliest occurrence of *fuck* in English occurs in a religious context. In fact, a number of the first references have religious links. Here's the first attestation we uncovered, from around the year 1500: "Non sunt in cœli, quia gxddbov xxkxzt pg ifmk." The quotation was supplied for the dictionary's files, in the time-honoured way, by a scholar reading a book published in 1848 which contained this text, and then sending it to be filed in the dictionary's word store. The original *OED* knew this 1848 anthology of early English well enough—and cited it regularly—but had not been able to use this crucial evidence.

Now, some of you will doubtless say that this sentence is not English but Latin, until you reach the fifth word, where the whole thing dissolves into gobbledegook. Up till then, we have a perfectly reasonable piece of Latin which translates as "They [that is, the monks] are not in heaven, because . . . " In fact, it does not dissolve into *gobblede-gook* (American English, 1944, possibly meaning to represent a turkey's meaningless gobble—well, meaningless to us, but maybe not to another turkey). Rather, it turns into cipher, and probably into a "Caesar cipher," so called because Julius Caesar used this type of code in his private communications. The trick is systematically to replace each letter by another one a certain number of letters away in the alphabet: in this case, just one place after it. So, in writing "gxddbov xxkxzt pg ifmk," the late fifteenth- or early sixteenth-century cryptographer really meant "fuccant uuiuys of heli" (*-ant* is a Latin third-person plural ending added to an English word), or, "they are enjoying sexual intercourse," as we might say, "with the wives of Ely" (in Cambridgeshire). Ely was then, as now, a religious centre in East Anglia, and apparently in those days—at least in the minds of the local monks—home to numerous compliant housewives. It seems likely—from the fact that the whole expression was encrypted—that it wasn't the word itself that had to be hidden from public view, but rather the insalubrious activities of the monks. Other evidence from slightly later suggests that *fuck* was boisterous but not yet taboo, as it became in subsequent centuries.

If *fuck* can be used unselfconsciously in a manuscript from around 1500, then the word must occur earlier—but how much earlier? Is it early Middle English, or does it perhaps date from before the Conquest, in Anglo-Saxon times? At present we can't tell.

The entry demonstrates changes in how we handled various components. Firstly, we can look at etymologies (word derivations). The First Edition of the dictionary had been rather cryptic in the construction of its etymologies. It wasn't that they were only written for etymological scholars (though there may have been an element of that), but that the editors were constrained to abbreviate whatever they could in order to keep the dictionary within reasonable bounds. But with the dictionary on computer, our boundaries had relaxed—though I always wanted to retain a tight structure and elegance to the entries—and we could expand many of these contractions in the interests of comprehensibility to the reader. So, as well as drawing on much better, more recent information about our words, we standardised and expanded the names of languages and other aspects of the scholarly apparatus mentioned in these etymologies in full. The First Edition's etymology for *fuck* ran, almost in its entirety: "Early mod.E *fuck*, *fuk*, answering to a ME. type **fuken* (wk. vb.) not found; ulterior etym. Unknown." It was almost telling you that this was going to be too difficult for you to understand—that if you wanted to venture into the etymology of old words, then you generally needed to obtain specialist training and gloves.

We were dealing with complex data, but the old editors had embedded it in another layer of cryptic complexity. Our new etymology was much longer, and more informative, but reads as natural—though scholarly—English. We also wanted to help readers understand the passage of the word from the Germanic precursors of English through to our language, so the new policy permitted us to specify in detail (where we could) the meaning and approximate dating of the meanings of these precursors in the old Germanic languages. That's very important if you want to gain a 3D picture of the word through time. We also included discussions to interpret spelling and grammatical points, shifting the concept of a dictionary slightly towards that of an encyclopaedia. We wanted to make the text readable and (as far as possible) understandable. And the fractured contractions of old etymology-speak were a good place to start.

As regards *fuck*, we looked in the Germanic languages first of all, because they seemed to have echoes of our word. Since the publication of the First Edition of the dictionary, many scholarly dictionaries of the Continental languages had been prepared, and the modern *OED* could benefit from all of these. There isn't a direct line of descent for *fuck*: the Dutch (from the fifteenth century) had a word *fokken*, which is recorded at that time as meaning "to mock," and later "to strike," "to outwit," and "to have children," and finally, in 1657, "to have sexual intercourse with." But this Dutch use occurs considerably later in time than our meaning in English, so maybe they just borrowed it back from us. You always need to check which way the influence is going. We can find similar verbs in the Scandinavian dialects—but they are late in time too. Ultimately we and others don't really know, but we think it's Germanic, and maybe goes back a step further, to Indo-European (no written records of this, sadly), in the general meaning "to strike." After all that, comparative philologists will then tap you on the shoulder to remind you that the Germanic form *fuck* parallels the type of word evidenced by Latin *pugnus*, "a fist" (for *flp*, compare Germanic *fish* / Latin *piscis*). There are numerous other suggestions, but they do not help the story forward.

The changes we made to the dictionary's illustrative quotations were equally about openness and readability, about broadening the scope of the dictionary by drawing in less formal sources and therefore trying to reach a new level of vocabulary in the present and in the past, and about imposing modern critical standards to the way in which texts were cited. In the revised *fuck* entry, for example, we now cite a *Sopranos* script, and a reference to the magazine *Sniffin' Glue*, one of those punk mags I had so proudly read in the 1970s. Previously, various short titles (abbreviations) had been used for the names of some of the texts cited—Robert Louis Stevenson's title *Treasure Island* had famously existed in numerous abbreviated manifestations—and we standardised these, so as not to confuse the reader and the searching computer. The online text even allows us to link titles to online bibliographies (for more information) and, for many authors, to their own biographies in the *Oxford Dictionary of National Biography*. The concept of the dictionary is already changed, just by this. It becomes the starting point of a voyage of exploration through the language.

What did these changes in style and policy tell us about *fuck*? We start off—unusually, as we have seen—with cipher evidence, but also with clear Early Modern quotations of the word in unembarrassed use: unabashed, straight up, in full. Close your eyes while I cite an example of this, from the sixteenth-century Scottish poet David Lindsay: "Ay fukkand lyke ane furious Fornicatour." Lindsay wasn't just a poet, but an official Herald, and the Lyon King of Arms at that. If society was squeamish about the word, he would have known. We normally think that many words sometimes considered offensive today (*fuck*, *arse*—I could continue) were not—or were much less—loaded terms in the Middle and Early Modern English period.

Then, following the evidence trail, when we reach the eighteenth century the forces of darkness start to frown at occurrences of the word in public, and the typographer's granny, the hyphen (or sometimes the dash), crops up. A new edition of the *Frisky Songster* of 1776 has: "O, says the breeches, I shall be duck'd, / Aye, says the petticoat, I shall be f—d.," following a tradition that had afflicted the word since the start of the century. Society in the eighteenth century was split in several ways. On the one hand, authoritarians came to want their language and their society to mirror the perfect elegance of the classical world. On the other, rakes sought more colourful expressions for their thoughts and actions. At the same time, society's poverty concentrated many people's lives around the business of keeping healthy and out of trouble, rather than worrying about the propriety or impropriety of language. There was room for canting orthodoxy and extravagant activity. In the case of *fuck*, the word was enthusiastically used but often formally obscured in print.

If a word is printed with letters omitted, the cautious lexicographer is not always happy to assume that it is his or her word. It might be some other word that the reader desperately wants to interpret as *fuck*. The danger is always that you interpret something as what you want it to be, rather than what it is. But with the *Frisky Songster*, we (the editors) were prepared to accept that "f—d" was our word *fuck* because of the fact that it rhymes in the 1776 text (as fellow detectives will note) with "duck'd." We always had to go right back to the earliest edition of these texts to ensure that the word was really there, and didn't start off as some euphemism or ambiguous collection of punctuation marks. By examining different levels of sources, we were now able to pinpoint much more precisely, and with far greater confidence, the life that this lively entrant to the language led in its early days.

By the mid-eighteenth century, as the search for a model of classical refinement and style in society and language gained ground, society began to impose a growing sense of taboo on printed matter. The more lusty dictionaries of Nathan Bailey had included entries for *fuck* in the early part of the eighteenth century, before the sense of refined politeness struck hard into civilised society. The Great Cham, Dr Johnson, however, avoided entering the word in his touchstone dictionary of 1755. To be truthful, he was a bit squeamish of "low" speech, and hoped to offer more of a polite model to his elegant readership.

The word *fuck* disappeared all but completely from the print media during the reign of Queen Victoria, when anything thought to promote social disorder was suppressed. The word went underground, appearing only in privately printed publications that members of polite society would not be able to purchase without a subscription and a business address for discreet mail-order acquisitions, in the manner of the day.

The Pearl and *My Secret Life* were two such gentleman's resources which the *OED* cites when all else fails, and sure enough, there they are in this entry. *The Pearl*, subtitled "*a Magazine of Facetiae and Voluptuous Reading*," was a pornographic magazine published in 1879 and 1880, after which it was banned; it contained erotic serials, parodies, and poetry; *My Secret Life* was an erotic memoir of over 1 million words, written by the anonymous "Walter," and published privately in eleven volumes in the late 1880s. It documents the supposed sexual adventures of the writer. Both works use the vocabulary of sex to describe their subject. I could list the other entries in the *OED* which cite words included in *My Secret Life*, but I think I'll leave them for you to discover: forty-three entries from *cock* to *spunk*, showing the Victorians in full flow.

Fuck starts to see the light of day again in texts soon after the First World War. In his novel *Kangaroo*, D. H. Lawrence stated that "it was in 1915 the old world ended," and certainly people started wanting at that time to be freer in their published articulation of coarse slang and taboo words. Printers were subject to the regular censorship laws and could be imprisoned for publishing obscene or pornographic material. In the early twentieth century they seem to show a predilection for using the asterisk (covering a single letter like a fig-leaf) rather than employing the carpet-bombing hyphen, but the effect is the same and they remained out of prison. James Joyce's *Ulysses* was published and banned in Britain and America in the early 1920s for its excessive sexual content. But Joyce, too, was a sign of the times—he wanted to write what people really said, and others did, too. D. H. Lawrence in *Lady Chatterley*, Philip Larkin, Henry Miller, Ernest Hemingway, all squeezed the word into print. But the secret in the early twentieth century was not to publish in the United Kingdom. Larkin kept his profanities to his private letters; and Joyce and Miller published in Paris, while Lawrence published in Italy, to avoid the British censorship laws. The literary set published abroad unfettered, and the *OED* needed to look abroad for its English evidence of a word which was thriving in the 1920s and those other decades before the *Lady Chatterley* trial. The dictionary's editors now had to call in all of their resources to ensure that those non-British publications were checked for the word—it wasn't enough to rely on later British editions.

We also made changes to the presentation of meaning in the dictionary, and we used our new policies to explain and display the meaning for the word *fuck* in our entry over its five centuries of use. And how did *fuck* move semantically over those five centuries?

The ride starts, as you now know, around 1500, with the basic senses "to have sexual intercourse" (intransitive, to be technical) and "to have sexual intercourse with (someone)" (transitive, ditto). The *Supplement* had thrown these two meanings together, perhaps so as not to drag the reader down with excessive documentation in an entry over which it was still feeling nervous. But we disagreed. In the interests of openness and accessibility it was necessary to let both meanings stand independently, with their own supporting documentation. And so we did. I've mentioned that we'd moved away, in our definitions, from "copulation," and we carried this policy out elsewhere in the entry.

We spotted evidence for a meaning of *fuck* not in the earlier dictionary: it started off as a fairly crude meaning in the early eighteenth century, where the object of the verb was not a person but a part of the body (the backside, breasts, etc.). But it is still well-attested today. So we added this use to the formal record.

After that, we were in the realm of phrases and exclamations. The *Supplement* had rather squeamishly rushed through these, piling them all into a single, short sense No. 3: "Const. with various adverbs: *fuck about*, to fool about, mess about; *fuck off*, to go away, make off; *fuck up*: (*a*) *trans.*, to ruin, spoil, mess up; (*b*) *intr.*, to blunder, to make a (serious) error; to fail; cf. screw *v.* 12c." Apart from the contractions here, the structure requires all of the evidence for each of these usages to appear in a single sequence of quotations. Yet again, in the interests of openness, we broke these up into their component idioms, supplied a much more thorough level of documentation to the new subsections, and tried to accord each of the usages the full scholarly but transparent treatment that they demanded. We did exactly the same with the other phrasal uses of *fuck*, opening everything out for detailed forensic inspection—should the reader so want.

We also watched the progress of *fuck* through the ages by way of its quotations. From the sexual usages at the head of the entry, we saw the eighteenth century—renowned for its classical posturings and secret naughtinesses—grab the word and shake it down. That *Frisky Songster* of 1776 contained the first example of an extended, non-sexual use (at least, not explicitly sexual), which had been allocated its own subsense: "to botch," "to ruin," "to spoil." That meaning existed in the eighteenth century, but it is not particularly well recorded until into the twentieth century, as the forces of convention prevented printers from running away with themselves in the nineteenth century. It seems that American English is responsible for another development, in the mid-nineteenth century, when we find evidence for the meaning "to cheat" and "to betray." In general the extended meanings are aggressive, tending towards disorder and chaos.

There's more of this exploding aggression in the oaths and swearing that hit print in the 1920s. It is quite noticeable that this decade experiences a loosening-up of sentiment with relation to *fuck*, at least along the borders of polite society. James Joyce leads off in *Ulysses* ("God fuck old Bennett!"), but once out there this broadening continues up to the present day. Phrases using adverbs build from the 1890s (*to fuck about*, in *My Secret Life*), but take a firmer hold from the 1920s (*to fuck off*, *to fuck up*), as the fringes of society become more verbally adventurous. The level of change and variation expands up to the 1960s, by which time we have most of the stock expletives and colourful expressions we know today (*to fuck around*, *to fuck over*), and a phrase with a preposition, *to fuck with* (someone). Our data collection had majored on phrases involving *fuck* which had evaded previous dictionary readers. We were at last able to approach more closely to a realistic picture of the word's history.

It's a strong word. Not much dies away. By now we have four or five main strands of usage whirring away and showing no sign of fading: the basic sexual usages, extended meanings such as "to mess or botch (something) up," phrasal verbs (*to fuck about*, etc.), exclamations and swearing ("go fuck a duck"), and examples where *fuck* is woven into existing oaths as a stronger alternative to another word ("Fuck the expense" might be such an example).

One contemporary issue with *fuck* is whether it has lost, or will lose, its taboo status. That, like most other language change, would be something that happens over several generations. For one tier of society (by age, gender, ethnic background, national economic power, geographical location, social class, etc.) it will retain its power to shock, whereas for others it will tend to lose this. Words can become taboo (as *fuck* once did), or they can go the other way and enter the mainstream. Which one wins out depends on how our cultures move. Often the significant vector is age, and so as the generations pass, the meanings that the older members of society know and have clung to will disappear, and the younger strains of the language will assert themselves. But it doesn't have to be like that. The usage of a dominant economic power can influence the language of its less dominant cousins, and vice versa (Australians or others might be attracted to some American usages, such as the filler *like*, because of the attractions of the culture it represents, or the reverse may occur). Normally there's some conflict between a number of vectors, so you can't claim to know precisely what is going to happen. It's too complex for that.

The updated entry differs from the old one very considerably as a result of the policy changes we had introduced. The definitions were no longer shrouded in Victorian reserve, abbreviations were expanded, and more standardisation was introduced at many levels; the etymology brought in the latest information from other scholarly sources— such as Jonathan Lighter's *Historical Dictionary of American Slang*—and tried to explain the progression of meaning before the term entered English. Critically, the quotations were found in a far broader range of sources than previously, and were tracked back to their first editions— often in libraries abroad—to ensure that we were not using corrupted secondary data. The structure of the entry was opened up, so that each possible subsense was separated out—and its "biography" could be seen and compared with that of other subsenses—and the range of informal expressions was extended to cover more of the real language with which English speakers are familiar.

It took us a long time to get there, but as the work went on I became more and more proud of what the editors were achieving. What had seemed to some like an impossible project was finally starting to come into its own.

TEN

At the Top of the Crazy Tree

The Third Edition of the *OED* was now approved and funded by the University, and a draconian deadline of 2000—only six years hence—had been attached to the project. Someone clearly thought that the easiest way to ensure that the project did not overrun was to set a target date, as loudly as possible. I once even heard 1999 suggested as our target. Had these guys ever looked into the *OED*? If we were to stand any chance of approaching that goal, we would need to recruit more lexicographers. Unfortunately it is hard to recruit good lexicographers. They are not available on supermarket shelves.

From time to time I would imagine famous writers and scholars from the past finding their way to the dictionary offices for an interview. Charles Dickens would have been exasperatingly fond of lengthy, indulgent, and detailed description. Lexicographers need to be concise. Keep your definitions to a single sentence and don't continually launch off into secondary clauses. We don't need a paragraph of introduction, scene-setting, and certainly not four paragraphs. I appreciate your handling of music-hall evidence—do you have an interest in the theatre? Are you familiar with Word? No, well, we have other systems too. Have you been keeping up with post-nineteenth-century usage at all? Like you, we are thinking of serial publication: What are the upsides and downsides? Thank you, we'll be in contact with your secretary.

How about philosophers? Immanuel Kant? Mr Kant, had you considered the language barrier when framing your application? Do you speak any languages other than German and Latin? No, we no longer write our definitions in Latin. In the aptitude test you demonstrated a weighty command of large abstract concepts, but do you feel comfortable reducing these to simple, approachable terms? What do you mean when you talk about the "transcendental formula of public right"? How would you critique the prospective definition of an intellectual as a person who speaks at the same time as he thinks? What other interests do you have? "None" is an unusual answer. We are looking for candidates with a top-class English style and the ability to pinpoint and clarify problems, not leave the reader more confused than when they started.

And then there was Archimedes, over on a graduate scholarship at the moment in Oxford. In my imagination, we had high hopes for this candidate, as he might handle some of our scientific terminology as well as the simpler non-science vocabulary. But we weren't expecting the hair, pretty unkempt; normally those guys from research centres have got it nailed down in a pigtail. Fortunately, he started to pull things back with the first few questions: he'd seen a bit of the world, had done some teaching and (we hoped) had got that out of his system. He was direct and to the point. But overall he seemed a numbers man, not a letters one. We'd mention a word or two, and he'd reduce it to how many letters it had; what the frequency of those letters was in normal written British English; and the maximum Scrabble score you could achieve with its constituent letters. He was bony and angular, too. Sometimes went off at a tangent. That's not something you want in a lexicographer.

Agatha Christie was careful with her words, picky almost. We ask the normal questions: for example, "How does your previous life prepare you for dictionary work?" She jumps on that one quickly, and wonders if we believe she may have had a previous life, and what it might have consisted of. Sadly, that's one of the over-literal ways lexicographers would respond to that question. "What aspects of working on the dictionary appeal to you most?" She informs us that she believes she has a penchant for detection. (Do we want someone who believes they have a "penchant" for anything?) "Etymology," she informs us—as if we were relaxing unsuspecting in our armchairs as the murder is unfolded—"Etymology is the science of fingerprinting words to establish their whereabouts during history." This is certainly a new angle. "Definition is the ability to say what you mean in fewer words than you intended." She tells us of a Belgian friend of hers who would also be just right for this job. We thank her and put her on the maybe file—which is two stages further than the earlier candidates got.

There is always a succession of Woolfs and Wildes, and sometimes even a fiery Shelley. Some ask if they can bring their dog. They've not succeeded yet. Mainly they are worried about the pressure: Will they have their own office, or is it open-plan? There are some lovely little words they would love to see in the *OED* and would there be any chance that they might be able to draft them? Would they be able to take a desk by the window, because they like to listen to the water dimpling—or the traffic roaring? One had written a little story about what it would be like working on the *OED* and would we mind if he left it behind for us afterwards. That hit the nail on the thumb for us. As if we haven't already got enough paper. Lexicography isn't for budding writers who just want an atmosphere of books and industry.

When we might be just about turning in for the day, James Joyce turns up. He's slightly late because he's decided to take a walk round Oxford. He might write about it. He hasn't visited the city before, but has a couple of mates who put him up the previous night. On the face of it he looks austere, with those wire-rimmed specs. But we're pretty used to that look, too. He asks about the hours—Will he be able to take time off in the afternoon if he needs to? He can make it up way into the night. No. But he doesn't really like that sort of negative response. We get the impression that he's used to having his own way. We try him on a few words that had amused Archimedes: *leatherette*, *gumption*, *selfie*. He picked up on *selfie* but wasn't too sure what it meant. "Is it a hyper-referential term for introspective monologue?" he asks. We ask him in return why he thinks that. "Because that's the way literature is moving. You must see that in every word and phrase that you define." Has he ever used the *OED*? Yes, he's currently working on a long novel and he's peeked at a few entries. It's, like, an epic reference book, yes? He'd be glad to help out for a bit, but he might be a bit ahead of us all most of the time. He's not endearing himself to me or my colleagues. Fortunately he's got a ferry to catch, so we say our goodbyes.

The author Julian Barnes (*Flaubert's Parrot, A History of the World in 10½ Chapters*, etc.): well, he really did turn up for interview, but before my time—and his. Julian was even a member of the *OED Supplement*'s editorial staff in the late 1960s, but moved on early.

With the ever-present deadline of the year 2000 looming, we needed to take serious action to recruit staff. What we needed were good editors, and preferably excellent, qualified, historical-dictionary editors who would just slot into the work and power ahead indefinitely, giving us perfect, publishable dictionary text meeting the highest scholarly standards. There were a number of trained editors elsewhere in the Oxford Dictionaries department who were emerging from their previous assignments and might help us out. Some wanted to, and others didn't. (Curiously enough, not everyone wants to commit themselves to a long-term historical dictionary project, when there appear to be more exciting things in the world to set your sights on.) We did manage to bring into (or back into) the fold several colleagues willing to give it all a shot. But we still needed more hands on deck, and we needed them quickly.

Generally speaking, people ask one of two questions when they hear about the dictionary and what it does. The first is, "How does a new word get into the dictionary?" (remember: usage over time and normally evidence from various genres). Once an editor has answered this question, and has described what a remarkable document the *OED* represents, the second question often is, "How can I get a job on the dictionary?"

When we advertise for editorial posts, we have to be very careful not to open the net too wide. We did once, in the early days, and received over a thousand applications for three jobs. It's not worth the time spent reading through those applications. If the job is described in too open a fashion, you just encourage anyone who thinks they "love words," or who wants an excuse to extend their adolescence in Oxford, to throw their hat into the ring. Those are our two biggest **bugbears**: people who dote on words, and people who want to stay on in Oxford. And yet these are the last people we need working on dictionaries. In my humble opinion. Though there are doubtless others who beg to differ.

I should state it outright: lexicographers are not people who "love words"—at least, not in a schmaltzy, sentimental way. Years ago, I had an aunt who once asked me if I loved books. I don't think she received a very helpful answer; I think I managed a hopeless stare, as if I couldn't even understand the question. To tell you the truth, lexicographers veer as far away as they can from people who claim to love words. What is the point of loving words and at the same time expecting to analyse and classify them? It's a grumble of mine, and I know it's a rumbling grumble of other lexicographers too. I've even listened to one lecture on lexicography where the final PowerPoint slide ended, "I HATE words." Okay, so that's a bit extreme, but it reinforces the point.

The meaning of words can "weaken" over the centuries. What was once a very forceful way of expressing an idea can be watered down so that the original power evaporates. A *crime* can be a "criminal event" or a fashion fail. An action can be *life-saving* if it saves a life, but also if it saves you from embarrassment. *Bugbear* went the same way. What do you make of it: Is it something really scary, or just (in its weakened use) just a minor irritant? It feels like a word from around 1600: you can imagine it in the drama of the day. It doesn't look Anglo-Saxon, and it's not French—so sometime after around 1600 would seem to fit.

The "annoyance" and "irritation" sense of *bugbear* is very much secondary. The stronger meaning, which dates from around 1586, as it turns out, is "an object of dread," "an imaginary terror"—something that frightens the living daylights out of you. That sounds about right for all of those dire Jacobean tragedies that were just over the horizon then.

But even that isn't the primary and original meaning, which is stronger still. Star-date 1581 and we have *bugbear* in the sense of (according to the *OED*) "a sort of hobgoblin (presumably in the shape of a bear) supposed to devour naughty children." Apparently nursery nurses would tell innocent and yet inherently mischievous children that these sprites would creep up and scare them. So a *bugbear* was a *hobgoblin* (a mischievous imp, again from the sixteenth century). And how is the word constructed? The *OED* isn't 100 percent sure, but its best guess is that it's the old word *bear* (grizzly animal) latched on to *bug*. This *bug* isn't the insect, but is an older medieval word meaning "an object of terror" or a "bogy," or even—as the *OED* sometimes throws in for good measure in cases such as this, a "bogle." There's a Welsh word *bwg* which means a ghost, and the *OED* currently places its eggs in that basket as regards the origin of this *bug*.

So how do we weed out these word-lovers? We give them an aptitude test. The reason we do that is that Hilary said we should, back in the 1980s when I started having to recruit editors for our New Words group. I might have got round to it anyway, but at the time she was in HR and fighting against the inertia which leads interviewers to decide in the first few seconds of an interview which of the candidates is their favourite. A neutral but job-related test gives you a much better assessment of the candidates' capabilities.

Mind you, we had a Plan B for identifying likely lexicographers. This is the left-handedness test. Instead of marking scripts at the end of an assessment session, you just look around the room and see who is left-handed, and then appoint them. It's a scandalous approach for a professional, but it's backed up by real data. There was a time when the whole staff of the *Concise Oxford* was left-handed, as was the chief editor of the *OED* (that's me), of the *Australian National Dictionary*, of the *Dictionary of South African English*, and several more. I've heard ruminations that there is a correlation between left-handedness and programming/analytical skills: creativity, lateral thinking. Still, Ed Weiner is right-handed, so that's a good call for the opposite view.

Perhaps surprisingly, we would allow candidates to complete their aptitude test in the comfort of their own homes, with whatever reference books or (nowadays) computer resources they had at their command. Back in the days of my own interview I remember boasting to the chief editor that I mightn't know everything but I generally knew where to look for anything, and that was the line we took now. It didn't matter what resources the applicants secretly used, because if they became editors they'd have access to just the same resources anyway. Knowing how to use the resources was the key part of the job. We didn't really want their clever friends to help them, but we guessed that if they did phone a friend to help with the test, we'd catch them out anyway because they'd come unstuck when we talked them through their test at interview.

So we'd publish ads in the national papers—and more recently internationally, too, and on the Internet—inviting prospective lexicographers to try their luck in the words lottery. We'd tell them they would have to complete a test, and hoped that that would put off some of the more left-field candidates. We knew that out of every five hundred applicants, only around two would be any use to us, and a fair number might not be any use to anyone.

Stage one involved receiving the letters of application which eager job-seekers from all corners of the academic world decided to send us. We had several rules of thumb.

Short letters were better than long letters, even if they only consisted of three sentences—as long as they were crisp and intriguing. Some candidates seemed to think that we were interested in the remoter details of their thesis and of their personality, but generally speaking we weren't. Handwritten letters were more helpful than typed or keyboarded ones, because clear handwriting, as well as clear thinking, was, at the time, part of the job. We normally asked for handwritten letters, but some people seemed unable to comply. It can normally be taken as a good rule that we didn't need to know whether an applicant had a clean driving licence, though we were often told. The job doesn't involve driving. Similarly, we came to expect that every sensitive applicant would claim an interest in reading, film, and walking.

Occasionally candidates would suggest that they enjoyed crosswords. I'm not sure if that was for my benefit or for theirs. Personally I've never been any good at cryptic puzzles, but they weren't to know that. The *OED* knows *crossword puzzle* from America in 1914. It took a while—into the 1920s—before the crossword craze hit Britain. But, as I say, it passed me by: I'd rather be sorting out real problems. So I'm not sympathetic to crossword-solvers. We were not playing games on the *OED*, we were researching language history. Some of my best friends are crossword compilers: I tend to steer the conversation in other directions if they want to talk about their clues. Still, I don't think I held this one against starry-eyed applicants.

Spelling mistakes are best avoided in application letters to dictionaries. When we are hunting for reasons to jettison an application, that is just playing into our hands. But what I looked out for most was the word ***hone***. I'm surprised how often people had apparently spent their whole lives *honing* their skills to be ready for this particular job application. Probably one in three application letters offered *honing* in some form or other, in much the same way as any novel written since around

2005 has to include the word *heft* somewhere along the line (watch out for it). That is, if they have forgotten to include *hunker* (watch out for it, too). I doubt whether the applicants ever used *hone* at any other time in their lives. They seemed to think that it gave their previous life some sort of developmental focus, as if all the time they were sharpening their skills for the very point at which they encountered the *OED*. It just felt false. Look for it if you are ever scanning through application letters: it'll be there. In my book, the appearance of the *hone* word certainly helped to shift their letters over towards the growing reject pile.

Homonyms (or words spelt or pronounced the same, but coming from different origins) can be problematic for non-native speakers, but the English language often has a way of dealing with them. It allows one of the homonyms to become dominant, and the others sometimes fall away from use. There are four verbs *to hone* in English, according to the *OED*. The oldest one has already fallen into obsolescence: that's *to hone* meaning "to delay or dawdle." It couldn't stand the pressure applied by the three remaining *hones*. Verb number two means "to hanker after or pine for," or just "to grumble or moan." Nowadays it's a dialect word (the West Midlands and the southern United States), not in general use. The most recent verb *to hone* (to "hone" in on something) is just a mid-twentieth-century garbling of *home* (in on).

Our verb *to hone* (to sharpen a blade and hence your wits and skills) is a fairly late arrival in English. It wasn't around when people were applying for jobs on Dr Johnson's dictionary in the 1750s, so he would have needed some other word to trigger the interviewer's trap-door (and I doubt he would have found that too hard). Our first known use of *hone* in the sense of "to sharpen (a razor)" occurs in the works of the seriously under-examined poet Ebenezer Picken (1769–1816). The curious thing about Mr Picken, who died quite young and in poverty in Edinburgh after a brief life of literary endeavour, is that he wrote a short dictionary which was important in the lives of later Scottish lexicographers. So I am sorry to have to relate that at this moment another lexicographer must be held responsible for the popularity of the word *hone*. The meaning of sharpening your skills—as opposed to sharpening an object—dates from the twentieth century, however, so Picken receives a partial reprieve.

One or two people may ask about the word's origin. In case you are one of them, I should say that the verb *to hone* derives directly, without deviation, from the noun *hone*. The noun *hone*—back in the Anglo-Saxon, Old English period—meant "a pointed or overhanging rock," and especially one that marked a boundary. They rather liked stones which acted as boundaries in those distant early days of the language, as one of the main activities in Anglo-Saxon villages was checking where your boundaries were and keeping other Anglo-Saxons (and sometimes Celts or Picts or Vikings) on the other side. But for us, the relevant meaning arose in the fifteenth century (so just back into the Middle Ages), when a *hone* started to mean a "whetstone," on which you might sharpen your razor of a morning. It's surprising that we had to wait so long, from the fifteenth to the late eighteenth century, for someone to find a use for *hone* as a verb. But nowadays, as I believe I've said several times already, we use it too much.

Once we had read through all the application letters and scanned through all the handwritten and printed CVs, and once we had filtered out all the honers, holders of clean driving licences, lonely cinematophiles, and ramblers, then we had to boil the remaining applicants down to around thirty by considering hard whether their experience, personality, and life skills warranted our moving them through to the next round. Those who satisfied most of these requirements were sent whichever version of the aptitude test we were currently employing.

The whole point of the aptitude test wasn't to ensure that the candidates failed, but to give them some idea about what work on the dictionary might be like. We started from the assumption that, whatever they thought, they really had no idea what working on a historical dictionary meant. We also started from the assumption that about a third of the people to whom we sent the test would disappear off our radar into the ether, laughing raucously to themselves at the stupidity of anyone wanting to do that sort of thing for a living. That's okay. They'll find a **niche** somewhere.

It can be instructive to watch the struggle for precedency of one pronunciation over another through the years. When we first adopted the word *balcony* from Italian in the early seventeenth century, we didn't immediately pronounce it BAL-co-ny; we adopted the Italian style of pronunciation, with the stress on the second syllable: bal-CO-ny. The *OED* says that the modern pronunciation was winning through by 1825, but it adds that the English poet Samuel Rogers (1763–1855) said that this newfangled way of saying the word "makes me sick."

Do you pronounce *niche* as /nitch/ or /neesh/? If you say /nitch/, then you are probably old-fashioned and proud of it. Most people pronounce it roughly /neesh/ these days. I suppose I do now, too, but I wouldn't have fifty years ago. The word derives from French, but developed its old-fashioned pronunciation in English quite early on. English speakers have used the word, according to the *OED*, since around 1610—so it's a late French borrowing influenced by Renaissance architecture and design. With such a strong cultural force behind it, it found its way into most of the European languages—even German (*Nische*) and Russian (*niša*). The First Edition of the *OED* (the letter *N* was published in 1907) gave /nitch/ as the only pronunciation option. Even up to 1977, most of the big pronouncing dictionaries gave /nitch/ as the standard and /neesh/ as a newcomer. Now, they have mostly decided that /neesh/ is the dominant form, and that /nitch/ (sadly) has had its day.

It is clearly pertinent to ask why these pronunciations change. And there are clearly different reasons. We began by using an approximation to the Italian pronunciation of *balcony*, but clearly came to feel that it was not consistent with English pronunciation norms. The derived form *balconied* (stressed as an English word on the first syllable) may have helped shift the accentuation of *balcony*, as might the more familiar word *falcon*. In general, there has been a tendency in English for stress sometimes to move forwards towards the front of words over time.

It is different with *niche*. The older pronunciation may have been influenced in the first place by late Latin and Italian use, or users of the word might have wished to make it sound more Italianate and rather snobbishly adopted this /nitch/ variety. But there are other possibilities, too. As usual, there is no one answer to questions such as these.

Niche wasn't a word you needed very often in the old days, unless you lived in a stately pile or spent your summers in Italy with friends who owned villas. This eventuality may lend weight to the snobbishness argument. A *niche* is a hollow recess in a wall where you might place a small statue. In English it has been a busy word. New meanings have been recorded in these years (divided by century): 1662 / 1725, 1733, 1749, 1756 / 1822 / 1911, 1913, 1963—so it's been good to lexicographers. I've separated the meaning shifts by century so that it is easy to see that the period of greatest activity was in the eighteenth century; and if you divide the centuries further, by quarters, you can see that the busiest period for the word was the second quarter of that century. That makes sense. That was a period of great classical influence amongst the style-blazers in Britain, so a word for an alcove in which to display your classical statue probably would have had a reasonable profile. But people were also interested in how individuals fitted into a society that was rapidly developing a class system—where their own position (or *niche*) in life was along the wall of society. That's the 1733 date, filled by Jonathan Swift (*Epistle to a Lady*: "If I can but fill my Nitch, I attempt no higher Pitch"). Also in the eighteenth century it came to mean a hole or lair for an animal (1725), or a natural recess in a rock or a hill (remember the celebrated faux-naturalistic landscape gardener, Lancelot "Capability" Brown?) (1756). We had to wait for 1913 for *niche* to develop into the place of an organism within an ecosystem, and as late as 1963 for consumerism to bring us the *niche market*.

Whatever home that one-third found who didn't attempt our aptitude test, it was the two-thirds who did have a go at it in whom we were now interested. First of all, they will have been surprised at how low-level and data-oriented the test was. They didn't need to know complex linguistic formulas, but how to analyse data sensibly. So we gave them a set of, say, thirty sentences, all containing one keyword. And we gave them a copy of the *OED*'s entry for that word. The task was to tell us which subsense of the *OED*'s long entry each quotation fitted into. On one occasion we used the verb *to list*. The verb has had about ten different meanings in English.

As with most things, it's easier to understand if you have a go at it yourself. So here is a quotation from Samuel Pepys's diary of 1668: "The persons therein concerned to be listed of this or that Church." You are not given any extra context, though you might check online to see if that helps, or go to your local library to extract a copy of Pepys's diaries. Now, you have to read that quotation carefully, and decide under which of the existing dictionary definitions it fits. Here are three possible ones (all abbreviated, and you would normally have around ten to select from):

(1) to set down together in a list;
(2) to include or enrol in the number or membership *of*;
(3) to enter on the list of a military body.

Read the quotation and the definitions carefully, and trust your instincts (just this once), or you will never finish. Samuel Pepys is not talking about enlisting in the army, so you can discount No. 3. Nos. 1

and 2 are more tricky. What do you think? Pepys means that his "persons" are put in a list, but that could be either No. 1 or No. 2. So what distinguishes these two definitions? Pepys is talking about people listed in separate lists ("of this or that Church"), so they are not being "set down in a list *together*" (No. 1), which the dictionary exemplifies (amongst other quotations) with: "About one hundred species of butterflies have been listed." Here the butterflies are all written out in the same list. But Pepys is talking about people being listed in the membership rolls of different churches, so it's No. 2. I hope you followed that. This sort of puzzle is one of the reasons I enjoy reading sixteenth- and seventeenth-century text.

Mostly the candidates got these questions right. Sometimes we would throw in an example of another verb *to list* (such as "to listen," or "to please or delight," or "to enlist"). Sometimes we'd throw in a noun, to see if anyone was concentrating. Sometimes we'd include quotations that might be attached to two or three different subsenses, depending on how you read them. There were other tricks, too.

Once they were starting to feel that everything was simple, we'd chuck them in the deep end with question two: a copy of a full dictionary entry, as compiled in, say, 1904, and not yet updated. And we'd just ask them the simple question: What would you do to update this in line with modern-day usage and scholarship? Their hearts should have shot through their mouths then. This was the big one (at least as far as I was concerned). We were giving them just enough rope to hang themselves, and we'd sit back and watch. Obviously some people had no idea what to do—despite having honed their skills for this precise day in their lives—and then wrote a short paragraph of waffle, before meandering on to the next question. Others set about it with gusto. It was all too easy to unseat yourself by sticking to generalities. What we needed were concrete ideas on updating the vocabulary of definitions, ideas for how to find new documentary evidence (quotations), and most of all some sense of the overall structure that the entry should have in its revised form.

Lexicography is pretty sharp-edged. There's no place for wobbly or brittle thinking. You see a problem and leap in to solve it; you don't wallow in it, indulging yourself in the beauties of the language. It's necessary to compare the usage you are addressing with hundreds of other examples from the same semantic area, to see what is special about your use. Or if you are trying to write or update a definition, you assume all of your source material is wrong until it proves itself not to be. You need a scientist's sense of distrust and a writer's sense of elegance.

People often think lexicography is easy: it's not. It involves qualities most people don't have. Stamina, for one. There are times when I think that's the most important quality for a lexicographer. Mental, and also physical. Mental is obvious; physical—well, it's not factory work, but it wasn't static desk work. All the time you were up and down stairs, carting huge books from shelves on to tables and back again, lugging open heavy filing cabinets that should have been power-assisted but weren't—relentlessly, because you had to hunt out that last piece of evidence. There is less of that to do now that the basic work is on computer, so maybe the profile of the lexicographer will change as time passes. Lexicography is a long haul, and you need to stay with it. It's not something you can jump in and out of, or you will never build up the necessary expertise.

And other people think that lexicography is hard: it's not. It's easy—if you remember to keep things simple, that normally things happen as you might expect them to, and that you just need to follow the data and not try to impose grand schemes on it yourself.

From the test we normally settled on about five or six applicants to interview. On the big day, two or three of us would be gathered together in one of the dictionary offices awaiting the arrival of the future generation of *OED* editors. We knew how the candidates had done in the aptitude test. But that wasn't everything—it was essential that people could fit in (fairly) easily with the other editorial staff that we already had. We wanted people to be very ordinary and quite extraordinary at the same time, and sometimes we got it right.

In general the applicants were just leaving university—either after a first degree or a higher degree. We didn't require doctorates, as we'd heard was the case in American dictionary houses. What we wanted was promise and competence. We hardly ever appointed people trained in linguistics, as we found they tended to come to us with theories of their own, and wanted to work from the top down—whereas we lived in a world of data, trying to piece the jigsaw together from within, or to dig ourselves up towards the light.

Once someone had reached the interview stage, they had a pretty good chance of being appointed. They were the cream of the crop. Obviously we couldn't use all of them, but they were all on short odds.

What sort of people were we looking for—what sort of temperaments and personalities? We wanted people who could listen, observe, and not necessarily just sound off—as some of them appeared to have been encouraged to do at university. The job is to hear language, to absorb it, think about it, and analyse and classify it. That's not really the sort of thing you can do if you are talking all the time. Let me mark myself on these criteria, to see how I'd fit in. Listening, not talking (nine out of ten). Sometimes I don't think I expend more than two hundred words a day, but I'm listening hard and monitoring what I hear.

We need to ensure that the candidate will fit into a team. There's a place for loners, but they make things more difficult for everyone else. It goes without saying that you can't tell everything about someone's social adeptness at an interview, but you have a chance to gauge it. I think I scored really low here when I started—maybe a three. You'd have had to see past that to employ me. But I just needed a year or so to integrate. I'm up with the eights by now.

Are you a rambler or a finisher? Do you prefer to research for research's sake, or as a means to an end? You'd be surprised how many of the ramblers there are. It is rather fun sniffing them out. You ask a leading question and see how long it takes them to bring their answer to a definite conclusion. And sometimes you add to that how long they have been working on an unfinished doctorate. The higher the aggregate climbs, the less likely they are to land the job. I would have done reasonably well here—maybe six or seven. I wouldn't have rambled, but I may have dried up prematurely if I didn't feel I knew what I was talking about.

I've already mentioned stamina. Lexicography is slow and involved; the excitement comes as the fuse burns slowly towards the answer. But it's not always climactic. So can the candidate demonstrate any achievement that would not qualify as gnat-like in its longevity? Concentration. Think about that one, and then think about it again. But don't waste time thinking; it has to be productive. We need slow-burning but explosive bursts of concentration. It may not be possible, but perhaps that gives you the idea. I get a nine for that.

What about the aptitude test they have all done? Well, we need to bring them back to that too. We need to see how they take criticism, because sure enough (if my experience was anything to go by), you'll come in for plenty of that before you're done. Do they sulk? People don't usually sulk at interview, but they can go into themselves and seem happier avoiding the issues. Can they dig themselves out of any holes they jumped into during the test? Are they ready to change their mind? If you spot a weakness, you have to try to explore it—bring it out into the open. Eventually even your fellow interviewers will see the point.

From time to time we wouldn't find any suitable candidates after two days of interviewing. If that was the case, it was best not to appoint second-best, as that would only cause problems down the line. What was exciting was when you could see glimpses of the strange potential a candidate needed to become a lexicographer. It could come when you didn't expect it, but it always left us on an up when the interview ended. Sometimes we thought we had a fantastic candidate, based on the aptitude test and the CV, but with some deft questioning things started to fall apart. At others, borderline interviewees pulled it round from a low base. You couldn't second-guess who would finally make it.

They might come from any discipline, any level (bachelor's to post-doc), any university or college. And any of them might be the next chief editor in fifteen or twenty years.

There are good things about dictionary work and there are bad things about dictionary work, and the higher up you go the more bad things there are. The best thing was the work—detective, creative, important, as we liked to think. The bad things involved spreadsheets and budgets and frowns from our senior colleagues, who thought we were overcomplicating a problem that a couple of sparrows could sort out while chatting at a bird-table.

One day in 1993, Ed and I had a short conversation. Our little discussion went along the lines of:

> ED: This will surprise you, but I'm more interested in writing
> the dictionary than managing its composition.
> JOHN: Okay.

The end result of this brief but considered exchange of views was that rather than remaining co-editors of the dictionary, I bravely took over as chief editor, with Ed as my deputy. I heard that some people thought I was now at the top of the crazy tree; the expression "poisoned chalice" was heard in the dictionary halls, as we were still battling against a completion date of 2000. But I fondly thought I could fight the dictionary's corner whenever the necessity presented itself, and Ed intended—sensibly—to nestle down to the excitement of editorial discovery and creation. As it happened, I planned to be there, too, and to spend only a little while on other matters. We did, after all, have the Admiral, whose job it was to steer the ship round any rocks that reared their ugly masses.

I mention the change of title to chief editor because you'll only ask if I don't. It didn't make any difference to my relationship with Ed. We were still both firmly behind the dictionary, and its editors, and looking forward to ploughing through the text as rapidly as we could. What it meant on a day-to-day level for me was that I was the editor everyone in the University Press, the University, and the outside world turned to for anything to do with the dictionary. We had to convert a series of policy proposals into a project plan, and I was responsible for establishing all of the editorial milestones, objectives, and work rates. Most of this would be guesswork until we had actually done a substantial amount of work, but I soon discovered I was best advised not to broadcast this. The Admiral fed all the figures into his spreadsheet, and we scratched our heads whenever the output seemed problematic (i.e., we'd need to request a big budget for a longer time, etc.). Being chief editor also meant, at least to my mind, that I should fight for the highest practical editorial standard, whatever the implications for resources. So I did. I wasn't always popular upstairs at the University Press. The University itself was much easier to deal with—academics knew that the *OED* was extraordinary, though they didn't quite know how. But as they didn't have to pay for it, they didn't really care.

I most liked dealing with the public, who were usually amazed if we so much as replied courteously and rapidly to their letters. Since 1983, we'd coordinated the way the *OED* replied to letters about language from the general public under the umbrella of the Oxford Word and Language Service (OWLS, as the witty acronym continually reminded us). People liked the friendly face of the dictionary that OWLS presented. When it was launched, I had to appear on the BBC1 early-evening TV show *Nationwide* to answer questions about language rung in by viewers. Later, we shared the task of answering readers' questions around the dictionary department, and then a couple of my colleagues wrote a book containing many of the most common Q&As (*Questions of English*, written by Jeremy Marshall and Fred McDonald, and published in 1994). We weren't swamped by correspondence, but word got around that OWLS was an approachable service which came up with reliable answers.

The questions were often straightforward, if you were a lexicographer—questions about spelling in *-ize* or *-ise* (*realise/realize*), about the name for a cat-lover (*ailurophile*), the name for the part of its back that an animal can't scratch (*acnestis*), the word for the channel under your nose (*philtrum*), the history of *sorry*, the etymology of *O.K.* (old Boston slang for "orl/all correct," as the evidence so far indicates), whether someone's daughter's new word can go straight into the dictionary (not unless it catches on), and so forth. Once people realised that there were real people answering their letters, they would send back thank-you notes. Someone once said he was so pleased and proud to receive a letter from the chief editor of the *OED* that he had had it framed and then pinned it up in his shed. That was going well until we reached the "shed" bit. Being there when the public thought they were probably writing to a brick wall in Oxford was worth the time spent responding.

The one thing that people couldn't seem to fathom, I discovered, as time went on, was how I (well, anyone) could handle the responsibility of being the chief editor of the *OED*. "I wouldn't be able to get out of bed in the morning," they'd say, or "I just wouldn't be able to decide which words to include and which to leave out," or "I would just panic." It's difficult to answer that one, but I had to fairly often. I'd calmly explain that we had rules and regulations, and guidelines and advisory reports, and had an excellent text to work with in the first place, and so decisions such as these usually made themselves. But despite my logical explanations, some people were still overawed. One senior lady librarian in America even curtsied when we first met.

W e were still learning how to edit the big dictionary. We had our policies, but policies cannot answer every eventuality. At home, we were also developing strategies, but this time for looking after Ellie. Strategies were good, but they didn't necessarily help you break new ground. Although teachers' reports on Kate were always positive, with Ellie it was a different matter. She was fast approaching three, and she definitely wasn't following the expected plan.

She was slipping behind her peers developmentally: I think we secretly hoped for years that she would "catch up," but all the time she was losing ground. Hilary and I just took one day at a time, relied on our instincts, tried to do our best for Ellie, and defaulted to the rules unless we thought they were wrong. We recognised by now that she had some form of serious developmental delay, and we had to accustom ourselves to a whole new side of bringing up a child and navigating the education system. We had more questions than answers. What was her condition, and how quickly would she develop? Would she have a drastically reduced lifespan? How could we accelerate her development? Were we the best people to do it anyway? What we both badly needed as parents of a disabled daughter was information and hope. Reliable information was in very short supply, and hope was something you invented for yourself.

One major worry we had was that she would never walk. She crawled a little—late, slowly, without much sense of purpose. Eventually we did see her trying to lift herself off the floor on to the edge of furniture, and even more slowly to propel herself towards whatever her objectives were. But it was late before she could walk—and even now she is a very careful walker, as if she knows she might easily trip up. It was all part of her long struggle, which little in our own backgrounds helped us to alleviate.

We took the view that we would be more use to Ellie if we remained as far as possible in full-time work, and employed people who were more able than us to provide the educational stimulation that she needed, either at home or in a nursery setting. At one point my parents offered to pay for any medical treatment she needed. They had some idea that there were clinics in America and Poland that had done wonders with profoundly disabled children. But as we didn't have a firm diagnosis, there wasn't any cure.

Ellie's day-to-day objectives were basic: food, the door (for a buggy-ride outside or a drive in the car), a person (probably an indeterminate person—but not always) for warmth, sound, texture. She was big on texture, and on action. Not that she initiated any, but she liked things happening to her. The main one was being driven in a car and watching things go past the window. That made her happy, and still does.

I desperately wanted to hear her speak, and to speak to her. There was a period of about eighteen months when we used to return home from work every day hoping to hear that Ellie had spoken her first word. It never happened. We'd look for signs of comprehension, and try to transmit ideas to her by action, tone, if not by speech. But it was no use. There *was* communication and comprehension happening, but it was at a very low level: she seemed to understand about five words. But was it even that? Was she just picking up on situations in which they might be used ("car," "food," "drink"—not much else). Then at times she'd burst out laughing: it's always been clear that she has a quiet sense of humour. And she liked the colour yellow for some reason.

I think our friends didn't quite understand the depth of her problems. They would have understood "blind," or "deaf," but not "wordless." Somehow they thought we were exaggerating the issue, and that she was just holding back until she was comfortable with speech. Her wordlessness stood in such dramatic distinction to the rest of my life. My family was so intensely literate. Hilary's PhD and interests lay in the modern novel, and in the interplay of male and female fiction; Kate (by now ten years old) would spend most of her spare time hammering the keyboard of our personal computer, creating stories of queens and princesses and witches communicating freely in a world of faery enchantment. At work I was surrounded by people who couldn't stop talking about words, analysing them, making clever linguistic connections, and we encountered fresh waves of brains every time we advertised for new editorial staff for the dictionary.

But at home, our evenings were spent worrying and trying to think how we could get through to Ellie. She'd look at you directly, eye to eye (she still does), and you'd think that there must be something preverbal passing between you. Maybe she thought the same. Maybe she thought

I had the problem if I couldn't work out whatever cognitive system she was employing—but I couldn't. You learn to cope, but you always hope that the next day there will be a change—in you or in her. There never was. She changes very, very slowly, and sometimes so slowly that you miss it.

Where I failed, professionals tried. They encouraged her to do activities that were supposed to develop a link between actions and words. Sometimes little things sank into her memory, and we'd be surprised how she could remember a face, say, after months. But nothing coordinated remained, nothing that could be a cognitive platform from which easy communication might develop. In the end, we found that gestures and tone—leading, guiding, directing, assisting—were all we could use, and we hoped that she was happy with our efforts. We were an excessively "wordy" family with a wordless newcomer in our midst: at times she dragged us into her silence, and we couldn't think how to help her.

ELEVEN

Shenanigans Online

Most lexicographers, if you ask them, will tell you that the letters of the alphabet each have their own individual characters. They will say that consonants are pretty straight-up, and that vowels are the problem letters. Vowels can go off anywhere at a tangent—they are volatile elements in the periodic table of the alphabet. You can track this volatility through pronunciation. The consonants are generally pronounced as you might expect, but this is not the case with vowels. The letter *a* is pronounced differently (depending on your variety of English) in *man, name, father, bath, village, comma, wan, war,* and *many,* and that doesn't take account of vowel pairs such as *ay, au,* etc. Historically, a long *a* (as in Old English *stan*)—when written—can be the predecessor of our long *o* (as in *stone*); some varieties of English use *aesthetic* and others *esthetic*; an *ambassador* could be an *embassador* (as in *embassy*). I never feel that an *A* word gives you a hint of what it means until you are some way into it—it doesn't explode, or insinuate, or stutter from the very start.

When you pass beyond *A* you hit the simple battering aggression of *B*—*break, bunch, bewail, beleaguered, bite, bump*. It's a rough ride, but *B* doesn't throw anything unexpected at you. *C* is calmer: *cat, cylinder, cool, cold, crystal*—you can't generate too much energy with a gentle *c*-sound (*ch-* is different; *cl-* can be noisy). *D* is explosive, like *B*— *danger, death, dredge, dungeon*. And then you are back with another difficult vowel: *E*. The letter *E* is the commonest (that is, the most frequently used) letter in the English language, which does make it something of a handful. Rather like *A*, it is not always pronounced the same way—though varieties of English differ: *be, here, there, acme, bed, alert, eh*, and even *clerk*. Since the early Middle Ages we haven't even pronounced it in—for example—*love* and *name* (the non-philological "magic E"). It introduces major prefixes, which add to the lexicographer's workload: *em-, en-, endo-, epi-, eso-, ex-, extra-*. In general, it's always there.

The alphabet, therefore, is inconsiderate enough to start with a problem letter—*A*. As we prepared to revise the entire *OED* in 1994, we needed to decide quick sharp whether to begin our revision here, or somewhere in the alphabet where the editing would be less alphabetically turbulent.

I've read something about the characters of the letters of the alphabet before, in my favourite book about the *OED*: *Reading the OED: One Man, One Year, 21,730 Pages*—Ammon Shea's blog-like account of reading through the dictionary from *A* to *Z*, published in 2008. What is important for me about this book is that it actually responds to the content, not to how the text was stitched together. So we hear someone else's view about what it feels like to read the letter *A*, and how the letter *A* differs in its character, for example, from the letter *G*. At the same time we are introduced to the engaging parallel narrative of Ammon's life whilst he was reading each letter: where he lived, what he was doing, why he struggled with some parts of the text. It actually starts to bring the dictionary to life in a way that almost all other books about dictionaries fail to do.

These were very early days for the revised *OED* project. We moved into new, open-plan offices at the University Press, taking possession of the ground once held by the Press's great printing machines. It heralded for us the beginning of a new era in publishing. Our general plan for this comprehensive revision of the dictionary was simple: work through the entire text of the *OED*, updating all aspects of each entry (many of which were unchanged since the Victorian period) according to the best information available to modern scholarship. While we were charged initially with completing and publishing in the year 2000, it soon became plain to everyone that the target date would have to be reset to 2005. Later, it was reset again, to 2010. One of the original *OED* editors, Sir William Craigie, used to tell anyone who asked, at whatever stage the project had reached, that it would be completed in about five years. As 2010 approached, and the end was not in sight, our arguments changed: we were online, the *OED* was in future going to be in a continual, dynamic state of change, and any completion date was less meaningful now than it would have been in past eras. That was my argument, at least. Rather like William Craigie, I'd say fifteen or twenty years whenever asked. It was the quality that mattered; quicker publication would impair the dictionary. As time passed, so much newly accessible information about the history of the language became available through the Internet that it made sense to reassess our scope and time constantly.

As well as thinking about the scope of the work, we also had to buckle down to do some of it. And the first question to arise in this department was where we should begin. After due consideration, we decided not to start the revision at the letter *A*, as any normal person would have done, but to kick the whole **shenanigans** off halfway through the alphabet, at the letter *M*. In the following years I was continually asked—by journalists, managers, editorial staff, and by myself—why we had started at *M*. The easy answer was so that we could get to the end more quickly, but only a few people swallowed that. The real reason was that Ed and I both thought the early part of the original dictionary was somewhat unkempt editorially. The first editors—back in the 1880s—had been struggling to find a style when they started off in *A*, and even to find enough data to fill their pages. It was going to be particularly hard to update that material. So why would we want to make life difficult for ourselves?

Shenanigans is another of those nonsense words of unknown or debated origin (like *bloviate* and *absquatulate*) which contains enough implicit suggestions to make you think it might have arisen amongst the self-confident braggadocio of mid-nineteenth-century Irish America, when the Wild West was being won. And most of that turns out to be true. We have already seen a number of strange and fanciful formations arise in early nineteenth-century America (to which we might add *discombobulate*). We don't know the origin of *shenanigans* with any certainty, but we know it hit our screens around 1855—in California. Most of the early references for the term come from the San Francisco area, so that might be a hint. That's like the fact that most of the early references for *O.K.* come from Boston, in the late 1830s and early 1840s. Again, it gives the detectives amongst us a geographical clue to its origins. Words can grow like cultures: the first records cluster in a particular place for several years, before people—via the media, or just the transport system—take them elsewhere.

An odd thing about *shenanigans* is that when it first appeared it was *shenanigan*. Not in the plural. That would sound very odd today, and you might be given an old-fashioned stare if you used it in the singular—and be corrected. Here's Mark Twain using the word rather uncertainly in a letter he wrote in 1862: "Consider them all guilty (of 'shenanigan') until they are proved innocent." The *OED* carries references to this singular form until around 1960. Maybe it still exists: most things do, even if you think they are well and truly obsolete. The dictionary presents 1926 (yes, as late as 1926) as the first time someone thought the word should be plural *shenanigans* (trickery, intrigue; a plot, a carry-on), and that was the American writer Edna Ferber in her novel *Show Boat*.

There were plenty of other good reasons for beginning the editorial work later in the alphabet. The order of the letters in the English alphabet isn't significant, so it doesn't matter in what order you edit them. *M* was a friendly letter. That is one of its characteristic properties. Mmmmmm. Umm. Yum yum. When the letter *M* was originally edited, in the early twentieth century, the dictionary was on a stable course and the results made for impressive reading. It was not going to be excessively difficult—we thought fondly—for us to test our mettle on it before heading back to the choppier waters of *A*, *B*, and *C*. Also, it contains a nice mix of words from the Germanic and Romance streams, which form the bedrock of English today. Generally, it gave us a good variety of editorial issues without presenting us with anything problematic. Obviously we hadn't noticed that after a few pages of text we would hit the verb *make* and all of the problems involved in updating a deceptively short and ancient word with viciously sharp teeth. The verb *make* slowed us down somewhat. It dates right back to the earliest tiers of Anglo-Saxon English: our revised entry gave it over 300 separate senses, illustrated by almost 3,000 quotations; we had found 200 ways it could be spelt over the ages in all of its tenses and persons, and our new etymology took up more than one and a half standard computer screens, rather than the previous ten lines or so. Still, it provided a stern but beneficial test for us as we applied our new editorial policies.

We had also decided that although we would start at *M*, we would only proceed alphabetically until the end of the letter *R*, before turning tail and closing the gap between *A* and *L*, and then heading off into the sunset from *S* to *Z*. The reasons for this modus operandi were esoteric, and involved the unlikely named *Dictionary of the Older Scottish Tongue* (*DOST*). This is a thoroughgoing, card-carrying dictionary of early Scots from the twelfth to the seventeenth centuries, initiated by that former *OED* editor, Sir William Craigie, in the 1920s. A sample of entries includes words like *schalange*, "a variant of challenge"; *schald*, "a sand-bank or shallow"; and *schalk*, "a man, a fellow"—two of which are also in the *OED*, and the other one probably should be. After years of slow progress, work on it had reached the letter *R*, and because of the significance of this dictionary to the *OED*'s etymologies and documentation for early Scots vocabulary, we didn't want to edit on ahead of it. (In the end, the *DOST* editors put on a major spurt and had their material ready for us to look at just when we needed it.)

To say that we started the revision of the *OED* at the letter *M* isn't exactly true. We decided to leave the big entry *M* (containing all the abbreviations and initialisms beginning with *M*) until later, as that was a seriously irregular entry and needed to be done with other seriously irregular "initial-letter" entries in mind. The First Edition of the dictionary had followed the *M* entry with lots of other fractured pieces of toast: *m'* and *ṁ* and other very similar grunts and hums which we rightly thought we could leave for later. So without further ado, we ran our heads into *M-A*.

You would have to have been very alert and to have concentrated very hard in school to know that there are—according to the *OED*—four nouns spelt *M-A* in the English language.

M-A noun-one is the oldest word *ma* in English: it's the letters *M-A* used as an abbreviation or shortening of the word *master* (like the modern "Mr.") when it's prefixed to the surname of a man (who might be a friend, a gentleman of higher status, the lord of a household, etc.). So instead of saying "Master Harvey," might you, in the sixteenth and seventeenth centuries, say "Ma. Harvey"? You wouldn't, as it's only a graphic abbreviation—one used in writing: you could write "Ma. Harvey" if you wanted to, and no one would have thought you were talking about his mother. The *OED*'s revised entry has that fateful dagger hanging over it, the printer's symbol used to indicate that the word is now obsolete or deceased. It has been deceased, as far as the dictionary knows, since 1602—the date of the last record of its use.

There are thousands of these daggers (or "obelisks," as the professional printers used to call them) dotted around the dictionary (†). They are visual marks on the page for anyone who needs reminding that the abbreviation *obs.* means "obsolete." It is helpful to the reader to know whether a word or a meaning is still in use, and if it isn't, the lexicographer stamps it with the dagger. In general the working rule is that the dagger is wielded if we have found no documentary evidence for a term for the past one hundred years. So *sword-fencer*, a seventeenth-century word for a "gladiator," is marked as obsolete, whereas *sword-hand* (still current, though mainly in historical contexts)—the hand in which you wield your sword—is not, even though it dates from the sixteenth century, earlier in history than *sword-fencer*.

Marking a term as obsolete if it no longer matches the criteria for active life is one of the most curious jobs that today's *OED* lexicographers have to do. A term may have been current when the First Edition of the dictionary was written, but still not meet the hundred-year rule nowadays. Lots of old words are now being labelled "obsolete." And just occasionally, we have new evidence for a word formerly regarded as dead, and we silently remove the dagger. One such example is *nut*, in the sense of "a revolving claw that holds back the drawstring of a crossbow until released by a trigger": the original *OED* labelled this as obsolete on the basis of its evidence, but renewed interest in archery apparently brought it back into specialist use. We use one hundred years as the required period of disuse before a dagger is applied because of human lifespans. People might remember words from childhood into their dotage a hundred years later. In that case, we would be premature to mark it as defunct. But we don't dismiss obsolete words from the *OED* altogether, because it is a record of the linguistic living and the linguistic dead. I don't really like the concept of obsolescence, as it's a false marker. Words can easily fall out of use and then return again. But readers like it.

It turned out that our very first revised entry—for the word *Ma.*— was unbundled from another entry with which it should never have been associated. The original dictionary had placed the abbreviation *Ma.* = "master" in the same entry as another abbreviation: *Ma.* = "majesty." They had no good reason for that, except the desire to save space. It is against all lexicographical principles to merge together two words from different origins. I think the old editors didn't really think these broken-up abbreviations counted as real words, and so the normal rules could be dispensed with. Our principal heroics as far as *Ma.* = "master" was concerned were therefore to drag it out of the *master/majesty* jumble and set it up on its own account. We couldn't find any earlier evidence, so we went with the old *OED*'s 1579 reference (the introductory epistle to Edmund Spenser's *Shepheardes Calender*). In general we added all the trimmings: a proper etymology, a fuller definition, and a new illustrative example—that one from 1602 (from the playwright and pamphleteer Thomas Dekker's *Satiro-mastix*).

I have never heard anybody mention this entry outside the dictionary department, but for us it was a tiny classic. This was the very first time we had applied all of our new policies to an entry which was going to be published, rather than just scrutinised by a committee. All the policies had to work, even on an entry most people would regard as inconsequential. Because if they didn't work here, they certainly wouldn't work on anything more challenging. Like every other entry, it was a cameo with which the artist must be pleased or the effort is wasted.

We then moved swiftly on to *Ma.* (number two) = "majesty": first recorded in 1584; last recorded in 1679; a graphic abbreviation and a shortening of *majesty*; daggers drawn again to show that it is obsolete.

The third *M-A* noun was *ma* = "mother." Here at least we had something of real interest. It's a word with a history, as in the nineteenth century it was ridiculed "as a mark of vulgarity"—as the *OED* carefully says (it would doubtless have preferred *mother*, *mamma*, or—if you had been to the right school—perhaps even *mater*). Early spellings include *ma'* (the apostrophe showing that it was taken as a shortening of another word). It can be hard to research words which are essentially children's words, because—by definition—children didn't record their lexical usages when they were bawling their eyes out in the Victorian nursery. There is a suggestion that *ma* might have originated on the east coast of England, in Suffolk. But one little piece of evidence from 1823 doesn't count as conclusive. *Mum* is earlier (late sixteenth century), and is probably a variant spelling of *mam* rather than a shortening of *mummy*—which wouldn't work, because *mummy* appears to be the later term (mid-eighteenth century). American *mom* is later still (around 1850), shortened from *momma*, itself a variation of *mama*.

These words live in word families. We shouldn't really have worked on *ma* without editing *pa*. They both come from the same era: *pa* crops up first—as far as we can tell—in one of Benjamin Franklin's letters, from 1773: "He . . . grew fond of me, and would not be contented to sit down to Breakfast, without coming to call *Pa*." Obviously that won't be the first-ever use of the word, but it's the first we've found. *Pa* is short for *papa*; *ma* turns up a bit later (1829) and is short for *mama*. But bear in mind that these two common affectionate terms for mother and father don't go back to the dawn of time.

Why didn't we edit the set *ma, mum, dad, pops*, etc. all at once? There are several reasons. Firstly, the editing system we had then only let us revise entries in alphabetical order (though we could insert new entries wherever we liked): it was the editorial equivalent of an ocean liner—you got on and cruised along without looking to stop at unscheduled locations. All the necessary checks and balances in the software depended on entries being completed in alphabetical order. It would have been, we were told, a "non-trivial" exercise to change this, even if we had wanted to.

Secondly, these small sets can become stupendously large and unwieldy when you add in all the possible members: in this case we also would have had to consider *mammy, marm, mater, maw, mums, mumsy, muvver, bab, bap, da, dad, dada, daddy, papa,* and *pops*—and others, too, if you wanted to expand into informal names for siblings, aunts, and uncles. And thirdly, it is stultifyingly boring (and therefore leads to error) just to work on one type of word. One of my colleagues, Sara Kirkham, was asked to work on the names of all of the muscles in the human body. When she'd finished, she asked politely never to be scheduled to edit a close thematic sequence ever again, as repetition on this scale was exhausting and not conducive to the necessary levels of concentration required.

There was one final *M-A* noun for us to process, and this was one for our scientific colleagues. Back in 1925, a group of scientists was casting about for a name for chemical element number 43. These scientists were in Germany. The existence of the chemical element had been predicted over fifty years earlier by Dmitri Mendeleev, who perceptively noted a gap in his periodic table. Mendeleev called the element *ekamanganese*, not because he was a poet, but because he predicted it would be chemically similar to the element manganese. Our German scientists begged to differ, and called it *masurium*, after the name of Lake Masuria—now in Poland—near to where the family of one of the scientists had originated. So much for linguistic reasoning. The *OED* was involved because scientists internationally had decided to use *Ma* as the shortened name of *masurium* in formulas, in the periodic table, and wherever else they might need a neat abbreviated version. We were grateful, of course, as it gave us yet another *M-A* word. The scientists, it seems, sadly became less enamoured of the name *masurium* over time, and in 1947—looking around for an even uglier name—invented *technetium* as the name of our old element 43, and this one seems to have stuck. Needless to say, element number 43 has provided a fair amount of work for lexicographers, but presumably more for chemists.

Tens of thousands of dictionary entries had to be edited in the same painstaking way we edited the *M-A* words. Even the simplest words require scrupulous attention to detail, though lexicographers become adept at making the right editorial decisions very fast. Nevertheless, even with our new recruits, we were not going to pull this off by the year 2000.

Despite *Ma* (masurium), our most complex definitions were normally those for scientific terminology. Science had always been problematic for the *OED*. The members of the Philological Society and other senior academic advisers involved with the fledgling dictionary in the late nineteenth century had been firmly of the view that they should sit on both sides of the fence where scientific vocabulary was concerned. The dictionary, they blared loudly to anyone listening, was going to contain the entire English language. Not a jot or a tittle was going to be omitted, and when it was completed, the British Empire would have a dictionary to be proud of. "What about the vocabulary of science?" Well, mumble-mumble-mumble, yes, it's very important but we certainly didn't mean that the dictionary should include all of that incomprehensible verbiage describing things the average educated chap didn't need to know about.

The editors themselves were more enlightened, and favoured the systematic inclusion of as much scientific vocabulary as would be of interest to the educated reader, rather than the eccentric or even mad scientist. In the end they included more or less all the scientific vocabulary they wanted to include, but on occasion took to defining terms in ways that only other deeply involved scientists could understand. So a definition of a scientific word might read like this:

> *acrolein:* a colourless acrid liquid, of pungent irritating odour, formed in the destructive distillation of glycerin (from which it is derived by the abstraction of two molecules of water, thus, Glycerin $C_3H_5(OH)_3$, Acrolein C_3H_4O"). It is the aldehyde of allyl, produced by the oxidation of allyl alcohol, and itself rapidly oxidizing to acrylic acid.

It is reasonable to assume that complex chemical or biological terminology cannot always be defined in a way that makes sense to ordinary people, but this entry (from 1884) is on the end of the jetty as far as abstruse is concerned, and was typical of the issues confronting our modern-day editors.

One day a while later, when revision had been proceeding for several years, the *OED*'s band of scientists working on the current revision met at one of their regular meetings to discuss science editorial policy, and came out of their huddle with the suggestion that they might consider making their scientific definitions more understandable to the general reader, and in fact that this should be the aim of their work. This notion ran counter to the drift of much scientific editing until this point in dictionary editing generally, but any suggestion of change had needed to come from within the fraternity to have any likelihood of success. Rather than let this suggestion fade, I encouraged it, and after a series of further meetings we developed a new science definition policy, driven through by a new breed of enlightened scientist led by my colleague Bill Trumble.

In essence, the *OED*'s science definitions would no longer be quite so classificatory (at least when it led to absurd results); if we needed obscure information, we would extract it from the main definition and insert it in a small-print note for Nobel-level scientists. The purpose or use of a term would from now on always be prominent in the definer's mind.

An example is worth a thousand words. The substance *rosenbuschite* was defined in the *Supplement to the OED* as "a fluorine-containing alumino-silicate of calcium, sodium, zirconium, and titanium occurring as radiating groups of slender triclinic crystals of an orange or grey colour." Most people would have picked up from this definition that this stuff (whatever it might be) was coloured orange or grey. As a result of the policy change, the comprehensible part of the definition was front-loaded to the beginning in the revised definition, and the most abstruse data, with the smaller readership, appeared last, in an associated note. The full definition now read: "A rare rock-forming mineral containing zirconium, occurring as slender orange or grey crystals, esp. in nepheline-syenites and pegmatites. [Note] Rosenbuschite is a fluorine-containing silicate of calcium, sodium, zirconium, and titanium, $(Ca,Na)_3(Zr,Ti)Si_2O_8F$. Crystal system: triclinic."

Democracy invaded our scientific definitions from this point on. Simplification for the reader made things more difficult for the editor, naturally—which was one of the reasons why it had not happened before. To write a complex definition, the editor needed to understand—at some depth—a complex issue. It is much easier to explain the issue using the terminology of complexity. It is another thing entirely, and requires yet another stage of experimentation and thought, to reduce that complexity to something simple. But from my point of view the dictionary always had to look simple, whatever intricacies it was hiding.

H ilary and I had been living in Oxford since I had started the job on the dictionary as a ragged-trousered young lexicographer back in 1976. But things were gradually reaching a critical point with Ellie. If events had run their normal course, she would have started attending the local primary school around now, as Kate had done before her. Up until this point, we had looked after Ellie ourselves, and she had been cared for privately at home and at a regular day nursery.

She had had numerous assessments over the years, and the end result of these was that we knew that her development had plateaued at an age of around eighteen months. Since then, there had been no measurable improvement. She was stuck, and we (along with the medical fraternity) had no idea what to do about it. But we did know that she was not "able" enough—in the jargon—to attend a "mainstream" school, even with extensive support.

At this point we began one of our battles with the education system to find a "special" school suitable for her. We didn't think of ourselves as the sort of parents who wanted additional support. We were quite able to cope on our own, and we didn't need support groups and state intervention and extra help. Probably Ellie wouldn't have minded where she went to school, as long as she was safe and loved.

We set about investigating the special schools in the area and chose one that seemed to fit most closely with her needs. It also had a pioneering reputation: let's try to give these youngsters a great start together—not apart, in a school that was "special," but in a school that was as integrated as it could be with the "mainstream" school on the same site. For me this meant driving a few miles out of Oxford each morning, to deliver Ellie to school, before turning round and heading back to the dictionary.

Time is different in the world of disability. You can't just turn up at roughly the right time, and wave goodbye as your child enters the playground. You need to be there at a very precise time to hand her over, and you need to observe the same time tyranny at pick-up time in the afternoon. In due course, we realised the only viable option was for us to move several miles out of Oxford to the village of Wheatley, where the school was located. That solved the deliver-and-collect issue, even though it threw up logistical problems for the rest of us. Fortunately, one of Ellie's classroom assistants, Teresa, lived near to us, and she brought Ellie home with her each day from school and looked after her until we returned from work. I'm not sure what we'd have done without her. She stayed with Ellie until Ellie left the school at sixteen, and we gave her a flying lesson as a present. I think she landed okay.

I hadn't abandoned my attempts to communicate with Ellie verbally, but we had found it was more helpful if we provided additional context through actions and signals—directing her with an arm towards the table, or opening our hands if we wanted her to come to us. We became adept at recognising nonverbal signs—the sort of signs that normally accompany and consolidate language, but in Ellie's case are all she has. She would push a person away if she didn't want company. She might cry out briefly, but not in pain (we assumed—and still assume), when she wanted a change of activity. But she can't tell you if she's hungry or thirsty or has a headache. You just have to know. But maybe she didn't need to communicate as much as we thought she did. She was happy, after all. At school the teachers would often write in her home diary "lots of smiles," "Ellie loved the music," "She just watched contentedly out of the window as we drove to the wildlife park." She was responsive, but not interventionist. For me it was frustrating, and continually pointed up a failing in my own power to communicate. But no one else seemed to be able to offer advice. I was used to going to books to find answers, but there were none here. It wasn't like language, where the obscurest point has been mulled over by linguists across the world. There was a resounding silence if I looked for mechanisms by which I could communicate with her. There was nothing. Compared to this, the dictionary work was easy. It used to remind me that often the meaning of the words we were defining was unclear without context: the surrounding words provided the equivalent of the gestures and nonverbal signs we had been developing with Ellie. But Ellie lived in a world with so little context that traditional meaning was largely irrelevant. In the end, it was more of a problem for us than for her.

Her doctors told us that even if researchers did find a cure for her condition, it was too late for her—she was already living with it, and cures only worked before the condition became embedded. So she had to live with this, as did we.

I n those days a strange thing was happening in the world of lexicography: research was moving online. Since time immemorial we had collected our data on index cards, from things called books. Back in 1989, when the Second Edition of the dictionary was published, we started collecting data (still from printed sources) on computer, and then filing our discoveries in what became a huge electronic database. As the 1990s took shape, things changed again, and we started to notice the possibilities that the World Wide Web and the Internet offered us from the perspective of routine historical dictionary research and publishing.

For a hundred years the dictionary staff had researched words on foot. Editors swept around the departmental library, and researchers padded softly around the wooden floors of national research libraries, in search of historical evidence for the language. But the earth was shifting. The Second Edition of the *OED* had been available on CD from 1992, and scholars were growing used to being able to search for information in the dictionary other than by "dictionary word." The *OED*'s editors were themselves becoming more familiar with this type of research just by having the searchable *OED* on their desktop computer. We soon discovered that the mass of historical text in the dictionary itself made it a remarkable research resource when we were searching for material on the history of words. To our amazement, we found hundreds of new first uses there, hidden away in other entries, and unlockable before digitalisation. Just one example: we found our first reference to *militia* as a locally organised fighting force of civilians (not professional soldiers) tucked away in a quotation for *folkmoot* (a local general assembly of the people): "Commanders of the Militia in every County were elected . . . in a full Falkmoth" (1642).

There had been signs of activity in the real world of electronic text in the late 1980s and early 1990s, and the *OED*'s editors were very early adopters of this trend. In the 1980s, editors had been accessing the Lexis/Nexis databases of American newspaper text and British legal material. The access system was quite primitive at first, and it was expensive to use, but we probed it cautiously. Results had to be printed out for the editor's perusal.

The Chadwyck-Healey English Poetry Database appeared on CD in 1992. That helped to excite people about the possibilities of text searching for research, but didn't shake our bones too much. The database offered access to an enormous mass of poetry written in English over the centuries. But adding quotations from poetry was not core business for the *OED*.

By 1995 we were using the huge Making of America (MoA) database, a collection of early American books and magazines published online—originally from texts held at the University of Michigan. This was one of the first online reference resources we picked up on as reference works began their shift away from the old-style CD format. We searched and searched this database, always surprised at how much new information we found about the *OED*'s words from the nineteenth and twentieth centuries: one first attestation out of hundreds we discovered (or recovered) was—somewhat surprisingly—for *magnetic compass*, from Michigan's *Biblical Repertory* of 1838. You never know where you will find useful material.

Over the course of the late 1990s, more and more databases became publicly available online, often through huge grant-funded agencies in America. We worried that American money was going to make American text more accessible than British, Australian, and other regional varieties of English, and for a time that was certainly the case. I worried that human library research, too, would become a thing of the past. But our library researchers hung on. It turned out that although we could extract remarkable swaths of historical material from the electronic databases, we sometimes needed the raw brainpower and ingenuity of a researcher to track a problem right down to earth: there was room for both research techniques.

As we became more familiar with this new research technology, we appointed research assistants to work exclusively on finding useful online material, so that it was already in place when an editor came to work on a word. Milestones included the availability of the Chadwyck-Healey Literature Online (LION) database in 1998, and the extraordinary Early English Books Online (EEBO), a collaboration of a consortium of universities including Michigan and Oxford in 1999. EEBO gradually made more and more books and pamphlets from the beginning of printing in the late 1400s until 1700 searchable or readable in facsimile online. It has been a stunning resource for historians. One example amongst thousands, again, was the new first example of *radiancy* (the fact of being radiant), from Michael Drayton's *Endimion and Phoebe*, published in 1595: "Her richest Globe shee gloriously displayes, / Now that the Sun had hid his golden rayes: / Least that his radiencie should her suppresse." How did the original Victorian readers for the *OED* miss that? Were they dreaming? But it is far harder to recognise first uses than you might think. Google Books appeared in

2004, offering lexicographers new worlds of words to search through; Britain fought back in 2007 with the British Library Nineteenth-Century Newspaper Collection: our first use of *Red Bank oyster* (found off County Clare) now comes from the Dublin *Freeman's Journal*, thanks to the British Library collection.

Did we trust these sources? That was tricky. Most of the early texts were scanned on to computer, and the scanning software often found old typography hard to understand (you'll remember that the *OED* had been keyed on to computer, then proofread, and so was a virtually faultless digitised representation of the original). To overcome scanner problems, databases soon started offering links to facsimile versions of the documents they had scanned. That was good—you could rely on facsimiles you could see. But however good your search software is, you cannot search successfully for something that has been garbled in the first place when scanned. It's still a problem with some sites.

Did this online material let us work faster? No—the sheer quantity meant that we had to apply pragmatic rules to the number of databases we accessed, or risk being swamped. That was parallel to the old rule from the regime of library research which said that you could spend twice as much time on a word, but only improve your research by 1 percent—so at some point you hit steeply diminishing returns and had to call a sharp halt.

What happened to all of that material collected for well over a century on index cards? Well, we operated a hybrid system. Editors had the old cards on their desks alongside the computers as they searched the new online data.

I used to ask myself whether we were in danger of being mesmerised by these treasure troves of historical quotations, to the extent that we would begin to neglect our definitions and etymologies in the search for better and better documentation. But better documentary evidence worked the other way—every aspect of each entry received a boost from this new data. The dictionary's traditional "readers" have largely survived the transition, too. They find earlier and better uses of terms which computers can't (in the jargon) disambiguate—distinguish from other similar uses. A human reader can understand nuance in a way that the computer cannot always recognise.

Most of the entries we researched benefited from the data accessible through the Internet. By the time we revised the entry for *hotdog*, in 2008, those incremental Internet discoveries had changed the face of our understanding of the sausage.

There was no entry for *hotdog* in the original edition of the *OED*. If there had been, it would have been published in 1899 in the letter *H*. In fact, the expression did exist—as we now know—at that time, but only on the streets and in the colleges of North America, a long way from the collection bowls of the *OED* researchers. And in 1899, *hotdog* was only just starting to make its presence felt.

It wasn't until 1976, a couple of months after I joined up with the *OED*, that it crept into the second volume of the *Supplement to the OED* (no thanks to me). In those days, we, or at least my immediate predecessors, were firmly of the view that the word *hotdog* had three meanings. The earliest, dating (it was thought) from 1896, was "someone who is skilled or proficient in some activity" (someone, presumably, who was pretty "hot" at it). The second meaning, chronologically, was the sausage in a roll (recorded since 1900). The final sense was some kind of surfboard smaller than a "big gun," known from the 1960s. Beyond that, the entry didn't seem to offer much in the way of a coherent explanation for the word's chronology or semantic development.

When we came to update the *hotdog* entry in 2008, the Internet caused us to reconsider it from the ground up. We knew (because we subscribed to his journal) that an American scholar had been busy publishing earlier and yet earlier examples of *hotdog* for several years, and of late most of his discoveries had been made online. These discoveries would have a big effect on our entry. Other online researchers had been at work on the word too. Earlier examples than the ones the *OED* knew about had been discovered, for the most part, in old issues of local American newspapers of the sort that had been pouring on to the Internet in recent years, for those who knew how to find them.

What became clear was that the *OED* had got it wrong in 1976. Online historical research into the hotdog revealed that the "sausage" sense was really top dog. Constant research for hotdogs in earlier American newspapers by editors and researchers throughout the world had resulted in an example being found as early as 1884, from an Indiana newspaper called the *Evansville Daily Courier*. (I wondered whether the people in Evansville knew about this, whether they were proud of it, and whether they were desperately hoping that someone wouldn't find an earlier example in a newspaper from, say, Des Moines or Milwaukee.)

Worse still, once our lexicographers had looked closely at the earliest recorded examples of *hotdog* in our possession, they realised that in these early examples the word didn't mean "a frankfurter" or "a sausage laid to rest in a bread roll," but "sausage-meat." Here's the Evansville reference: "Even the innocent 'wienerworst' man will be barred from dispensing hot dog on the street corner." That's "sausage-meat," however it is dressed up, even if it is dressed up as a hotdog. If you don't see a difference, that's one of the reasons you're not working on the *OED*. One is an individual thing (a sausage) and the other is a type (sausage, or sausage-meat).

Editors' ears were pricking up, as we would now have official sanction to break the meaning into two. We had identified the collective "sausage-meat" meaning from 1884, and the "frankfurter" meaning from a few years later (not unreasonably) in 1892. For this second meaning, the Internet had provided us with a reference from the *Paterson Daily Press* in New Jersey: "The 'hot dog' was quickly inserted in a gash in a roll, a dash of mustard also splashed on to the 'dog' with a piece of flat whittled stick, and the order was fulfilled." (Surprisingly, I haven't heard that the inhabitants of Paterson have been out on the streets celebrating, but there's still time.) One more thing: some jokesters suggested that *hotdog* first meant "sausage-meat" because it was sarcastically (I hope) first said to have consisted of warmed-up dog meat. You can decide whether you believe that. Pass the sauce.

This earth-shattering news about the sausage-type hotdog is bad news for the "skilled or proficient" meaning. That is bumped down to second place, dating now from 1894. This time, the reference—captured online—is from a University of Michigan "humour magazine" called *Wrinkle*. I'm sad to report that nothing much has happened to the surfboard sense; it is still bringing up the rear from the 1960s.

Access to the Internet, by dictionary editors and by any other interested party, could have profound effects on any one of the *OED*'s entries. That made working on each entry even more of a challenge than it had been before, but it also meant that the rewards were far greater. There was such a clatter of text available for analysis that you could almost feel that you were with those eighteenth-century ladies discussing their hair-styles, or inching forward with the Cavalier forces during the English Civil War. You always had additional context to whatever you were defining, and sometimes it seemed as if you were caught in the middle of a novel whose storyline involved the tracking and capturing and unmasking of your word. It was a race against time, too. If you missed a clear antedating, and the entry was published online, then someone else would pick it up and email the dictionary. You didn't want that to happen if you could help it. On the other hand, that was a safety net: the dictionary was dynamic, and it would change like the language whether you wanted it to or not.

The *OED* moved online in several stages. It would have been enough of a change if the dictionary had only benefited from the availability of the astounding pools of raw, historical materials that these new databases brought us in the 1990s and beyond. But that was not all. Right at the time when those first databases of online text were becoming available in 1993—and the *OED*'s new North American reading programme was up and running efficiently—my colleague Jeffery Triggs, in New Jersey, was able to turn his attention to other things, and in this case it was how to put the *OED* on the Internet.

In Oxford in 1993 the suggestion that the *OED* might migrate away from being at heart a printed book would have been sacrilege. There are lots of things that Oxford University and the University Press (beyond the dictionary) were extremely good at, but at that time, foreseeing the value of the Internet was not at the top of the list. Jeffery, however, realised that it would be possible to write software to publish the *OED* as a fully searchable online database. He started coding, and he liked coding. After a few weeks he had thousands of lines of code, and he told me what he was planning. We had the *OED* on CD, and it was proving a great success with scholars and researchers, not just in the field of language, but across the spectrum of disciplines. What Jeffery wanted to do was to transfer the search and display capabilities of the dictionary on CD to the new Internet, so that it wasn't just accessible to the CD user, but to anyone across the world. We didn't really know where it would end, but no one else seemed to have managed to do this with a massive, complex reference text. This was off-plan. No one had agreed to it yet, because no one knew about it. The *OED* had led the way in the past, and perhaps this was where it had a chance to lead again. At the same time, it could draw a new generation of users into its net.

To start with, we didn't tell Oxford what we were up to. We wanted to get just a bit further along to see how practical the whole plan might be. So by day I was a regular dictionary editor, as we progressed through *M* into *N* (fortunately a very short letter), and then into the vowel *O* (full of awkward prepositions, adverbs, and prefixes that take ages to edit—try *on*, *off*, *out*, and *omni-* for size); and in the evenings Jeffery and I were exchanging ideas across the Atlantic on how best to replicate, on the Web, the functionality of the *OED* on CD, and how to do new things with the dictionary—things that no one had thought of doing before—such as linking the *OED* quotations to the texts they came from.

This seemed to me the most important thing I could do for the *OED*, after hammering out its editorial policy for the future. We were battling to keep the *OED* relevant by updating it editorially, but we saw that the updated dictionary would be twice as powerful if it could be accessible to a new and wider audience online. Jeffery and I didn't keep our experimentation to ourselves for long. Soon I let Ed in on what was happening, and he, too, was excited by the opportunities. We trooped along to the dictionary's business director, the Admiral, who could also—fortunately—see the possibilities of this new vision for reference works. A bit later, in 1995, once we had a prototype of the *OED* online and running smoothly, we showed it privately to some decision makers in the University and the University Press; sadly, they didn't seem to be able to imagine how an online dictionary fitted into a traditional book-publishing outfit like the University Press (the inability to see beyond the past is known to lovers of punctuation as the "Oxford coma").

Naturally, we thought we were right all the same, so we carried on. Soon we had an online prototype that anyone around the world with online access could visit and use for their research. The only problem was that it was in secret development; no one knew it existed except a handful of us in Oxford and a few friends and acquaintances in computer science departments in America. It was one of the first five hundred sites on the Web, so in reality, not many people had the faintest idea how this sort of technology worked in the first place. Nowadays there are over 3 billion Internet users; when work started on the OED Online there were only 14 million, and they were mostly using email, discussion forums, bulletin boards—and a bit of e-commerce.

Back in the dictionary offices, we were getting used to our new open-plan environment, which seemed fitting for the collaborative expansion and scholarly openness we were keen to promote. Several huge pillars holding up the ceiling stood in the centre of the office. On these—in keeping with our low-tech coloured progress strip of the 1980s—we plastered paper progress charts which the editors marked in pencil as they reached the end of a task. Somehow it meant we were still in control of things and hadn't ceded responsibility. Once we had become adept at researching our words in an expanding online environment, we started to turn our attention towards online editing of dictionary entries. Up to this point in the early 1990s, the extensive changes to the text of the Second Edition of the dictionary had been marked by editors on double-spaced printouts, which had then been passed around the various editorial groups (etymology, bibliography, science, new words, etc.) who needed to review and revise different aspects of the text. We had text-editing software from the old days in the 1980s for merging *OED* and *Supplement* text, but this wasn't available to all the editors, and our marked-up printouts were keyed to our dictionary database by specialist keyboarders.

Later in the 1990s our text-editing software became resilient enough to allow online editing by all editors. For the publisher, online editing meant cutting one step in the publication process, with the possibility of saving money; for the editors it provided a higher level of control and satisfaction. There were academic arguments at dictionary conferences over whether lexicography was an art or a craft. It is both, but the online text editor gave us scope—depending on the particular editor and the particular word edited—of foregrounding either the artistic impulse to present a beautiful and coordinated entry, or to weave— craft-like—the complex threads and skeins of the entry into a pleasing whole. The computer screens containing the text of a dictionary entry were themselves a mass of vivid colours. Each slice of information (the definition, the etymology, all of the parts of a quotation, etc.) was allocated its own personal colour—maybe to help us remember which section of the entry we were working in. Most editors quickly became adept at **online** editing.

We have had the word *line* in English since the earliest days, when it mainly meant a length of string or rope. But it's been around long enough by now to have developed many sub-meanings and new branches. One of those new branches is the word *online*, and because we have so many different "lines" (telephone, shipping, air travel, consumer products, etc.), it's hardly surprising that *online* can live in various contexts. Obviously the digital use of *online* is a fairly recent innovation. *Online* started life as a railway term. In fact, the *OED* says we have to start our investigation with *offline*, back in 1919. I suppose that's not really surprising, as more things are offline than are online. In early twentieth-century railway days, a warehouse was *offline* if it was not immediately connected to a railway, and you had to trans-port goods for a distance by lorry to get them to the freight train. If you were *online* (recorded from 1926), then things were a lot easier, as your manufacturing facility was right next to the railway track and all ready to ship freight by train.

If we move on to the 1940s, we find a similar distinction happen-ing on the airlines (most early air-flight terminology comes from ship-ping, sometimes via railways). We had shipping lines well before we had airlines; pilots guided boats before they guided planes. In 1940s' flight jargon, a stop was "online" if it was one of the authorised stops used by an airline, and "offline" if it wasn't.

The big jump to computing happened soon after this. The *OED* records both *offline* and *online* from 1950 in relation to operations or processes that take place while connected to (or not connected to) a computer system. As with our editing, you could be "online" just by being connected to a computer system. Our research and publica-tion was online in the slightly newer sense of being connected to the Internet.

For the newer editors, who hardly knew the old ways, online edit-ing was the only way forward. They were used to manipulating their mobile phones and SMS communications in a way that the old guard, such as Ed and myself, were not. One or two editors were unhappy with the way things were going. You could see that they wouldn't last.

But I was excited by the possibilities, and with working out how to make those possibilities into realities. In all areas of our work (editing, research, publication), I wanted to find ways of retaining the standards of the past, and maintaining the intellectual rigour and discipline of what we were achieving, while making the process of capturing those standards easier and extending exponentially the profusion of ways we could display, present, analyse, and reuse our data by storing it online.

Researching and editing online created new issues, of course. New editorial and logistical problems arose daily that we had to address and solve. Different research databases had different kinds of search software and held their text in different ways. Working with them wasn't simply a question of keying your request into an anonymous search engine. Take a simple example: when researching words, we continually wanted to search for two-word compounds in modern and historical text. But the problem was—or at least one of the problems was—that they could be found in print in any of three different forms: e.g., *table cloth*, *table-cloth*, and *tablecloth*. The quick-eyed amongst you will notice that sometimes the term is written as one word, and sometimes as two, and sometimes gracefully split by a hyphen. And surprisingly enough, this doesn't only happen with the word *tablecloth*. It happens all the time. So when dictionary editors were searching computer text in those old days, they typically had to perform three separate searches to find all the relevant examples they needed. This was before we were all familiar with repetitive-strain injury.

Some of the high-use research databases were controlled by us (our reading-programme database, for example). For these databases, it seemed a small thing to write a tiny computer program to allow us to search for all three formats at once, and indeed it was. But as with any simple but crucial development (I'm giving this one more credit than it's due, as I devised it), it's not the program that is important, but the very first spark of the idea. I remember the jaw of the editor of Toronto's *Dictionary of Old English* bouncing on the ground when I explained to her that we could do this. She put her programmer on to replicating it that very afternoon.

Alongside the innovations in research and editing, we were still promoting the transfer of the full *OED* to the Internet, both as a means of searching and displaying its contents, and as a way of publishing our new and revised entries incrementally. These ideas would involve the University Press in a major change of plan, and one where failure might prove embarrassing, if not catastrophic. But over the previous decade and more, the *OED* had attracted risk, and had survived. We argued that online publication was a new and justifiable risk, and in fact a risk that the dictionary had to take to survive.

The prototype online *OED* devised in the mid-1990s was our starting point. We drew up plans to rewrite the software to industry standards (about which I knew nothing, but which was clearly the way to go). The plans involved selling the online version, as the University Press had to recoup some of its massive investment. Would universities, businesses, the public, take up a subscription scheme? And now at last we had our own marketing director, Susanna Lob, dedicated single-mindedly to convincing the universities of the world (and anyone else who wanted access) that they needed to subscribe to the OED Online. This wasn't the sort of thing that university libraries at the time wanted to do with their annual budgets, but even they could see the wind was changing. From our point of view, we weren't used to marketeers who understood and appreciated what the *OED* was up to in the way that Susanna did. But she used to say that selling the as-yet-non-existent OED Online to librarians was the easiest job she'd ever done. It more or less sold itself. People immediately sensed the possibilities—librarians could see that this wasn't just a dictionary, but an opportunity to introduce their users to a journey through language and through the different chambers of knowledge. It was considered—by those in the know—that, rather than try to attract all types of users in the first instance, we should concentrate on whole-university and whole-college subscriptions, which would be purchased by librarians. We were experimenting as much as they were, and starting there would give us valuable experience on how to market the dictionary online in the future.

We went on a focus-group tour across the United States in 1999 to demo what we had and to seek comments for last-minute changes. It will be a long time before I forget the audible gasp that erupted from a focus-group audience in America when I clicked a key and linked from one of the *OED*'s millions of quotations to a page showing the relevant passage of the book from which the quotation was taken. That sort of thing is easy now, but back in 1999 it was cutting edge.

But the biggest change for us, editorially, was that we would no longer be running a project where nothing was published until the whole work was completed. It was hard to motivate editors who might not still be on the staff (through old age or infirmity) to see the fruits of their labour. By publishing online, we could now be publishing incremental updates to the dictionary at quarterly intervals for the foreseeable future—even after the main revision was done. No other dictionary had plans like this. It was what we should have been doing, and at last the University Press was behind it.

Our plan was to go online in March 2000 with the full Second Edition (1989) and the very first instalment of newly revised entries. With a growing sense of concern, we looked at those early entries from *M* which we had edited in draft over five years earlier. Sure enough, it was clear we needed to rework them significantly before publishing, as much more information about the *M* words was now available on the Internet. We needed to find that data before our reviewers and users did. We had about a year left to bring this about, and so we had to get our skates on.

Fortunately we had a cupboard full of skates, and we set about brushing up those old *M* entries. We decided that the first instalment would only include a thousand new entries, which didn't take us far into *M*, but would serve as a clear indication of things to come. The Internet was transforming what we knew about our words, and I enjoyed pushing *mad scientist* back from 1940 to 1893, and finding the *Mafia* in Sicily in 1866 (rather than 1875, as *The Times* had formerly led the editors to believe). In the changed world, we could never have published those entries as we had first left them—although they had seemed fine at the time. There were new standards now.

We were also drawn down some curious sidetracks. Since the publication of the Second Edition of the *OED*, the whole project was becoming more visible to the public, and some companies had done their best to clamber on to the bandwagon of the dictionary's success. A couple of these ambushes were quite extreme. At one point, the University Press's offices in Oxford were the object of a small demonstration by the British Potato Council on behalf of their wards (the potatoes themselves). The argument—such as it was—ran along the lines that the *OED* was disrespecting the potato by including an entry for *couch potato*. Clearly, the demonstrators were people, not potatoes, as the potatoes were far too idle to get off their sofas in their own support. But things died down once the company had achieved whatever publicity it was after. We fearlessly refused to budge from our position that people had the right to read an entry for *couch potato* in the *OED*, and we returned to our lairs wondering whether to seek revenge by downsizing our entries for *chip* and *spud*.

We had a similar altercation with some purveyors of lettucy salads. The organisation's representatives complained that the *OED*'s definition of *salad* regarded it as a cold collation, whereas they (marketeers of salads of all kinds) wanted us to recognise the existence of the *warm salad*. Our entry for *salad* had not been updated since 1909, so it was not surprising that it was a bit out of date. Updating it was, after all, the purpose of the new edition we were all working on. This time we deflated our demonstrators by agreeing with them.

When I had first taken up my desk at the *OED* in 1976, life was very much as it had been in Victorian Oxford. Editors researched the history of their words by pacing around the reference shelves and the card indexes of the dictionary department, and wrote hopeful little research-request notes to colleagues working in libraries in Oxford, London, New York, Washington, and elsewhere. Definitions were written out on index cards, and batches of cards were sent off at fairly reasonable intervals to the printer to be turned into *OED* pages.

March 2000 arrived, and the University Press's publicity machine geared up for the *OED* going online. The University Press had little or no prior experience of running a campaign around an online product, but its marketing and publicity specialists were never short of new ideas. Our publicity campaign was led by me discussing the dictionary with a somewhat precocious five-year-old descendant of the original editor of the *OED*. The small Murray had nothing new to say about the dictionary, but he smiled cheerfully for the photographers, and demonstrated continuity, and friendliness and charm, and whatever else the publicity machine had hoped for.

We had wanted to open up the dictionary—to make it easier to use. We had wanted to open up access to a wider readership. We had wanted to incorporate the newly accessible information about language from the Internet. We had wanted to publish the Third Edition of the dictionary. It's not as if everything we had ever wished for had come true, but we were on the way—and we had to let the dictionary find its place in this new world. I had spoken to the tiny descendant of the original founding editor. It was March 2000, and the dictionary was at last launched on its new life online.

TWELVE

Flavour of the Month

O nce we had gone online, we suddenly became **flavour of the month** within the University Press. The dictionary was certainly not making a profit, but we were at last returning a ripple of revenue to the organisational coffers rather than sustaining the generous losses that the dictionary had traditionally delivered ever since it was first published in 1884. The fact that almost every university in the known world—or at least the English-speaking part of it—was subscribing to the OED Online meant that the future of the dictionary suddenly felt more secure. I should really have realised that we were starting to be regarded internally as another "brand," rather than as a research project, and that this might in future make us susceptible to "brand management." But as usual I missed this.

It is not unusual for expressions to arise quietly in particular contexts, but then to attract public notice to the extent that they drift into the mainstream. According to the dictionary, we have the Illinois Association of Ice Cream Manufacturers to thank for the expression *flavour of the month*. The *Ice Cream Review* for September 1946 (yes, we read everything) reported that the Illinois ice-men were giving "serious study" to a proposed "flavour-of-the-month" programme for 1947. Apparently it wasn't until the 1970s that we even thought of using "flavour of the month" in any context outside ice cream.

Although the OED Online had solidified our position within the University, it also created new problems. By daring to publish and update the dictionary online—and especially by keeping entries continually up to date once they had been revised and published—we were taking something of a gamble that people would be brave enough to accept that there is no absolute truth about language; that as soon as we published an updated entry, it was out of date and liable to change. Scholars—or just ordinary members of the public—could mail us with even newer and better evidence that they had managed to squeeze out of their memories or their data-bases. And they did. No sooner had we announced to the world that the earliest record of the word *numismatics* dated from 1803 than we were informed that it also had occurred in 1790—as we hadn't thought to check in Adolf Ristell's *Characters and Anecdotes of the Court of Sweden* of that year. But this didn't annoy us—it was what was supposed to happen. We had initiated what was effectively an international challenge to beat us—and at the same time improve the record of the language. It was the sort of democratic user engagement I thrived on. We didn't seem to attract time-wasters, either. So we made these changes to the database as soon as we could, to keep the dictionary dynamic. The alternative was to stick our heads firmly in the sand, draw a firm line of demarcation (once again in the sand), or do whatever other things people did with sand to show they didn't want to move with the times.

This race to keep up to date created an enormous amount of editorial spade-work for us. While the Internet had made certain kinds of research much easier and quicker to accomplish, there were still a great many issues that couldn't be solved by the Internet. Sometimes we just had to pull on our old detective leggings and venture out into the real world in search of information. One day we were working quietly away in the letter *P* when we came to revise the entry for *pal* (in the sense of "a friend" or "mate"). The *OED* had published its original entry for the word back in 1904. It had found that, in the vocabulary of the day, *pal* was a "Gipsy" word that had reverberated across Europe as the travelling community had spread it generously around, taking it into other languages as well as English. It had, the *OED* told us, entered English in the late seventeenth century. First of all, it had been used for the most part in quite disreputable company: a *pal* was a highwayman's accomplice, for example, or a thief's associate. It was only later, in the late eighteenth or early nineteenth century, that it settled down to have the "chummy" sort of meaning we know today.

The very first quotation example for the word *pal* in the dictionary proved to be a problem. It dated from 1682 and was supposed to mean "a criminal accomplice." This example didn't come from a printed book, but from a set of legal depositions or statements kept in a manuscript in the Hereford Diocesan Records. At some point in the dim past, a Friend of the *OED* had sat for hours with his slippers and pipe in a comfy armchair in the vestry at Hereford Cathedral, or wherever these records were kept in those days, and had read through legal deposition after legal deposition looking for word usages that might be of interest to the *OED* editors back on dry land.

Reading diocesan records is a praiseworthy activity, though it's not a pastime I've ever toyed with. In fact, I positively encouraged lexicographers to consult non-traditional, non-print records. But I was suspicious about this one. Here it is—see if it strikes you as odd:

> Wheare have you been all this day, pall? . . . Why, pall, what would
> you have mee to doe? (*Hereford Diocesan Register: Depositions* (1682),
> 29 January, p. 51)

There's nothing obviously wrong with this example (*pal* might easily be recorded with a double-l at that time), but to me the conversation just didn't sound right. There was an edge of formality about what the

First Edition of the dictionary had analysed as a conversation between thieves.

Based on my hunch, I decided to pursue it. I was due a day out of the office, so one morning I drove off in the direction of Hereford. I had taken the precaution of ascertaining beforehand that the manuscript registers that I wanted to consult were no longer at the cathedral, but were now held for safekeeping and ease of research at the County Record Office.

I arrived at the Herefordshire Record Office just before lunch and outlined my problem to the archivist. He was both puzzled and courteous. I explained that I wanted to find the relevant deposition and to confirm from the context that the meaning of *pal* used in the 1682 example was the meaning (= "accomplice," or maybe "friend") assumed for it by the *OED* back in 1904.

He wandered back to his store cupboard and came back with a collection of books and boxes that were not what I was looking for. Obviously, the archive shelf reference had changed at the time when the Record Office had accepted all of these diocesan depositions from the cathedral, and there was no known finding-list which would tell us where this particular text was now located. After much head-scratching on my part, and continued puzzlement on behalf of the kindly archivist, I eventually found a reference to a document that I thought might be the holy grail. After another wander back to the store-room, the archivist returned with a further dusty offering. I sat down and turned to page 51, as directed by the *OED*, and (eureka) found the reference. (For those of you eager to get on your bikes and read it for yourselves, the archive reference in Hereford is HD4/4/3, and the depositions are filed under the heading "Hereford Consistory Court Records.")

You would hope that that would be the end of this story, but it simmers on for a while longer. I transcribed the whole deposition and drove back to Oxford to give it my full concentration. I showed it to

Ed Weiner, and we worked out the problem: this was a statement addressed to one Mary Ashmoore, who was accused of some hanky-panky (not the term used in the deposition) with a male friend. This male friend was recounting for the church court a conversation he had had with Mary. The context was not that of one shady type talking to his "pal," but of a man recalling a snatch of familiar conversation with a woman with whom he was having a relationship. He wouldn't have called her his "pal" or his "mate." But we knew that *Poll* was an informal variety of the name *Mary*, and that *Pall* is a regional by-form of *Poll*. (You get from *Mary* to *Poll* through *Molly* and *Polly*.) So the gallant swain was not calling Mary his "pal," but simply using a nickname that he might have used of anyone called Mary. Case solved, and that quotation had to go out of the *OED*.

That was a problem for us. We left a little note explaining what had happened in the *pal* entry, in case anyone was confused by the disappearance of what might seem an acceptable example. And then we set about validating the remaining evidence, to see what was now the earliest reference we had for *pal* in the sense of "accomplice" or "mate." We had to jump forward in time as far as 1770, to a "choice collection of songs" published under the name of *The Humourist*: "Let your Pal that follows behind, / Tip your Bulk pretty soon." But this was the right sense ("accomplice"); a *bulk* is another type of accomplice, in the same pickpocketing scam. Although the exploded 1682 example would have been acceptable chronologically (Romany words did enter English as early as that), the meaning and context there were wrong. By 1770 we had found our new first example, in the correct meaning.

We couldn't go on field trips every day, but this one is a reminder of the value of paper-based research, conducted in conversation with an expert who can guide you through an archive. It is also a salutary reminder that even something in the *OED* may have been misinterpreted—that lexicographers should never accept anything at face value. Beware of relying simply on yourself or on the Internet.

One unexpected side effect of the publicity surrounding the *OED* going online was that rumours of our existence somehow reached Europe. From the point of view of language, Britain (or the United Kingdom, as we are frequently called in Europe) is an anomaly. The Europeans just couldn't understand why the British government didn't take a controlling interest in the *OED*, given the apparent economic value of the English language throughout the world. Furthermore, if the British government had taken a lively interest in the dictionary, then the various European governments could have easily found someone official to bombard with letters of complaint about the expansion of English into their languages.

But the British government cleverly observed language from the sidelines. Whereas in Europe, language was the prerogative of every Department of Culture between Lisbon and Warsaw, in Britain language issues straddled various departments (Education, Health, Culture, etc.), without overall responsibility for the language settling anywhere. To us in Britain, there are Orwellian overtones to language planning, and we dismiss the model developed by some European countries of having state-authorised spelling lists and embargoes on incoming foreign words (regarded as stunting their language, as homegrown alternatives are unable to establish themselves). But we are oblivious to the wider language issues in Europe stemming from the widespread use of English, because these issues do not affect Britain: most graduate programmes in the sciences in European universities are nowadays taught in English, and theses are predominantly written in English; major international companies in some countries—Germany, for example—use English as their internal company language. There are two sides to every question, as the old proverb wisely says.

The British government leaves the English language largely to itself, at least on the face of it. Arguably, the language is so pervasive, with bases on almost every continent, and a worldwide presence as a second language, that it would be too difficult to control anyway. We could never achieve a universal agreement for even the smallest change from each of the main language varieties. It is confusing to many Europeans that the British government does not have any legal control of the English language: English is only a de facto official language in England, as it is in the United States at the federal level, Australia, and New Zealand. In other English-speaking regions the situation is different, and in Scotland, Ireland, Wales, Canada, and South Africa (as well as in numerous US states), the status of English as an official language is confirmed by legislation.

Europeans have been concerned about the aggressive advance of English into their languages. *Le Weekend.* O.K. Internet. Football. Eurostar. (Even if the last is not an English word, they probably assumed it was.) Different European countries take different views, and some are more liberal than others. So there is either consternation or resigned acceptance (and occasionally even satisfaction) that if three European citizens of different nationalities meet together, they will often converse in English as a lingua franca, as we say. Two, probably. You can see why it has been a worry in Continental Europe.

Around the year 2000, a group of European language specialists decided to sit down and work out how to counter the emerging global threat of the spread of English. The best thing to do was apparently to have a meeting, followed by another meeting. Gradually they formed an organisation containing two members of every member state of the European Union except Britain (as we were the problem). But gradually, light dawned, and they realised that if we were the problem, then it couldn't be resolved without involving us.

Here was the difficulty again. Britain didn't have an official academy charged with maintaining, improving, monitoring, protecting, or in any way supervising the English language, and so it was hard for this new organisation to decide whom to invite to represent English. They decided that in the absence of a government representative they might as well email me on the *OED*, as we had been in the news recently and appeared to have some involvement with the English language. *Faute de mieux*, as we say when we are trying to get out of a tight spot and don't want to involve the English language.

They asked if I would consider representing Britain in what they hoped would become a new trans-European language organisation, soon named the European Federation of National Institutions for Language, or EFNIL. The organisation had several objectives: it was a network of linguists and language-planners who met to exchange ideas and to hear about the changing language situation across Europe; it was available for expert opinion on language should the European Commission require such information; and it was a major proponent of multilingualism and the maintenance of the national languages of Europe.

I was initially extremely cautious about their offer to join. Insular Britain isn't known for its multilingualism; we have no language-planners; we aren't particularly concerned about the spread of English around Europe (though we didn't think it would eradicate any other language). Since Anglo-Saxon times, after all, English had done nothing else except accept words from the European languages—or so we felt—and it didn't seem to have done us much harm. So what was the worry? But I took the precaution of seeking advice from as close to the British government as my tentacles extended at the time, and was indeed encouraged to involve myself in the workings of the organisation, but to sit quietly in the corner, in true, diplomatic British fashion, and to observe, and be inactive.

Naturally, each country (including Britain) had its own idiosyncrasies and played up to its own stereotypes. The old countries of Europe (except, notably, Italy) generally wanted to preserve their languages free of incursion from abroad (i.e., English); the newer East European countries were still at a stage where they felt that the best way to secure linguistic independence and equality for their citizens was through strict legislation; the Dutch and some of the Nordic countries had regular spelling reforms, and were unable to understand the English position where spelling has veered so far away from pronunciation, and perhaps too far to pull it back. Most countries realised that the dominance of English today has more to do with the economic dominance of America than with the United Kingdom itself (and so were on occasions prepared to let Britain off the hook). And they consoled themselves that Latin seemed to have had a similar position of superiority in the Middle Ages, and where is it now? etc. But even in my concern about each country "defending" its language, I was conscious of falling into a national isolationist stereotype. Other big European languages—such as French and German—are protective not only of their own language, but of the languages of other European countries, whereas the British do not usually think to consider how Slovakians (for example) feel about incursions into their own language from English (or German). This issue of survival is a live concern for the smaller Scandinavian languages and for some of the languages in the EU countries of Eastern Europe. Was Britain too isolationist? Or is it the opposite: Is the British interest in language wider than Europe—does it have global perspective? The whole experience was challenging and at the same time satisfying, inasmuch as the British point of view was clearly better appreciated the longer I remained involved, and I think I understood other European views better by regular discussion of them.

In the end I played a more active role in EFNIL than I expected. In the early 2000s, I would regularly set off with my passport, a map, and a pocketful of Euros to innumerable meetings about stabilising and promoting the languages of Europe. Almost my first act was to insist that we talk not about "defending" one language from another—which was for me quite the wrong rhetoric—but monitoring language change and promoting linguistic diversity. The British are in general bad at learning foreign languages and the general concept of linguistic diversity, but I agreed with the multilingual objective that EFNIL and the European Commission promoted: that state educational systems should promote the knowledge of two languages as well as the country's native tongue. It's just that dotting the *i*'s and crossing the *t*'s on a European document doesn't mean the British will play the game and sign on for language evening classes.

After several years of shadow-boxing, and under the benevolent chairmanship of a German colleague from the Institute of the German Language (they don't, apparently, give it an English name yet), we started to make progress, or at least to understand each other's positions much better. The organisation is an excellent example of European specialists working very well together in an area (language) where they have traditionally been isolated from and suspicious of each other. That, at least, is a good start.

Although I was on the executive committee, it appeared that my main job was to represent the acceptable face of English. After years of practice in this earlier in my career, I found that I was entirely able to sit through long meetings in which Britain was (in the early years) implicitly criticised for allowing its language to creep like a vine throughout Europe, and yet at the end to propose a collaborative course of action to which others often assented. In due course, the undercurrent of linguistic antipathy towards English evaporated, and so my slow-burning efforts at collaboration and consolidation appeared to have worked. To add to the advantages, I made some close friends, and their advice on aspects of the *OED* and the English language over the years has been very valuable. Knowing many of the language planners in Europe has enormous benefits (well, obviously not to everybody).

The language issues in my family were of a quite different order than those I encountered at work or in Europe. Hilary had always regarded the dictionary with some amusement: if a request for funding a historical dictionary had come before her, as adviser to Oxfordshire County Council's chief executive, the amusement would probably have turned to an outright laugh. Kate was at university by now, at Bath, studying French and Italian, and with a preference for translation. Ellie was still at home with us, languageless and approaching the end of her years at the special school, and we were beginning to think once again about her future and how to provide the best for her.

We were used to Ellie being different by now, and we recognised over the years that she was regarded as one of the most profoundly disabled students at her school. The school at that time only took pupils up to the age of sixteen, and so, after considerable difficulties of the sort that all parents of disabled children regularly encounter—we managed to find a suitable placement for her in the special-needs department of a local sixth-form college. The downside was that the college was a forty-five-minute drive away from our home, and we needed the local authority to provide transportation for her (for which we had to argue vociferously).

Ellie still had a developmental age of about eighteen months, even though she was sixteen and looked like a normal, pretty teenager. In the end, she stayed at Henley College for three years and had a wonderful time. We didn't receive written reports of her progress, but her tutor—Mark—used to sing them to us and to Ellie on his guitar at her termly review meetings.

Ellie continued to live at home until she was nineteen. Every evening we'd welcome her back from college, feed her, play with her, change her as and when required, bathe her, and put her to bed. Sometimes I think neither of us could concentrate quite as much on our work as we might have, because we had to champion Ellie first and foremost and manage the rest around that. Sometimes we felt isolated; evenings out involved booking a specialist sitter, and holidays were always a challenge. Whenever we went on a self-catering holiday we had to photograph every room where we were staying and then remove any furniture that Ellie could knock over or climb on, and any knickknacks (including wall clocks and pictures) that she might accidentally dislodge, throw, and destroy. The photos allowed us to reconstruct the layout when we left, without the owner knowing that anything unusual had happened. There were plenty of other precautions we had to take after that, too.

Despite the difficulties, Ellie travelled with us all over Europe. Mainly she liked the sun, which has always delighted her. Brightness communicates itself to Ellie, and she becomes much more smiley. Chartres Cathedral would leave her cold, in numerous senses. A busy street with bustle and colour would lift her, as we pushed her around in her wheelchair, or let her walk short distances, firmly attached to us. And the French, for example, would show great affection for her— much more than the English.

Our greatest fear, of course, was about the future. Ellie was not developing, and she would be quite unable to look after herself, or even keep herself safe. She would need round-the-clock care. Hilary and I were attuned to this by now: I think of it as acquired wisdom, not resignation on our part. Someone has to fight for her. Ellie was not going to change, and we would need to find a way to create and manage the environment in which she lived.

I t would be nice to report that once the dictionary had gone online we could relax into automatic pilot, allowing the steady pendulum of progress to take the *OED* on its stately route through the alphabet. When we went online we were committed to updating and publishing at least 1,000 entries a quarter, but we wanted to get that up to 2,000 or 3,000 a quarter as quickly as possible. We had to maintain some speed through the remaining letters of the alphabet, which would not, it would seem, edit themselves. We wondered about asking external editors to try updating our Victorian material, but you can't find world experts on every little word in the language. And, in fact, we were those experts. So we decided it was more efficient to do it ourselves.

And so every three months from March 2000 we had to hand over a substantial quantity of text (sometimes the size of a large novel) for online publication—every word in the alphabetical sequence we were working on. Nothing was left for later—I didn't believe we would have any more time "later" than we did now. The book version was becoming—to us—largely an irrelevancy, and was slipping into the past. We thought that the dictionary might be published later as a series of book volumes, but not until the full cycle of update was over and not unless the book-buying market wanted it and made the publication economically viable. The dictionary's "centre of gravity," as we proudly explained to people, had shifted to the online version, which was where any change would in future take place. *M* had moved into *N* and *O*, and then we spent ages in *P* and *R*, which are both massive letters, dwarfed only by *S*—which the original dictionary had had to divide into two enormous volumes in order to prevent the spine from splitting. But each quarter the work was ready, and we never missed a publication deadline. There were no volume ends to worry about—we just closed the publication range after the end of whatever range of words surrounded our numerical cut-off point.

We were hampered, though, by our old system software, which was gradually sinking into obsolescence. We knew this because whenever something went wrong with the computer system, we were told that it couldn't be fixed properly, but that we would have to use a **workaround**. Eventually I think there were more workarounds than there were simple bits of code. As each programmer left, another piece of code became worthless, as each time it became apparent that no one else knew how to fix it.

When we started working with computer scientists, we heard for the first time quite a few words (such as the noun *kludge*: a makeshift software fix) to describe the process or result of encouraging a faulty computer program to work even though the computer scientists didn't really know why it was broken in the first place. When talking to real people, the technicians politely called these informal fixes *workarounds*. Even *workaround* was quite a new word in the 1990s, though the concept is age-old. This time the word does not derive from the world of ice cream, but from the aeronautical and the astronautical industry, where safety mattered in triplicate. By 1961, if a system wasn't working and the engineers couldn't go back to basics to fix it, they euphemistically employed what they blandly denominated "workarounds," so as not to frighten anyone—which doesn't really seem particularly good news for the customer, or the astronaut. As with the *OED*'s computer system, if you couldn't fix a problem, you employed a workaround. After a few years—and at least by the late 1970s—people realised that it was a useful word to get you out of any tricky situation.

Eventually all the pieces of string involved in holding together our software were stretched to breaking point, and in 2005 we took delivery of a brand-new system in which most aspects of the editorial and publication process were integrated, and which finally allowed us to edit wherever we wanted in the database. In addition, we used the opportunity to make further changes in the look of the dictionary entries, making them easier to read and understand by breaking up huge columns of quotation material and implementing thousands of backroom standardisations to the text.

When the software was ready for us to install, we had a small competition to give it a name. Old *OED* software suites had traditionally been allocated names based on any word that included the letter sequence *O-E-D*. Predictably, our first set of programs had been called "OEDipus." Unlike Welsh, English has only a few words containing the *OED*'s letters, especially if you leave out unlikely program names like "three-toed." The winner of the naming competition this time (radically) did not contain the letters *O-E-D*. It was "Pasadena," wryly named by my colleague Jeremy Marshall as the "Perfect All-Singing All-Dancing Editorial and Notation Application."

We argued amongst ourselves (maybe for the first time) and with the University Press's senior managers on whether it was right to revise entries out of alphabetical order. In general I was in the conservative camp, keen to edit everything in detail as we encountered it on our sequential pass through the alphabet, but in this I was apparently one of a dwindling band of druids. And indeed there was an argument to be made that it was worth making exceptions to our alphabetical progress in order to address the most relevant entries, those that our audience might be most eager to see updated—typically the big, core-vocabulary words, the sensitive words, words that "really mattered." For the editors, though, these were the tough ones to edit, and a constant diet of these would be crushing. I felt that editors also needed the small, surprising, intriguing entries that the alphabet throws up to counteract the unremitting gigantism of the "important" entries (*black, earth, field, ground, nation, self-, work*—all of which go on for pages). What followed was a sort of tug-of-love between the two ideologies—slow and careful editing in alpha order and slow and careful editing wherever in the alphabet we felt it was most needed.

In the end, we shifted our editorial priorities so that in one quarter we'd progress along the old alphabetical sequence that we knew well— further into *P* (the new computer system hit us around *panache*). And then in alternate quarters we devised ranges of "big" words, to which we'd give the full *OED* treatment.

I have to confess that, despite my inclinations to the contrary, it was rather exciting to put together that first range of non-alphabetical words. These were published—once we'd become used to the new system, in March 2008. We had selected some meaty, high-profile terms to update in this ground-breaking batch: *affect/effect, air, American, cancer, gene, heaven, hell, language, love, sad, thing*. These words all involved some heavy-duty editing—most had been in the language for centuries and had developed a multiple subsense-structure and numerous compounds.

At the top of the list was the word *gay*, a word we were at the time continually asked about by journalists, lecture audiences, radio DJs, and just about anyone else we happened to come into contact with. We set about updating this entry straightaway—most of the text still dated from the original instalment published in 1898. Let me take you through some of the issues that *gay* raised for us.

From at least the 1960s there had been extensive social advocacy for gay rights, and social change typically influences language. At first there was often a deep-rooted worry in conservative quarters that "we could no longer use a traditional old word," *gay*, because it had been hijacked by its new meaning. On the other side, there was a powerful cohort of language users who actively promoted the use of *gay* as a symbol of a new-found personal liberation. The opposing pulls on *gay* in the modern era, coupled with its extensive history in the past, made it a challenging and yet intriguing word on which to work.

We were updating a composite Second Edition entry consisting of the old *OED1* entry (first published in 1898) augmented by additions in the twentieth century—so we already had hints of the "homosexual" meaning from the days of the *Supplement* I had worked on in the less-enlightened 1970s. When the *OED* had first defined *gay* at the very end of the nineteenth century, it was a merry, lively word, and one that in its dotage had become slightly naughty. Its first use in English dated, according to the nineteenth-century editors, from around 1300, and had found its way into English from French *gai* (itself recorded from the twelfth century). The old *OED* was puzzled about how *gai* had got into French, so it offered a number of suggestions, only to distance itself from them all—as usual—in as polite a variety of English as it knew how.

Once *gay* had found its way into English, the First Edition of the *OED* described it in a number of meanings, mostly circling round the idea of "full of joy or mirth": people could be mirthful, and women (typically in poetry) were apparently particularly prone to being joyful or *gay*. Gay horses pranced, poetry was known as the "gay science" (apparently after an idiom from Provence). But by the mid-seventeenth century, *gay* veered off in a rather more dissipated direction: we start finding "gay lotharios" (and "gay dogs"), and the subtle vocabulary of laxness and incipient immorality. By the early nineteenth century things had become even worse, and it was possible to regard prostitutes as "gay women," leading colourful lives described by a word which allowed the sanctimonious middle classes to discuss but not condone them. By the nineteenth century, *gay* had two faces: on the one hand, happy, carefree, and joyous, and on the other, abandoned to pleasure and morally lax.

These two strands blended into the new meaning "homosexual," which the *Supplement to the OED* had identified only as recently as 1935, in an underground glossary published in Upland, Indiana, and this use has blossomed explosively since then. Our revised entry would need to tease out the process of how this new meaning, apparently promoted by the people to whom it applied, had come into being.

Dictionary work is not all about definitions: we also needed to clarify aspects of the etymology. For example, we found a bridging word *gai* recorded in Anglo-French (the variety of French used in the upper echelons of British society after the Norman Conquest). This discovery allowed us to document the progression of *gay* from French into English via an interim dialect. And that's important to us. We didn't get the word willy-nilly from Paris or central France—it came as part of the Norman hang-over package. Rather than limiting ourselves to around 1300, we could now plot an earlier use in about 1225, which is much more satisfactory for a working Anglo-French word. (You must forgive me if these niceties seem unnecessary to you.)

The First Edition of the dictionary had associated *gay* with immorality and louche behaviour, but too late. New evidence from online sources and elsewhere helped to focus the picture. With the help of the *Middle English Dictionary*, we found that the medievals also had given the word *gay* a lascivious spin (missed by the original *OED*), although only for fifty years around the early fifteenth century. Geoffrey Chaucer wrote of "som gay gerl" in the late fourteenth century: *OED1* thought this use of "gay girl" was—in its context—simply an expression of praise for a lady; more recent scholarship preferred the reading "lascivious girl." The usage now seems to lay the seed for the general sense of promiscuousness or immorality (the gay lotharios, etc.), which now dates not from 1637 and the time of playwright James Shirley (*The Lady of Pleasure*), but from William Shakespeare's time, with a first example weighing in from 1597 (in John Payne's *Royall Exchange*). At that time, you might *go gay*, if you wished to lead a life of licentious immorality. Even the prostitution sense creeps backwards in time from the early Victorian era into the late eighteenth century, in Richard King's long-forgotten *New Cheats of London Exposed* (around 1795). After research, meanings often turn out to be older than we had imagined.

But new forces were at work around *gay* as we moved into the twentieth century. The old dictionary firmly stated that *gay*, in the meaning "homosexual," dated from Noel Ersine's underworld glossary of 1935. That says explicitly, after all, that a *geycat* (or *gaycat*) is a "homosexual boy." But *geycat* is recorded, as we discovered, much earlier—from 1890s America, without explicit homosexual connotation, and meaning a "young or inexperienced tramp." We took the view that this 1935 use apparently only implied homosexual conduct contextually, and was not prima facie evidence for the equivalence of *gay* and *homosexual*.

One reason why *gay* was a tricky entry to revise was that readers could—incorrectly—read later meanings into earlier evidence. I don't think they had a political agenda here: it's just a natural tendency to wish that what you've found is what you were looking for. I've done it myself—everybody has. But editors are trained to reject everything unless it demands inclusion with a cast-iron certainty. If they start bending the rules, or letting in maybes and possibilities, then the dictionary's credibility is blown. It's better and safer to err on the side of caution and conservatism than to run with every idea that is sent along to distract you.

Because the "homosexual" meaning of *gay* had a complex history, and clearly attracted so much interest and misjudgement, we took the highly irregular course of printing a series of false quotations before the "real" ones. These false—or near-miss—quotations illustrated early halfway usages which might be interpreted in the "homosexual" sense, but which in fact only exemplified the older meaning "merry" or "happy," in contexts suggestive of homosexuality or lesbianism. Here is the first of these, from Gertrude Stein's "Miss Furr and Miss Skeene" of 1922:

> Helen Furr and Georgine Skeene lived together then. . . . They were together then and travelled to another place and stayed there and were gay there . . . not very gay there, just gay there. They were both gay there . . .

It's not hard for someone to think that this is a true example of the later meaning *gay* = "homosexual" (and specifically "lesbian" here), but it's probably just the older mirthful and colourful meaning, used in the context of homosexuality or close companionship. There are many examples like this, where the context suggests more than the word itself conveys. Here is another, from Noël Coward's song "I Went to a Marvellous Party" (1939):

> *Everyone's here and frightfully gay,*
> *Nobody cares what people say,*
> *Though the Riviera*
> *Seems really much queerer*
> *Than Rome at its height.*

You can see how this might be mistaken by the over-zealous for "homosexual." But we need to look at every aspect of the word and wait until the evidence is overwhelming. In this case, we waited until Gershon Legman's heavy-duty *Language of Homosexuality*, published in

New York in 1941 as part of George W. Henry's *Sex Variants*. We made this the new first example of the "homosexual" sense of *gay*, bravely five years *later* than the *Supplement to the OED*'s first use (the *geycat*)—which we now considered to be a misreading. You couldn't argue with Legman, and his explanation suggests that the term arose as a positive use amongst homosexuals (which fits its first appearance in a text which would not have had a general readership):

> *Gay*, an adjective used almost exclusively by homosexuals to denote homosexuality, sexual attractiveness, promiscuity . . . or lack of restraint, in a person, place, or party. Often given the French spelling, gai or gaie by (or in burlesque of) cultured homosexuals of both sexes.

One final observation on *gay*: we found that, as usual, the productivity of *gay* as a word in the second half of the twentieth century was marked not by new basic meanings (we added only two), but by the proliferation of compounds, and especially compounds involving the "homosexual" meaning. Whereas our starting-point entry had twelve compounds, we easily expanded this to thirty-three, and doubtless could have gone much further. Here are a few, though I dislike lists in language books: *gay bar, gay boy, gay day, gay gene, gay icon*, and *gay lib* (not to mention *gaydar*). **Sorry**—that's enough of them for now.

Sorry makes its appearance in English in the Anglo-Saxon or Old English period, before the Norman Conquest of 1066. Early manuscripts containing English are pretty thin on the ground, and so we have little surviving documentary evidence for that period of the language (about 3 million words of text, and even then often of a religious or a legal nature). From today's perspective it's remarkable that *sorry* is directly related not to *sorrow*, as you might naturally think, but to *sore* (the noun: bodily pain, a sore place, etc., etc.). So if you're *sorry*, you are not primarily displaying your sorrow, but betraying how much you hurt. But there *is* a secondary link with *sorrow*, as similar words often influence each other's development: it is probably from *sorrow* that *sorry* gets its short <o> (or else—after *sore*—we'd spell it something like *soary*).

To the Anglo-Saxons, *sorry* meant "expressing pain or sorrow," but even then it could also mean "penitent" or "apologetic." So you could say that you were sorry about something from the early days, but the emergence of the single word *sorry*, used on its own as an apology for something you have done, occurred much later than the Old English period. We don't have any records of Anglo-Saxon merchants saying "sorry" for overcharging an Anglo-Saxon peasant. In fact, we don't have any evidence for this particular lexical usage until 1843, in *Sargent's New Monthly Magazine*, an American periodical published by Epes Sargent, a Boston journalist and litterateur and a member of the American East Coast literary "Knickerbocker Group," which included the more famous Washington Irving and James Fenimore Cooper. Fascinating though Sargent doubtless is as a minor Boston literary figure, he's most important to us because, in March 1843, his short-lived magazine *New Monthly* included the short sentence "Miss Marion, good morning, see you tomorrow—sorry I'm in such haste," which (as far as the *OED* has so far been able to ascertain) is the first known occurrence in print of "sorry" used apologetically, and shortened from "I am sorry." It's a small thing, but it kept us occupied, and it's from these small tiles that the grand mosaic of the language develops.

Although the media profile of the dictionary was now consistently high, it was highest of all in the United States. By now the *OED* had a small editorial office within the main Oxford University Press operation on Madison Avenue in Manhattan, New York City. This was led by Jesse Sheidlower, the first port of call for American journalists contacting the *OED*. Jesse had been involved with the *OED* for about five years by then: a lean, super-smart, super-slick New Yorker with a passion for slang, words, and cuisine, both in the oven and on the plate. To his closest friends, he was the Jessemeister, ruling the word-waves of American English. He had previously been working with Jonathan Lighter on the *Historical Dictionary of American Slang*, and seemed to remember almost every fact he had ever read about language. Unlike most of his Oxford counterparts, Jesse would get up in the morning hoping that the press would ring him or email him, offering a "publicity moment." I even imagined he sent letters to himself at work to provoke publicity opportunities. The press was mesmerised by the fact that he'd had the temerity to publish a treatise on the word *fuck* called *The F Word*. That wasn't what got him the job on the *OED* **by a long chalk**, but it made our dictionary publicists sleep well at night.

Phrases live and die through the amount of use they enjoy. In order to survive, they often need to leap from a small world into the big one. But they don't always jump continents. *By a long chalk* ("by far," "by a long way") is an expression first recorded in the 1840s, just into the Victorian era. It is commonest in British English, with less evidence—for example—from Australia and New Zealand, and less still from America.

The phrase comes originally from the small world of bar-room games. If you were engaged in a long drinking session in a public house in Britain in the sixteenth century, the landlord might chalk up on a slate just how much you owed. In the seventeenth century, people found it useful to use chalk to keep the score in games (often also enjoyed in alehouses)—and each point you scored would be represented by a chalk mark. If you ran rings round your opponent in the game, then you'd win by a larger margin, or a "long chalk." So they say.

The lexicographical arm of the OUP in the United States was entrusted with updating the North American component of the *OED*. Jesse would broker contacts with many of America's most successful word-hunters, such as Fred Shapiro of the Yale Law Library, and we'd suddenly find early uses for jazz terms, film terms, and (as I had come to expect) baseball terms flooding into our electronic files and hence online for all the world to view. When we revised the entry for *jazz* we suddenly found that the network of American jazz historians had been encouraged by Jesse to let the *OED* into their secrets. The 1910s were a crucial time for the development of the word *jazz* (1912—energy or excitement; 1913—misleading talk, nonsense; 1915—the new popular music style; 1919—dance styles associated with this music; 1918—sexual intercourse). We discovered that the *Supplement* had made another mistake, claiming 1909 as the first recorded use of the word *jazz* to describe a type of music; the source should have been dated 1919 (a recut version of Cal Stewart's *Uncle Josh in Society*, which had originally been recorded without the word *jazz* in 1909).

D ictionaries and their editors are often not considered prime-time television material, so we were in for a surprise in 2005 when an upbeat London TV production company, Takeaway Media, was commissioned by the B.B.C. to create a television programme based around a national word hunt. The idea was to help the *OED* record the language better by tapping into the everyday experiences and reminiscences of the television-watching public.

The plan was for us to come up with a set of words—maybe fifty would do—for which the public would be asked to hunt out earlier evidence from the piles of special-interest magazines generally considered to be piled up in their houses. So we dutifully created such a list. We suggested a group of fairly serious words for which we thought a public appeal might help—*biodiversity*, *mega-rich*, *playlisting*, that sort of thing. Then we were told that the list had to contain the sort of words people might be interested in and might be able to discover hidden away on their bookshelves. So we went back to square one.

The sort of expression people might be interested in, apparently, was *the full monty*. It turned out that they would also be interested in *cocktail* and *codswallop* and *boffin*. In general, they would be interested in the history of curious, but everyday, informal words and phrases—nothing too serious, and only terms where there was a fighting chance that the public might turn up gold. That was fine by us—any new information would be useful to the dictionary, whatever sort of word it related to. So we pulled together a search list and launched it on the production company, which then launched it on the national media. People saw the list for the new TV programme (called—rather dismissively and against my lexical intuition—*Balderdash & Piffle*) in their newspapers, or on the radio, or on the programme's website, and they rushed off in their droves to try to help, and then began emailing or posting their discoveries to the programme's producers.

> *Balderdash* is intriguing because of what it used to mean, its possible correspondences with Scandinavian dialect, and the leap from its original meanings to the only one we know today. It is a word that defies etymology, at least in the eyes of the cautious *OED*. But the dictionary does draw our attention to the dialect word *balder*, which means "to use coarse language," as well as to various similarly aggressive Scandinavian words.
>
> The problem in English is that the earliest documentary evidence insists that *balderdash* was a drink. In the sixteenth century it apparently meant "froth, or foamy liquid" and, as things hotted up in the seventeenth century, "a jumbled mix of liquors," which might mean milk and beer, beer and wine, or brandy and mineral water. Only by the late seventeenth century do we start to find evidence for the modern sense of "a senseless jumble of words," or "nonsense, trash, spoken or written." The feeling of the nineteenth-century editors was that really this sense might turn out to be the original one, but they didn't quite have the nerve to assert this. In cases such as this, we need to await the *OED*'s update, to see if the tectonic environment of *balderdash* has changed.

The B.B.C.'s word hunt started to take shape. All of the programmes for the series were recorded on the same day, which gave us no chance to develop in the role. And we were given no advance notice of what relevant new information the public had turned up. The show worked like this: There were three *OED* lexicographers (Peter Gilliver, Tania Styles, and me) sitting behind the inquisition table, caped in immense learning. The programme's presenter and the leader of the word hunt, Victoria Coren (daughter of the languid, quick-witted humourist and writer Alan Coren), would sweep down upon us from her eyrie to ask us whether we would accept her word-hunt searchers' latest findings, and if we would promise to put them straight into the *OED* as the earliest evidence ever discovered for the word we were reviewing.

She was so forceful and decisive that we really should have collapsed and just put anything she asked into the dictionary, but deep down we had our principles. So when she told us yet another shaggy-dog story about the origin of *shaggy-dog story*, we were all (after learned discussion of its merits) prepared to throw it out the window, until we realised that she did have a point: the evidence she had in her hand was indeed earlier than anything we had in the dictionary, and someone had trumped us (or at least trumped the editors who last worked on that entry twenty-five years earlier). On some occasions we would dispute the evidence hotly (and we were pretty conservative—we couldn't just accept anything), but at other times we grudgingly accepted it, and doubtless made someone very happy.

As far as we knew before the programme, the expression *shaggy-dog story*, a long-winded rigmarole tale, amusingly pointless at best, dated from 1946 and an anthology enticingly called *A Collection of Shaggy Dog Stories*, published by a small company based in Hunstanton, on the Norfolk coast. It is inherently unlikely (though not entirely impossible) that the expression first saw the light of day in a seaside town in East Anglia with no apparent links to shaggy dogs, but the *Supplement to the OED* had no way of improving this data. No one really knows what the first-ever shaggy-dog story was. People make up stories about what it might have been, through some impulse to complete the picture. They say there was an archetypal rambling shaggy-dog story in which the dog's coat grows longer and shaggier, until at a pitch of excitement someone observes that the dog isn't shaggy at all. Fortunately the *OED* isn't too concerned with speculation of this order.

After the programme, we had better information, thanks to the avid watchers and word-hunters. Someone had access, at home or online, to a copy of *Esquire* magazine from May 1937. *Esquire* here offers helpful advice in techniques for separating sheep from goats—as you might say, or the sharp- from the dull-witted: "One of the more sporting ways of finding out which ones are not [sane] is to try shaggy-dog stories on them." When presented with this information, and a verified photocopy of the original, we had to concede, and after the filming we rushed back to our offices to add the new information to the dictionary.

It turned out that a few of the word-hunters had been cunning (or you might call it using their common sense) and had used big text databases to find better evidence than we had previously discovered. But that was fine. In the end, the dictionary benefited from the series, and the additional national publicity fed further interest in the dictionary. Once it was finished, the B.B.C. commissioned another series, and so more new findings trickled into the dictionary. Funding for entertaining cultural programmes then suddenly took one of its cyclical dips (or the producers realised that television wasn't the dictionary's natural milieu), so the second series turned out to be our last.

It was in fact a refreshing change to find people who were not simply interested in the new words that the *OED* was adding. Most of the *Balderdash & Piffle* words came from the twentieth century, and they were predominantly informal words or expressions, but they weren't froth. They were words, for the most part, that had seeped into everyone's vocabulary without being noticed, but they had left little unresolved issues for lexicographers which needed to be cleared up. Two of my favourite finds from the series were *nit nurse* and *pass the parcel*. I'd known one of these when I was growing up in the 1950s, but not the other.

Fortunately the one I knew was the game, *pass the parcel*, which in its original Spartan form was a staple of every birthday party I had attended when at primary school. For those too young to remember, a prize is wrapped in multiple layers of gift-wrap, the music starts, the parcel is passed round the circle of partygoers, the music stops, and the lucky holder opens a layer of wrapping. Mostly there is no prize there, but eventually the music stops with only one layer of wrapping left, and the lucky holder gains the prize. In its later form it involved unwrapping a prize from the parcel in every round of the game, but in my day you just sat through five minutes of passing the dreary parcel around and around the circle of your fellow partygoers, with occasional halts when the music stopped—until eventually someone else won the prize.

But the *OED* had clearly not been playing enough party games: it had only discovered evidence for the expression from 1980. That was very late, so we put it on our appeal list for *Balderdash & Piffle*. Sure enough, as the weeks passed, new evidence arrived at mission control, and when we came to film the series, we had a description of the game (which talked about "passing the parcel") from the aptly named *Foulsham's Fun Book* of 1932, plus a real, concrete example for 1953. The history of the expression now extended back at least as far as my memory allowed.

My other favourite find was *nit nurse*, an informal expression for the school nurse who would comb through the itchy heads of wartime children looking for head lice. We had often found this sort of informal children's term hard to pin down. It was as elusive as the lice themselves, and we had only discovered written examples from 1985. That was slightly worrying, as the expression had already drifted into childhood mythology by then: our evidence from 1985 actually read, "Whatever happened to the nit nurse?" So we threw it open to the word-hunters, and this one attracted the research community.

Someone with online access to the top UK medical journal, *The Lancet*, instantly took it right back to 1942 for us. All at once it had been demonstrated that *OED* research doesn't find everything, that words arise from the social environment that demands them, that there are always people out there who know more about particular terms than the *OED* editors, and that computers can save a lot of leg-work (though you shouldn't necessarily believe everything they say). It was also a reminder that *The Lancet* database was still too expensive for simple publishing companies such as Oxford University Press to subscribe to.

This increased publicity and interaction with the media brought another issue to the fore for me: the popular misconception that the chief editor of the *OED* doesn't edit, but spends the day organising things so that other editors can get on and edit. That would be easy to do. There were always meetings I could have attended to discuss organisational or publishing matters. But I wondered whether there was a point in being editor of the *OED* if you didn't spend the day editing. By continuing to edit, I showed the seventy or so other editors on the project that I thought it was the most important thing for me—and hence for them—to be doing. Editing is also (fortunately) what I enjoy doing most. Maybe I could have become a successful commercial publisher (well, you know me—I sort of doubt it), but I've always prided myself on the fact that I can edit, and edit pretty fast. It is the *OED*, after all. It doesn't deserve to have people using it to further their own ends. There are always enough people around who want to do that. But someone has to stand up for the dictionary. The editors don't want to be run by ciphers who creep from meeting to meeting discussing budgets and office moves. I always felt it was too important for that. Call me soft, but I did what I thought the chief editor should do, and that was lead the editing.

Even though the dictionary was now living happily online, there was still one general problem that I had with it: it still looked like a book (or at least a series of books) on computer. There was nothing wrong with that, and many people just wanted to look up a word and then move on with their lives. However, there are many ways of looking at data, and the book view is only one. Those of you with a predilection for classifying things, and I'm including all lexicographers in this catch-all group, will know that putting index cards in piles according to word meaning is only the bottom rung of knowledge. With all of the complex software behind the digital *OED*, we knew that there were new ways of visualising the language on-screen that could make the dictionary (and the language) come alive to a far wider set of people.

From the days, back in the early 1990s, when the *OED* had first appeared in its entirety on CD, we had been encouraging scholars not just to look up the meaning and history of individual words, but also to start exploring the language on a broader scale. We did this by suggesting that they take a look—as they then could—at comparative data, to search it for patterns and differences. This was a brave attempt to draw people away from using dictionaries simply to look up definitions, and to encourage them to glimpse all of that extra information hidden in the big, historical *OED*. I wanted people to be able to see charts, diagrams, animations, and videos that would give them further **clues** about language history, and also to be able to collaborate much more closely with editors, perhaps through the medium of wikis.

Clue is unusual in that it is a word that nicely knits together the Germanic origins of English and the fascination we have had—even from the days before the Renaissance—with classical mythology. The older spelling of *clue* is *clew*. The *OED* reminds us of other similar pairs in which the *-ew* spelling is the older one: *blew* and then *blue*; *glew* and *glue*, *rew* and *rue*, and *trew* and *true*.

We first encounter *clew* in Anglo-Saxon times, when it was spelled *kliwen* or *klewen* (with a final *-n*) and had widespread equivalents around Germanic Europe. It meant "a ball" ("a round ball"), and often a "ball of thread," so it was a domestic, homely sort of a word. As Geoffrey Chaucer and his contemporaries knew, various figures from classical mythology had used balls of thread to get them out of scrapes, and the most famous was probably Theseus, when on his

Minotaur-slaying quest. Ariadne had given him a ball of thread (a clew, to the medieval mind), which he fed out gradually when entering the Minotaur's Labyrinth, so that he could follow it back when he returned—at speed if need be, with the Minotaur at his heels. So strong was the connection between these myths and the purpose of the balls of thread that we formed the idea that anything that gave you a hint or a clue as to how to extricate yourself from a mazelike or perplexing situation was itself a clew, or—as had become standard by the seventeenth century—a clue. Although I don't like crosswords, I like the origin of clue and its labyrinthine simplicity.

Visualisations and animations had been on our to-do list for a number of years as we approached the year 2010, but we had little hope that we would find the resources to experiment in this area. With my realistic hat on, I can see that most people will always want to search for basic definitions, pronunciations, and etymologies. But we still hoped that we could increase the percentage of users who would be interested in carrying out more creative, global searches of the data. We had become quite familiar with seeing trends of, say, economic data predigested by way of graphs and other visualisations in the newspapers or on the TV news. Why couldn't the *OED* offer similarly inviting digests of language data?

We sensed that there was a latent appetite for this new perspective. We also knew that the way the *OED* appeared online when it was first published back in the year 2000 was not helping. However much we stressed that the text was a brand-new computer-searchable animal, it still just returned to you lists of words. But all around us people in their everyday lives were positioning themselves within a world of fluid, dynamic, visual data.

Everyone, not just the lexicographers, could see that the online dictionary needed a new look and a new feel: one that empowered the user more actively. Those with more of an idea of these things had cottoned on to the concept of filtering data. You looked up one thing, and you could then throw a second search at the data which refined and filtered your results until you had drilled down, in the technical jargon, to what you were looking for. Suppose you searched for all of the words in the category Visual Arts (2,768). Then, having found those, you decide you want to filter out all of the ones that didn't originate in the eighteenth century: you'd be left with 209. Then you might want to drill down further to discover how many of these words were of French origin. That would leave you with 29 of your original 2,768 Visual Arts terms, including *costume* (first appearing later than you might expect, in 1715); *fine arts*, from 1767 (and from French, inasmuch as it is a translation of the French term *beaux-arts*); and also *statuette* (1738). This methodology gives you the ability to decide what you want next as you go along, rather than having to predetermine where you want your searches to take you.

All of this work required money. There was no extra money, however politely we asked. Then, to our surprise, our luck changed. As a result of arguments initiated by us, but eventually rumbling through the highest quarters of the University Press, we heard that we would receive a considerable enhancement of our annual budget to relaunch the OED Online in 2010 with much-improved functionality. At last everyone realised that ten years was too long for a website to remain unchanged in a rapidly changing digital environment. So then we just had to work out in detail what "improved functionality" might mean.

It is never easy to shift people's perceptions and expectations, but we wanted to re-envision the dictionary so that people could experience both word-based results to their enquiries and visualisations and animations. I'm not always the sharpest knife when I come to new ideas, but I remember becoming increasingly frustrated back in 2009, as we were discussing how a relaunched OED Online might look. Filtering was fine, but it still resulted in screenfuls of word-based output, leaving the user to do all the brainwork of analysis (which was itself often rather a dangerous thing to allow some users to do, as I had previously discovered).

I was bold enough, at one of our terminally tedious meetings on the relaunch, to propose that we offer users visualisations of the results of searches alongside the traditional verbose, wordy views. I reasoned that traditional dictionary users were only familiar with word lookups, and didn't appreciate the wealth of underlying information that was stored in the *OED*. If we could redirect the results of searches into timelines, graphs, animations, and the like, then perhaps some of these users would discover that there was more to their language than they had anticipated. I knew the lexicographers would be in favour of this, as some of us had pondered about the possibility already. I discussed these ideas with my colleague James McCracken, who was just the person to lead the computational experimentation.

Meetings at OUP were polite. If you suggested something outrageous you would be told it was an interesting idea, but implicitly you would come to realise that, for whatever reason, its time had not yet drawn into the station. We had all experienced that many times before. But to give our chairman (the current successor to the Admiral) his due, he only gave me 50 percent of the normal response, and with a quizzical air wondered aloud if I might like to make a more formal presentation of my ideas at the next meeting.

There wasn't much time to put together a comprehensive document based on what I had learnt several years earlier was called "blue-sky thinking," as we had our regular word deadlines to hit for publication. But I sensed that this opening was important, so I started jotting down a few ideas. Soon they had marshalled themselves into some sort of order. The basic idea was hardly ground-breaking in a real-world context, but it was enough of a divergence from normal dictionary thinking to masquerade as radical. Instead of outputting only streams of words to users, we would offer an alternative view by which the data was re-expressed in graphs, pie charts, timelines, and any other visual medium we could think of. (I don't think I dared suggest sounds and colour, but they became part of the package.) In some ways this was returning to the discussions I'd had with Jeffery Triggs, when he was designing the prototype OED Online in the mid-1990s. We had tried to link entries together using whatever means we might have to hand—and the principal one now was a *Historical Thesaurus of the OED*, the result of a remarkable forty-year research project at the University of Glasgow, which we were engaged in binding into the main online dictionary. If we could achieve this, then we could actively start to promote the *OED* as an accessible repository for networks of words, not just of words existing purely in isolation.

The *Historical Thesaurus of the OED*, the brainchild of Professor Michael Samuels at Glasgow, began its association with the dictionary in around 1965. Like the *OED*, it was a mad idea that worked. The idea itself was that most of the words and meanings in the *OED* would be written out on index cards, then sorted so that all the terms that had ever been used for the concept of, say, "an instrument for poking a fire" would appear side by side, in the order in which they were first found in English (*purr*, 1357/8; *fire-purr*, a1451; *fire pike*, 1483; *poker*, 1534; *fire-pote*, 1638; *pote*, 1638; *teaser*, 1839; *kennedy*, 1864; *tickler*, 1881; *curate*, 1891; *fire stick*, 1896). The same procedure was followed for all the other concepts in English (love, hate, continuous stationery, frogs) until eventually an enormous reference resource of links and cross-references existed which allowed you to skip around the main *OED* historically and semantically in quite new ways. The original *OED* took forty-four years to move from *A* to *Z*; not surprisingly, the work on the Glasgow *Historical Thesaurus of the OED* also took forty-four years from *aardvark* to *zebu*, or whatever the relevant concepts were. Nowadays, if you look up a meaning in the *OED*, you are likely to be offered a button taking you through to all the other words for the same concept, in chronological order of their appearance in English.

By the time we arrived at our next online-planning meeting, I had primed a few likely types to support the plan to introduce visualisations into our search results, and we received a partial acceptance that we might perhaps investigate the possibility. This was as much as James needed, and he soon had a new working prototype in place which incorporated many of our ideas, and indeed several which sadly didn't make it through to the final live version. We had charts showing, for instance, the gradual advent of Japanese and Chinese words into English from the late sixteenth century—it was so much easier to see the outline of the story from a picture.

These charts made for a telling comparison. English traders and early tourists noted the Chinese *litchi* fruit, and as more Chinese words entered English, climbing steadily (rather than interruptedly, as in Japanese) to a peak in the late nineteenth century, we find many food terms (*bok choy*, *chop suey*, *oolong*, etc.), and music (*san hsien*, *se*, *ti-tzu*), but less "art" (decorative or martial) than in the equivalent Japanese set. The profiles of borrowings from these two Eastern languages are similar but distinct. As in the old and supposedly Chinese proverb, one picture is worth a thousand words.

In fact, for any search you carried out on the dictionary data, you had the option of receiving the results either as a list or as a timeline visualisation. A clever short visual animation prepared by James and showing words entering English from 1150 to the present day on a world map, according to their country of origin, later provided a stimulating ride-through experience documenting on-screen the emergence of English as a world language: whenever I give a talk about the *OED* this is always one of the sections people want to discuss further. If only we could do that for French, or German, or Spanish, too. As usual, you had to view the visualisations with some caution, as there were often outlying results which had to be excluded for one reason or another. But the basic package was in keeping with the direction in which I wanted the dictionary to be moving. It was only a start, but the first step, as they say—to quote another trite proverb—is the most difficult.

Offering visualisations was one way of engaging with a new, modern audience for the dictionary. But users were still fascinated by the idea that they might contribute to the dictionary, in much the same way in which thousands of people had contributed to Sir James Murray's original *OED* back in the nineteenth century. This desire takes us to wikis, by way of crowdsourcing—harnessing the goodwill of people internationally to contribute to the story of English captured by the *OED*.

We've made some advances in crowdsourcing since the early days of the first *OED* when readers in the nineteenth century sent in handwritten slips, but not enough. We are still presenting information to users without giving them the opportunity to make significant, wholesale contributions to the dictionary—for example, through wikis and other massive data-collection projects. It's still something we need to work on, but we've travelled a little down that road.

Around 2005, the dictionary formed a collaborative relationship with Jeff Prucher, an American author interested in improving the documentation of the *OED*'s collection of science-fiction words. The result, apart from Jeff's book, *Brave New Words: The Oxford Dictionary of Science Fiction*, was a website in the form of a wiki where readers could read details of the *OED*'s current coverage of the vocabulary of science fiction and enter their own findings (which were typically earlier references to specific terms: *alien, earthling, space shuttle*, etc.). Here's an example. The *OED* includes the noun and the adjective *anti-gravity* from the 1940s (for example, Arthur C. Clarke, in *Across the Sea of Stars*). If you know about early science fiction, you know that the 1932 spring edition of *Wonder Stories Quarterly* contains a use of the term by James Morgan Walsh: "But the antigravity apparatus will have to be capable of generating a greater repulsive force than is required for ordinary interplanetary conditions." And then if you know more about early science fiction than the *OED* editors, you'll know to look out for the equivalent term *counter-gravity* (not yet in the dictionary, but with evidence waiting on the wiki site from 1950). The *OED* editors were then able to turn to this ground-breaking intergalactic resource when updating their terms. Yet again, it reinforced the lexicographer's maxim that there are always people outside the dictionary offices who know more about any particular word than do the dictionary's editors themselves. By sharing this knowledge, we have been able to improve the coverage of science-fiction vocabulary astronomically.

This science-fiction pilot study suggested that there were at least two directions in which the dictionary might proceed. Firstly, we could establish wikis on a similar or enhanced model for a wide range of subject areas, collecting information from many pockets of interested users; secondly, we could open up a parallel *OED* in the form of a wiki where anyone interested would be able to suggest improvements to the editors over the whole range of vocabulary. I don't think we have ever suggested going quite as far as Wikipedia and leaving the final product theoretically in the hands of others.

Alongside all of these plans for the future, we still needed to keep the editorial chariot on track, maintaining our production targets and publishing more and more of the dictionary online at each of our quarterly website updates. We were progressing well through the alphabet by now, and we were producing remarkable entries, full of new and exciting information. Wherever the dictionary was going in the future, we knew we'd brought it through.

THIRTEEN

Becoming the Past

B y 2013 it turned out that, without really intending to, I'd been at the *OED* for over thirty-five years. In retrospect the time seemed to have flashed past in an instant, but that didn't erase the fact that it had passed. Employment law was changing, and it was becoming possible to stay on beyond the grave, but that idea had never appealed to me. Ever since I had met that dapper military personnel director when I was first interviewed for a job on the dictionary back in the 1970s, I had felt we shared an unspoken agreement that when I arrived at sixty or so I would leave the building. I don't think I'd told anyone else, and the Colonel had left decades earlier, but one of us still knew.

There's no best time to step off the *OED* roundabout, so I concluded that there was no worst time either. One of my earliest wishes, when we came to updating the big dictionary, was to ensure that, by the time I departed, the project should be far enough advanced not to be cancelled. It seemed to me now (pending a disaster) that it was as safe as it could be. We still had about 60 percent of the way to go to *Z*, but the direction of travel was firmly in place. I wouldn't see the update through to its completion, but I'd come to terms with that some years back. Even Sir James Murray had not taken the dictionary through to

Z himself: he had died while the original dictionary was working through the letter *T* in 1915.

It seemed to me that the *OED* was entering a period of consolidation—without any radical changes on the horizon—and so it might be a good time to give someone else a chance to step into my editorial shoes. I hope I left it in good shape, and I certainly wish the new chief editor, Michael Proffitt, all the best as he and his colleagues take the dictionary forward into the future. I had never found it a problem to maintain my **enthusiasm** for the *OED* project, and so leaving it was in some ways hard. But when you've been doing something for over thirty-five years nothing's too hard. You make the decision, and then you stick with it. There would be plenty of others things I could find to keep myself occupied.

Words can change to the extent that we no longer recognise their original component parts. In the case of *enthusiasm*, there will be few people who can see the Latin or Greek words for "god" hidden in there, but in the old days that semantic image was what drove the word. *Enthusiasm* looks, on the face of it, like an unholy scramble of letters, which suggests it derives from Greek. According to the *OED*, there are 144 words in English that end in *-asm*, and most of them involve *chasms*, *clasms*, *plasms*, and *spasms*. There are no prizes for guessing that those words all stretch back to Greek, too. *Enthusiasm* is not medieval in origin, as you might think, but entered English in Shakespeare's time, around 1600. The original senses of the word were rather negative. The nub of it is hidden in the first couple of syllables: *enthus-* means "possessed by a god" (there's a *theos*, "god," as in *theology*, behind the *-thus-*). So when the word was first used in English, *enthusiasm* meant "possession by a god," or at least acting as if you were in a state approaching divine madness or frenzy. As the years passed (1660), *enthusiasm* came to mean any misdirected religious fervour: not a frenzy that seemed to take you over, but one that you intentionally adopted. By the early eighteenth century (1716), *enthusiasm* had started to drop its religious colouring, and to develop its modern meaning of rapturous intensity or passionate eagerness. Once we got there, we were so excited that it hasn't really changed its meaning since then.

I'm not allowed to criticise words, but perhaps by now I can be excused for saying that the barbaric *enthuse* dates from the early nineteenth century in the United States, and has sadly been going strong ever since. I've used it myself earlier in this book, just to show that I bear it no ill will.

I do like a modicum of enthusiasm over words, but not too much. I come from a generation and a society where over-enthusiasm was deplored, and keenness was deprecated. Nonchalant, non-interventionist observation was the order of the day when I was growing up, and the perspective stuck. It turned out that that world-view worked well for historical lexicography, too—though it's obviously not the only one that would. I found that it was easy for me to stand on a still point watching words stream past in all directions, just noting patterns, changes, peaks and troughs, accidents.

If this propensity to monitor and report attracted me to the *OED*, I now realise that it's what attracts me to other things I've become involved with over the years, whether it's literary research, local history, or genealogy, and especially if it involves revealing long-standing misconceptions.

These misconceptions are never far from the surface. After my father died, I inherited a large Victorian oil painting of an Italian lake scene, which had originally been bought by my great-grandfather. It was clearly very competently done, and the artist had made a sterling effort to catch the colour of the light playing around the old houses on an island in the lake, which formed the centrepiece of the picture. The painting is entitled *Isola Bella, Lago Maggiore*, in black lettering, on the frame. So Hilary and I thought it would be worthwhile using the scene as an excuse to go there—at which time I could confirm the historical details, and perhaps write up some notes on the place. Hilary had her annual misgivings over whether this technically constituted a holiday.

We scanned the maps and found Isola Bella, one of three little islands along the side of Lake Maggiore, and we booked our tickets. It would have been useful to have had Kate along with us, as she was by then fluent in Italian, but she had other things to do. When we arrived at the lake, we immediately booked a trip out to the island. To our dismay, the scene that confronted us was nothing like my painting, and the island could never have looked like that to the mid-Victorian painter.

Nonplussed, we returned to the hotel and spoke to some locals. We had taken the precaution of bringing a photo of the painting. Eventually someone offered the opinion that the painting did not represent an island on Lake Maggiore, but one on the next lake up, Lake Orta. We didn't have any better suggestions, so we arranged to travel over to Lake Orta and visit its island. From a boat a third of the way round the island, we saw the scene of our painting, almost precisely as the artist had depicted it—misnamed, misdescribed, and misadmired by my family for about a hundred years.

The parallels with *OED* work were quite striking. The more closely you investigate the details of the past, the more you find that they have been altered slightly to suit the present, or have simply been forgotten or recorded in error. We—collectively—lose the information, for example, that a British English word comes originally from American English, and if we forget that, how can we remember from five hundred years ago that one word derives from French and another from Italian? Does it matter? I think it does, and that someone, and as many people as possible, should retain an awareness of the historical stages by which we have reached how we speak and live today. Small mistakes escalate: a misattributed date may cause us to misevaluate a larger variable, which in turn imposes a greater sense of inexactitude on our scaffolding of knowledge. This wasn't something the Simpsons had ever discussed at home, but I think the wrongly labelled painting confirmed

Hilary's suspicion that with my family there was sometimes less than meets the eye.

But these inexactitudes weren't restricted to my family. It was similar *OED*-related themes that warmed me to James Joyce, as I came to unbutton myself from the *OED*. Since I left the dictionary (and for several years before that), I've been researching Joyce's usage and perspectives. He's the obvious author for an *OED* editor to investigate, I think. I was rather surprised to find that Joyce used techniques in constructing *Ulysses* which were rather similar to those I'd become familiar with in constructing entries for the *OED*. Both texts are woven together from the shreds of the civilisations which the authors observed from a distance in time or space.

One of the *OED*'s contributors, Harald Beck—from deep in Germany—had cottoned on to the lexical implication of Joyce's method of composition several years before I did. We were discussing Harald's contributions to the *OED* (antedatings collected using the new and publicly available online resources such as Google Books) when he mentioned his interest in Joyce. Most people say they've read some of *Ulysses*. Some even wish they had time to read the rest. Harald, on the other hand, is translating *Ulysses* into German. He explained a couple of his current textual problems, which, using *OED* research methods and materials, I was able to solve rapidly. We continued to exchange ideas and encourage each other to further research, and in the end we decided to set up a scholarly online journal, the James Joyce Online Notes, as a forum for discovering and publishing more historically accurate information about the real people and the unfamiliar words of Joyce's novels than was generally available to the interested public. We spend a lot of time resuscitating forgotten lives and expressions.

Ulysses was first published in 1922. In it, Joyce merges together the collective memories of many people—his own memories and (particularly) those of his father, who moved to Dublin from Cork before Joyce was born, and who drifted several steps down the Dublin social ladder as the nineteenth century progressed. It also incorporates the collective memory of Dubliners, recalled by Joyce from his eyries of exile in Trieste, Zurich, and Paris. Joyce's Dublin, re-created on one day in 1904, never really existed, but it could have. Similarly, the *OED*'s re-creation of the language of the past did exist in a way, but we can never really appreciate what it was like back then. We create flickering images, and all the while we and our contemporaries forget more and more of our shared past.

One of the first of Joyce's silent and forgotten Dubliners whom I managed to revive was the real-life boxer Myler Keogh, just mentioned in passing in *Ulysses*, and of whom no one you meet has ever heard. He was a puzzle for Joyce scholars, but by consulting old Irish newspapers online I was able to pull together a bruising life for him as an Irish middleweight champion in the 1890s. The information about Myler arose by imagining he was a word, and employing the *OED*'s research methods to uncover the facts. I did much the same with Marcella the Midget Queen, a sideshow act above a World's Fair shop in central Dublin, and then again with Annie Mack, ringleader of the Dublin prostitutes—according to traditional Joycean commentary. It turned out she was a Scottish lady with a head for lowbrow Dublin business who ran a string of brothels along with some of her cronies. It's all there, if you care to look. I recommend the Dublin Registry of Deeds. House deeds, that is.

Not that I restrict myself to researching people. There are plenty of expressions and jokes in *Ulysses* that require unpicking. The typical problem is that because people don't know the expressions, they think that Joyce invented them. In fact, he was an avid magpie, copying down expressions he saw and heard, intending to reuse them in his novel. Here's an example: *kidfitting corsets*. Molly Bloom lusts after them, as advertised in the *Gentlewoman*, to restrain her generous figure. But what does *kidfitting* mean? It isn't in the dictionaries, and the annotators of Joyce are strangely silent. After a hunt around possible sources, it became clear that kidfitting corsetry meant corsetry that was held together (at least where it rubbed against the skin) by kid fittings, or fittings made of soft goatskin. At around the time *Ulysses* was published in 1922, you could buy these in Dublin: "Royal Worcester Kidfitting Corsets. The Corsets of Style Superiority. Light and Flexible. . . . There is a model for every type of figure—slender, medium, or full—in the Royal Worcester Kidfitting Corsets. Pim Bros., Ltd., South Great George's Street, Dublin." Please form an orderly queue.

The fact that the dictionary was flourishing, and finding that I could carry on researching and writing on topics outside the *OED*, were two things that made leaving the dictionary easier. But realistically there were many other factors as well. I'd always had a large extended family of aunts and uncles, but within a decade that whole generation of the family seemed to have been swept away. Then, at a family party in 2011, my sister told me she had to visit a cancer specialist the following week, and the prognosis was not good. She died of an inoperable tumour three months later. I think Hilary and I both felt that it was time to think of making a fresh start.

After considering things for a while, we decided to make an (almost) complete break from Oxford and move forty miles west to Cheltenham, where I had lived as a child and had been to school. It's a strange place, in some ways, as it's set right in the heart of the Cotswolds, but doesn't share much with the agricultural, county interests of the neighbouring towns and villages. Its life changed overnight when someone discovered a natural spring there in the eighteenth century and came to the conclusion that Cheltenham should become a **spa**. When the king visited a few decades later, he bestowed upon the place everlasting celebrity as a health resort. His courtiers mentioned it to most of their military friends in British India, and on retirement they all rushed back here to take the waters and expire.

When the *OED* decides to include place names as dictionary entries, it needs to know that the name has developed new meanings, and doesn't just refer to the one and only place of that name. American dictionaries don't follow these rules, and unusually the British are the purists here. Needless to say, it comes as a surprise to most people that the word *spa* derives from a place name. A *spa* is, according to the *OED*, "a town, locality, or resort possessing a mineral spring or springs." It comes directly from the name of Spa, a town south-west of Liège in Belgium. We spelt it *Spaw* in the early days. The Continentals liked to think it was called *Spau*, and so we altered this to what passed as English. Intrepid English travellers discovered the Belgian Spa in the mid-sixteenth century. Even Edmund Spenser refers to it rather cryptically in the *Faerie Queene* (1590): "Both Silo this, and Iordan did excell, / And th' English Bath, and eke the german Spau." Clearly he didn't know that the region was going to become Belgium, and thought of it as a Germanic stronghold.

The rise and rise of Cheltenham in the late eighteenth century coincides with the emergence of the word *spa* in the general sense of a health resort that capitalises on its mineral springs. We can date this, at the moment, to 1781, and Richard Brinsley Sheridan's play *A Trip to Scarborough* (another place where the Simpsons have washed up over the years). Sheridan's play was a polite reworking of John Vanbrugh's rather cheeky *Relapse*. I think nowadays a spa can be something you put your feet into, but that just goes to show the curative powers of language.

The more alert readers will have noticed that I have peppered the text with little discussions like this about the history and usage of words. Those are the bits, I discovered, that Hilary skipped over when she read the typescript, but it may be something she regrets. I'm sure she isn't alone, but I do believe it is a bad habit and won't get you very far. I mentioned in the Introduction that I had an ingenious plan in interspersing these discursive references throughout the text. Mainly I wanted to demonstrate the fascination of more or less any word in the language, if you can just settle back and look at it for a while without rushing on to the next thing. But more importantly I wanted to take you surreptitiously through a brief history of the English language, so that if you read the gobbets and snippets, you would at least have got something out of this book. If none of that interested you, then I tried to add in a few episodes from the Theory of Lexicography in palatable portions.

As we made our way along these ancient passages, you'll have wandered through the linguistic history of the Anglo-Saxons (also known as the Old English) over a thousand years ago. They were the first speakers of the Germanic dialects spoken on British soil, and they are historically blamed for chasing the incumbent Celtic speakers off to the outlying parts of the country. Although hardly any Celtic words are known to have been absorbed into regular English, the real situation was more complex. What feels today, in retrospect, like a linguistic takeover, (*a*) masks what was certainly much intermarrying and other inter-confusion between the resident Celts and the incoming Germanic tribespeople, and (*b*) obscures the fact that we don't have any substantial records for five hundred years after the merger began, so we don't really know what we are talking about anyway.

That seems to be the case with a lot of language study. One of the great unanswered questions about Old English is—why is it such a complex language, with streams of cases and declensions, while the later versions of the language are (on the face of it) so much simpler? How does something start complex, and end up simpler? Obviously it's not really simple now, when the complexity lies in word order and idioms and the disjunction between spelling and pronunciation (amongst other things). But those Old English words we looked at were intended to introduce you to some of these issues: the Germanic heritage, rural society, difficult-to-define little words like *same*, and then *hone*, the *queen*, and the concept of being *sorry*.

As we edged through the centuries (*hue and cry, marriage, apprentice,* etc.) we hit the Norman Conquest. We have a lot to thank Norman for, because he brought an element of bilingualism to Britain and forced us to shape up to the continental traditions of law and the modern world (as it then was). So here we encountered the cataclysmic meeting of two cultures, like the Neanderthal and the Cro-Magnon (or European Early Modern Humans) earlier: the Germanic philosophy of farming (and invasion) met the French (Romance) traditions of civilised authority (and invasion). It was even possible to find words which made their way into English from the northern French of the Norman invaders (as opposed to different forms which had developed in central and Parisian France), and we could investigate Anglo-Norman, the variety of Norman French that came to be used in the upper echelons of British society for several hundred years after the Conquest, until someone realised it wasn't English.

When we skipped over the traditional borderline of 1500 (and in reality, as we emerged from the pre-printing era) we started to see the English language peep into the contemporary world. By now English was shrugging off its inferiority complex as regards French, and it was becoming a language in which great literature could be written and in which business could flourish. The language once again echoed the preoccupations of society. As British travellers and explorers pushed their ships out around the world, they brought back new words and new ways of thinking to the British Isles, as we saw from the words discussed from the early sixteenth through to the mid-eighteenth century. This might be the time to interpose that it's my considered view that any two-word compound (like *tea cup*— 1700—or *shirt front*—1838) first found after 1600 will eventually be tracked back before 1600. Again, it's not a view everyone shares with me. But just wait and see who's right. There are exceptions. I'm prepared to admit that we won't find *telephone receiver* anywhere in the vicinity of 1600.

By 1750 we have a language that is recognisable as Modern English. And then gradually we discover words which fed back into English from the regions of colonisation and Empire, and soon those regions (especially America, Australia, New Zealand and Australia) are going through the same process of emergence from subjection and the recognition of nationhood and independence that English in Britain had done almost five hundred years earlier. The language sparkles with new inventions from around the word (*deadlines*, *blueprints*, and *buses*), leading into the preoccupations of the twentieth and twenty-first centuries.

The purpose was not to present a rounded course on the English language, but to try to instil the idea that if you took the time to investigate any word in the language, you would see that it had a history, and that that history matched the histories of many other words that entered or developed in English at the same time; that there is a patterning in the language over the centuries that mirrors and comments on the emergence of peoples and nations over history. Nothing exists on its own. It may not seem likely, but there was even a reason for *selfie*.

> It is a truism known only to lexicographers that every new word is at least ten years older than you think. You might think *selfie*, for instance, is as recent as this morning's newspaper, but its history actually does stretch back beyond the *OED*'s self-imposed ten-year inclusion rule. The first reference our bloodhounds tracked down for the term dates from 2002. It first appears—perhaps surprisingly—in Australia, and it seems that Europeans didn't take any particular notice for a while. Here's the original online posting from an Australian Broadcasting Corporation online tech forum (still there when I last checked): "Um, drunk at a mates 21st, I tripped ofer [that's there in the original—it's not my typo] and landed lip first (with front teeth coming a very close second) on a set of steps. I had a hole about 1cm

long right through my bottom lip. And sorry about the focus, it was a selfie."

One guess is that *selfie* was a shortening of "self-portrait," but we might need to be cautious. These days you can go straight from "This is a photo of myself" to "This is a selfie." So don't be too precipitate with your etymological ideas.

Selfie came to unnatural prominence in the world of lexicography when it was chosen as the Oxford Dictionaries WOTY in 2013. Despite its awkwardness as an abbreviation, WOTY is regularly used in lexicographical circles for "Word of the Year." You might imagine that as I'm never prepared to admit to a Favourite Word of All Time, then I am equally unlikely to have a favourite Word of the Day, Month, or Year. Although something called the Oxford Dictionaries WOTY sounds as if it comes with the imprimatur of the big *Oxford English Dictionary*, it never did (back in my day), as we always refused to play along. It was all decided elsewhere. I'm not sure what happens nowadays. Maybe the *OED* could have settled on a Word of the Year 1563, or something along those lines, but I'd probably have vetoed that, too. All the same, I actually thought *selfie* was a good choice. It was obviously an overused word in 2013 (the year it won the ultimate accolade), but even more it told us something about the sort of people and society we had become. Not thoughtful and reflective, but self-obsessed, capturing images of ourselves in rear-view mirrors, like selfies on sticks.

The OED today is very different from the dictionary I first encountered at first hand in the 1970s. The same is true of Oxford and its University Press. I might go back to the past for some things, if I could. There's a romantic aspect to writing out definitions late on a cold October evening, lit only by a bright desk-light, to the accompaniment of the shuffle of paper as your colleagues sort their index cards into order, ready to attack their next word. The smell of the loosely folded, freshly printed galley proofs returned to your desk from the printer and waiting to be corrected is something that editors won't experience again. That has all given way to greater accuracy, more and better evidence, and a sense that the dictionary is now accessible to so many more people. But those old ways should be remembered, because they were essential steps to the present, which will eventually be other editors' pasts.

In the end we had decided that Oxford itself might be best observed from a distance: easy to return to, but not the focus of everyday life. Hilary retired a few years before me, and since we moved to Cheltenham she has—amongst other things—become involved in running various local charities, as usual taking a strategic approach to any available problem.

Kate has two children, Laura and Evie, and she now works as a special educational needs and disability manager in a large secondary school. Kate shied away from the disability environment for many years, grieving for the mainstream sister she never had and for whom she somehow felt guilty. Ellie has made all of us more tolerant and caring. Laura talks of Ellie as her "very special auntie," without realising the significance of "special (needs, education, etc.)" in this context.

Ellie is a disabled "adult": really she hasn't changed a lot since she was two or three, but she's inspirational for me and I hope for other people with whom she comes into contact. She lives quite close by—in Oxfordshire, so we and Kate can visit her easily. She's in a house with three other young people with similar disabilities, and they are cared for by support workers from a local care charity. There are normally three or more supporters on hand when we visit, and Ellie and the others have a full programme of activities—far fuller than we would be able to give her these days: horse-riding, drumming and dance, wall-mounted digital iPads, sensory equipment, love, care, and entertainment. You hope it will all continue. . . . If there is something that chills me in the middle of the night, it's that something may go wrong for Ellie in the future, and no one will be there to fix it for her.

Even if I can't communicate with her verbally, spending time with her reminds me that interaction isn't only verbal. Seeing her takes you into a corridor where communication fluctuates with the passage of time: sometimes stronger, sometimes weaker. When it's weak, it seems almost to vanish away, and you wonder if you will see it again. When it's strong, it's the most important thing there is. Wordless, but powerful.

As for me? Mainly I'm just working on various projects that scoop up aspects of the past that we've forgotten and re-running them for a new age online. It took me a while to realise that that was what I liked doing, and was what I was best at. Not everyone's got the patience. But then Hilary says I'm just an ordinary bloke who's been lucky enough to do an extraordinary job. I suppose she's right. She usually is.

ACKNOWLEDGEMENTS

This book couldn't have been written without two things: my remarkable colleagues on the *Oxford English Dictionary* and more generally within Oxford University Press, with whom I've shared many years of lexicographical thrills and spills as we tussled the venerable *OED* out of its Victorian straitjacket and into the new, elegant garb it displays today on the Internet; and David Kuhn, the New York literary agent who saw a piece about my impending retirement on the *Time* magazine online site and—apparently able to see round corners—thought to pick up his phone and give me a ring. There are lots of other people and things without which it could not have been written, but these two deserve the lead-off places.

It had never really occurred to me that anyone might be interested in the thoughts I had while working on the dictionary. It's true that while I was being shown round the Library of Congress in Washington many years ago, my guide—listening to what I was telling him about my work—whispered, "Well, I hope you are keeping a diary of all this." Of course I wasn't. I don't think a journal would have served me much better, and you'll remember that my last diary ended up in the washing machine.

I've learnt a lot about how to write a book since I started. Thanks to David Kuhn and his colleague Becky Sweren for walking me through the early stages and for setting me up in the right direction, and then for critiquing my early naive efforts. Thanks, too, to my editor and publisher at Basic Books, Lara Heimert, and to her colleagues Michelle Welsh-Horst and Kathy Streckfus, for guiding the book through the publication process. I owe Lara a debt of gratitude for insisting that the book should have a sharper structure and that its text should follow a more logical trajectory than would otherwise have been the case, as well as for her infectious encouragement throughout. And many thanks also to Richard Beswick, publishing director of Little, Brown—calm and unflustered—who came along to a talk I gave about the *OED*, and then quietly and politely told me all the stories from my talk that I needed to add to the book. Also to Zoe Gullen, whose careful review smoothed over numerous infelicities and worse.

Finally, I'm grateful to Yvonne Warburton, Ed Weiner, and Robert Ritter, all at some time editors at Oxford University Press, and to Harald Beck, for reading versions of the text and improving it immeasurably by their comments; and to my wife, Hilary, for remembering with me.

FURTHER READING

My 100 Favourite Books on the *OED*

Fortunately there aren't 100 books on the *OED* (I hope). To make up for this, I've come up with a cut-down hit parade of twelve books about the dictionary which will help to fill in any gaps I may have left. I've slotted these titles into an imaginary ranking list, supposedly for ease of reference.

No. 43 belongs to Jeremy Marshall and Fred McDonald's *Questions of English*—a survey of FAQs about English from the postbag of the *Oxford English Dictionary* in the 1990s. The idea was that it might stop some enquirers from writing in to ask us the same "Questions of English" which other people were continually asking us. It didn't work, of course.

No. 37 is John Willinsky's *Empire of Words*—a good early effort at interpreting the online data which goes to form the dictionary, but probably a book to encourage others to leap over its shoulders rather than one which challenges for the lead itself.

Jumping up to **No. 32** in the dictionary charts we find Sarah Ogilvie's *Words of the World: A Global History of the 'Oxford English Dictionary'*. Sarah is a former colleague who can tell a fine story. It's down at No. 32 because although the story is well told, there are bits I don't agree with. Maybe that's my fault.

Just on the southward side of Sarah's book, at **No. 28**, comes Jeff Prucher's *Brave New Words: The Oxford Dictionary of Science Fiction*. See pages 327–328 above for the lowdown on this, and use it to help you contribute to the future of the *OED*.

We take a bit of a leap now to one of the old classics, at **No. 21**. Elisabeth Murray published a biography of her grandfather, Sir James Murray, founding editor of the *OED*, way back in 1977—just after I joined the dictionary staff. She had access to her grandfather's own personal papers, and also to dictionary archives held in the Bodleian Library in Oxford and at the University Press. She was fortunate in being prescient enough to include the word "web" in her title (*Caught in the Web of Words*), but too early to exploit that. To my mind this would be higher up the Best Books listing if it didn't contain such a long middle section documenting in enormous detail the arguments between Murray as chief editor and the managers of the University Press, in which the author leaps acrobatically between one footnote and the next. It's an important book, so you have to read it—but remember that things are really more interesting than that.

A little higher, at **No. 15**, comes Charlotte Brewer's *Treasure-house of the Language: The Living OED* (2007). Again, this is written by a friend and colleague in the University at Oxford, who also runs a website for *OED* investigators: "Examining the *OED*." Her book tells the story of the dictionary with lighter feet than Elisabeth Murray, and—by being more recent—is able to speculate on the future for the dictionary as a result of the ongoing revision. For me it slips down the table a bit because it doesn't contain unending, relentless, and uncritical praise of the *OED*. But then nothing does.

No. 10 is reserved for another of my former colleagues, Peter Gilliver, whose panoramic and thoroughly researched *The Making of the Oxford English Dictionary* (squeezed into a single volume) doesn't leave *OED* beachcombers with many more stones to turn over in future.

It's jostling for position with Philip Durkin's *Borrowed Words: A History of Loanwords in English* at **No. 9**. Philip's book was the first to make extensive use of all of the new information we found for the Third Edition of the *OED*, so it's a great leap forward in lots of ways. It's not just for the scholar of etymology, as it gives a picture of the emergence of the modern world through the interchange of words between nations.

We have a lot to thank Simon Winchester for, crashing into the charts at **No. 8** with *The Surgeon of Crowthorne*, the remarkable story of one of Sir James Murray's American contributors housed as an inmate in the Broadmoor Hospital, then an asylum for people classified as "criminally insane." The story goes that Murray went to visit him one day, assuming Dr Minor was on the staff of the hospital, and was alarmed to find himself conducted into the inmates' quarters to meet the unstable gentleman. Murray always vigorously affirmed that he knew he was meeting an inmate, as afterwards did any of his editors who wanted to remain on his staff. If it had not been for Dr Minor (it is said), the *OED*'s coverage of sixteenth- and seventeenth-century vocabulary would have been immeasurably poorer. Well, you take what you can. The book is a fascinating read, and of course prompted reviewers to ask if we had anyone like that on our books in modern times. We always said no. The title *The Surgeon of Crowthorne* was considered too opaque for the book's American audience. They were treated to the populist alternative *The Professor and the Madman*, which itself prompted reviewers to ask which was which. After you've read this, take a look at Simon's *The Meaning of Everything: The Story of the OED* (2004).

Places Nos. 2 and 3 are both the lexicographer's choices, not the people's selection. At **No. 3** comes Jürgen Schäfer's *Documentation in the O.E.D.: Shakespeare and Nashe as Test Cases*. German academic Jürgen Schäfer was interested in how good the *OED*'s Victorian readers were at finding first usages—so he retested their findings. What he discovered was, naturally, what any practising lexicographer knows already—i.e., that nobody is perfect and that things do sometimes get missed. But he was able to put a percentage on this for different authors and by implication even for different readers, and this is helpful. He was also able to send us details of what we (or our ancient predecessors) had missed. Which was also very helpful too, and something not everyone does today—despite the Internet.

No. 2 consists of two volumes that were published posthumously by Schäfer, along the same sort of lines: *Early Modern English Lexicography: Vol. 1, A survey of monolingual printed glossaries and dictionaries, 1475–1640* (1989), and *Vol. 2, Additions and corrections to the OED* (also 1989). Christmas stockings were bulging in Oxford that year. Although they were uninteresting to the general reader, they were more grist to the theory that the dictionary was—at that time—badly out of date.

I've already told you my favourite book on the *OED*, so if you missed the comments on page 264 above, please return there now. **No. 1**—to spoil the surprise—is Ammon Shea's *Reading the OED: One Man, One Year, 21,730 Pages*. Perhaps I'll re-read that now I've finished this.

INDEX

Note: Entries in ***boldface italic*** are the subject of extended discussion.

John Simpson is the former chief editor of the *Oxford English Dictionary*, where he helped move the dictionary online in the 1980s and led the editorial work on its Third Edition (2000–). He is an Emeritus Fellow of Kellogg College, Oxford, and writes and researches widely on language, literature, and history. John lives in Gloucestershire.